THE
SEWING

THE ART OF SEWING

ANNA JACOB THOMAS

UBSPD
UBS Publishers' Distributors Ltd.
New Delhi Bombay Bangalore Madras
Calcutta Patna Kanpur London

UBS Publishers' Distributors Ltd.
5 Ansari Road, New Delhi-110 002
Bombay Bangalore Madras Calcutta Patna Kanpur London

© Anna Jacob Thomas

First Published 1993
First Reprint 1994
Second Reprint 1995
Third Reprint 1995

All rights reserved. No part of this publication may be reproduced or transmitted in any form or by any means, electronic or mechanical, including photocopying, recording or any information storage or retrieval system, without prior permission in writing from the publisher.

Cover Design : UBS Art Studio

Lasertypeset in 11 pt. Times Roman at Alphabets, New Delhi and printed at Rajkamal Electric Press, B-35/9 G.T. Karnal Road Industrial Area, Delhi

To
My Parents

To
My Parents

PREFACE

Home sewing is popular even in today's world of ready-made clothing. It enables one to develop the ability to adapt basic drafts to suit individual requirements.

Since most drafting instructions are based on body measurements, it becomes imperative that these be taken accurately. However, taking accurate measurements requires a lot of practice, so in order to simplify the task, the drafts in this book have been worked out to help beginners.

An aspect of vital concern is the selection of fabric. Most beginners tend to use inexpensive fabric. This has two major disadvantages. First, one does not feel the need to be careful, and second, fabric that is inferior and loosely woven, tends to stretch.

On the other hand, good quality fabric hides defects in tailoring simply because it looks good, takes the required shape and hangs or drapes well. Fabric used by the beginner should be firmly woven, pre-shrunk and should not ravel easily.

The book has been divided into two sections. In Section I, sewing fundamentals and basic concepts have been detailed. Section II provides the actual drafts for age groups ranging from infants to the various adult sizes. Furthermore the adaptations for different styles, suitable for each age group have been detailed using these basic blocks.

The drafts for adults have been tried and tested successfully on the students of the Clothing and Textiles Department, Faculty of Home Science, Maharaja Sayajirao University of Baroda.

Anna Jacob Thomas

CONTENTS

Section I

CHAPTER 1
The Importance of Clothing 1

CHAPTER 2
Common Sewing Terms 3

CHAPTER 3
Dressmaking Equipment 15

CHAPTER 4
The Sewing Machine : Its Use and Care 21

CHAPTER 5
Sewing Construction Details
(Basic Sewing Techniques, Seams and Seam Finishes, Neckline Finishes, Linings and Interfacings, Pockets, Waist Bands and Plackets, Preparation of Fabric before Cutting, Precautions to be taken while working with Different kinds of Fabrics) 25

CHAPTER 6
Fabric Selection 70

CHAPTER 7
Colour 74

CHAPTER 8
Understanding Your Body 77

CHAPTER 9
How to Take Body Measurements 79

CHAPTER 10
Alterations to Fit Different Figures 84

CHAPTER 11
Design Elements 95

CONTENTS

Section II

Drafts

CHAPTER 12
Collars — 102

CHAPTER 13
Sleeves — 112

CHAPTER 14
Children's Clothes — 122

CHAPTER 15
Drafting for the Adult — 143

CHAPTER 16
Adapting to New Styles Using the Basic Bodice Block — 150

CHAPTER 17
The Sari Blouse — 153

CHAPTER 18
The Skirt — 179

CHAPTER 19
The Sari Petticoat — 189
Measurement Chart — 191

CHAPTER 20
The Salwar — 192

CHAPTER 21
Shorts — 195

CHAPTER 22
Trousers — 197

CHAPTER 23
Sewing Tips — 200

SECTION 1

Section 1

CHAPTER 1

THE IMPORTANCE OF CLOTHING

The desire to decorate or beautify the human form has existed since the stone age when early man painted his face and body. Though standards of beauty have changed, the desire remains.

The evolution of clothing has been closely interlinked with the social, economic and industrial progress of each period in the history of mankind. The compelling demands of the environment, along with the dictates of fashion and the driving compulsions of the human personality have had immense influence on clothing styles.

Initially what one sees and reacts to in a person is his or her clothes. Clothes reflect a person's age, sex, nationality, occupation and socio-economic status. Clothes are also the outward symbol of a person's attitudes, values, interests, taste and so much so that they are often instrumental in the conscious evaluation of personal characteristics. They also fulfil important psychological needs of conformity and self-confidence.

This desire for social acceptance through dress and behaviour is greatest during adolescence. As a person matures and grows in self-confidence, it is replaced by the need to be individualistic. This can be expressed outwardly through selection from a range of choices in fabric, colour and design, while yet conforming to basic fashion lines.

Awareness of one's physical attributes and drawbacks as also awareness of one's personality is the essence of acquiring good clothes sense. Whether one is beautiful or not, it is possible to appear well dressed and well groomed by selecting clothes that bring out one's best features. The ability to select the right clothing, colour, fabric, design and accessories to suit the individual and the occasion, is an indication of a person's good taste. Some individuals are born with this ability whereas others have to acquire it. Fashion designs are really meant for model figures and have to be adapted to suit one's figure and personality.

For a garment to be truly attractive, it should fit well. To achieve a good fit, it is necessary to give attention to finer details such as individual proportions and contours, which only home sewing can cater to. Home sewing also provides a means for creative expression.

Sewing beautiful clothes is an art in itself. It is essential to be adept at this art with tailoring costs soaring and also because tailoring seldom provides a satisfactory fit.

Above all, home sewing gives one the freedom to choose from a variety of fabrics, colours, textures, and styles, giving clothes that slightly different look which is the mark of a well dressed woman. Achieving this more than compensates for the many hours of labour spent in sewing.

CHAPTER 2

COMMON SEWING TERMS

A-line	:	A garment with sloping sides, the widest part being at the hemline.
Alter	:	To change a pattern so that it corresponds to body measurements.
Allowance	:	Extra fabric outside the seamline or within the garment to accommodate gathers, ease, tucks and pleats.
Appliqué	:	Decorative pieces of fabric applied by hand or machine.
Armhole	:	The opening in a garment for the arm.
Armscye	:	It is commonly known as Armhole.
Back stitch	:	A small hand stitch that looks like machine stitching on the right side, but with stitches overlapping on the wrong side.
Bagging out	:	To stitch two pieces of a garment together round the outer edge leaving a short section free, through which the two pieces are then drawn out to the right side. This method is used to fix lining to a skirt or jacket.
Bands	:	Strips of fabric, ribbon or bias applied to edges or set into garments to finish or decorate.
Bar	:	A group of cross threads used to stay the ends of a button hole.
Basque	:	A woman's tight fitting dress-waist made separate from the

skirt and having the waistline finish attached to the waist portion.

Basting	:	A long, loose termporary stitch made by hand or machine.
Bell sleeve	:	A straight sleeve flaring at the bottom.
Bermuda shorts	:	Tight, narrow shorts reaching the top of the knee.
Bertha	:	A wide, flat collar usually rounded at its outer edge.
Bias	:	Any direction in the fabric which does not follow exactly the selvedge or weft yarns. A true bias makes an angle of 45° across the lengthwise and widthwise grain. It has maximum stretch.
Binding	:	A bias strip of material used to enclose a raw edge as a finish or trim.
Bishop's sleeve	:	A long, full sleeve gathered onto a narrow cuff.
Blend	:	A mixture of different fibres in one yarn or different yarns in one fabric, each lending its own characteristics to the fabric.
Blind stitch	:	A form of hemming made by catching only one thread of the outer fabric.
Bolero	:	A Spanish jacket of short length with or without sleeves and without lapels. Worn open in front, over a dress or blouse.
Braid	:	A woven novelty trim, finished at both edges.
Breakline	:	The roll line of a lapel when it turns back from the garment.
Brettelle	:	A sort of cape or decorative shoulder strap extending over the shoulder from the belt in front to the belt at the back of the waist.
Brides	:	The threads of warp or weft connecting parts of the pattern in lace.
Buckram	:	A stiff fabric made by impregnating a light-weight open cloth with adhesives and fillers.
Bustle	:	A pad or frame worn by women on the back below the waist to distend the hip.

The Art of Sewing

Cap	:	The top part of a sleeve which is curved to fit the armhole.
Capsleeve	:	Extension of the shoulder and upper armhole to cover the top of the arm.
Casing	:	A hem with an opening so that ribbon or elastic may be drawn through.
Centre front	:	The position of a pattern or garment at the exact centre of the front section of the garment.
Chic	:	Originality combined with good taste.
Chinese cord	:	An ornamental knot made of cord and used as a trimming on coats or dresses.
Classic style	:	A style which is re-used with only minor modifications through many changes of fashion.
Clip	:	A small cut in the seam allowance of a garment which allows a corner or curved area to turn and lie flat.
Closing	:	A placket or any garment opening.
Collarette	:	A standing collar with a wide ruching around the top.
Construction lines	:	Basic seams that give shape to flat cloth.
Co-ordinates	:	A number of garments which match and can be worn together in different combinations.
Cord piping	:	A cord which is encased in bias fabric and used to finish and decorate edges, waistlines, button holes and furnishings.
Cord seam	:	A seam with a corded effect which is produced by turning both seam edges to one side and then stitching through the three thicknesses of material.
Corsage	:	The waist or bodice of a dress. Also a bouquet of real or artificial flowers worn at the waistline.
Cossack collar	:	A high stand band collar fastening at the side.
Costume	:	Dress belonging to a given country, time and class.
Count of yarn	:	A number indicating the mass per unit length or the length per unit mass of a yarn.

Cowl	:	A neckline cut on the bias and which drops into soft U-folds generally on the front of a bodice.
Crease	:	A pressed fold line as in trouser legs.
Crowfoot	:	An ornamental stitch having three points and a raised triangular centre and like arrowheads used on tailored garments to give strength to certain parts and provide a finish.
Culotte	:	A combination of dress or skirts and shorts, often with centre front and centre back pleats to hide the crotch seam. Sometimes known as a divided skirt.
Dart	:	A fold of fabric stitched to a point at one end. Used to fit fabric to body curves.
Design lines	:	Lines or seams that add design and make the garment different.
Dickey	:	A small decorative apron-like attachment to the front of the bodice, sometimes used to fill a low-cut neckline.
Dolman	:	Style with a very low, loose armhole. The seam runs from the waist out to the wrist.
Double breasted	:	A blouse, jacket or coat with a wide overlap at the front and fastened with a double row of buttons.
Drape	:	Soft folds of fabric controlled by pleats or gathers.
Draped	:	A style in which the fabric is gathered or folded into unpressed pleats to create a soft effect and provide shaping.
Dressform	:	A duplicate of the human form which is useful for fitting or draping a garment.
Drop	:	To lower a shoulder line.
Ease	:	(a) Extra measurement allowed for comfort. It is the difference between actual body measurement and the size of the garment.
	:	(b) To work in excess material that has been allowed for comfort.
Edge stitch	:	A line of stitching placed along an edge, usually for a decorative finish.

Edging	:	Narrow lace having one finished edge and the other, usually scalloped or indented. Used for trimmings.
Emery bag	:	A small bag filled with an abrasive powder used to sharpen and remove rust from pins and needles.
Empire line	:	Style with no waistline, but with a seam placed high under the bust. This style was started in France.
End	:	An individual strand of yarn.
Eton collar	:	A flat collar with a very slight roll.
Extension	:	Additional fabric jutting out beyond a seam or a centre line.
Eyelet	:	A small hole in a garment finished by hand or a metal ring to hold the prong of a buckle. Also for lacing with ribbon and cord.
Facing	:	A shaped or bias piece of self fabric applied to a garment edge as a finish.
Faggoting	:	A trim placed between two seams, it is either handmade or machine-made.
Fastenings	:	Hooks and eyes, press buttons, and zippers used to fasten garments.
Fichu	:	Piece of fabric draped softly in folds around a low neckline.
Figure types	:	The classification for various figures according to height and body proportions.
Fish dart	:	A dart that tapers at both ends, generally used at the waistline.
Fittings	:	Adjusting the pattern or garment to fit the individual figure.
Flap	:	A piece of fabric that hangs loose and is attached at one edge only, usually on pockets and shoulders.
Flared	:	A style which is much wider around the lower edge.
Flounce	:	Flared bands of fabric, sometimes gathered and used to decorate edges of garments or used in tiers to make a skirt.
Flouncings	:	Wide dress lace having one edge scalloped and the other straight, it is usually about 10-12" in width.
Fly front	:	A closing which conceals buttons or zippers of trousers.

Fray	:	The threads which come out during the handling of fabric.
Frog	:	Decorative closing formed by looping braid. Usually associated with oriental style garments.
Gauging	:	Fullness drawn up in uniform sized deep folds of fabric where a long length of fabric is to be gathered into a small length. This forms a decorative effect.
Gathering	:	One or two rows of stitching, either by hands or machine, that are drawn up to form even fullness.
Gingham	:	Plain weave fabric constructed with coloured woven check pattern.
Give	:	The ability of a seam or fabric to withstand pressure without breaking or tearing.
Godets	:	A shaped or pleated section of material inserted into garments.
Gore	:	A skirt section that is shaped upto the hip level and then flared out to the hemline.
Grain	:	The direction of threads in a woven fabric. The lengthwise grain runs parallel to the selvedge and the cross-wise grain runs from selvedge to selvedge.
Grey goods	:	Woven fabrics as they leave the loom before being bleached, dyed or finished.
Gusset	:	A shaped piece of fabric inserted usually at the underarm of the garment to provide comfort.
Halter neck	:	A garment without sleeves, the bodice being supported by a band or string passing around the neck or tied at the back of the neck.
Hand finishing	:	The details sewn by hand to finish the garment.
Harem trousers	:	Very full trousers gathered tightly at the ankle.
Hem	:	The finish formed by folding back the raw edge of a garment to the wrong side.
Hemline	:	The line designating the finished length of a garment.
Hipsters	:	Skirts or trousers which start at the hips instead of the waist.

The Art of Sewing

Invisible hem	:	Hem stitch for attaching facings and interfacings.
Insertions	:	Lace having two straight edges, used for inserting between the edges of two pieces of material.
Interfacing	:	An extra piece of cloth placed between the garment and the facing to impart strength, shape and stiffness and to prevent stretching.
Interlining	:	An extra layer of fabric placed between the lining and the garment for added warmth.
Jabot	:	A flounced decoration in fine fabric or lace attached to the neckline of a bodice.
Jersey	:	A smooth, plain knit fabric of wool, cotton and synthetic blends.
Kick pleat	:	A short pleat at the lower edge of a skirt. It is formed by an extension cut on the centre or side seam and is stitched across the upper edge to hold in it in place.
Kimono sleeve	:	Sleeve cut all in one with the bodice. May be of any length. It gives folds of extra fabric under the arm. It may be cut with or without a shoulder seam.
Knife pleats	:	Series of pleats that turn in the same direction. They are usually equal in width and are pressed straight down to the hem.
Lapel	:	Upper edge of a coat or blouse front that turns back.
Layout	:	The arrangement of pattern pieces on the material so as to ensure economical cutting.
Leg o'mutton sleeve	:	Long fitting sleeve with high, gathered head.
Lining	:	A fabric used inside garments. Its edges may be attached to the garment at the seams with slip stitch or it may hang loose from the neck or from the waist in the case of skirts.
Loop	:	A fastening which extends beyond the finished edge, used on closings with no overlap. Can be made with thread, cord or fabric.
Machine basting	:	A temporary machine stitching using the longest machine stitch.

Mandarin collar	:	A narrow, high standing band, divided in the front, generally with the corners rounded off. Same as the Chinese collar.
Marking	:	Transferring all necessary pattern lines or markings to the wrong side of the fabric.
Mitre	:	Diagonal joining of material at a corner to reduce bulk, by avoiding overlapping.
Nap	:	The word means "pile". Pile fabrics should always be cut in one direction only.
Notch	:	A small V-shaped mark or cut, on seam allowance of the pattern pieces.
Opening	:	Term used interchangeably with closing.
Overblouse	:	A long blouse reaching the hips.
Overskirt	:	A skirt or drapery worn shorter than the skirt of a dress.
Panel line	:	Seam lines running from the armhole or waist to the hem.
Peg top	:	Trousers or skirts that are made wide at the hips and narrow at the bottom.
Peplum	:	A frill or flaps attached to the waist and covering the upper part of the hips.
Picot	:	Loop stitch along the edge of the fabric to form an edging.
Pile	:	Weave of a fabric with upright surface yarns such as velvet or velveteen.
Pin tucks	:	Tucks as fine as the width of a pin.
Pinking	:	Jagged cut finish for a raw edge.
Pivot	:	A method of turning a sharp corner while machining. With the needle in the fabric, the presser foot is raised, the material turned to the desired angle, the foot lowered and the stitching continued.
Placket	:	A closing or opening in a garment.
Pleats	:	Folds of fabric used to control fullness.
Polo neck	:	High, rolled collar worn close to the neck.

Princess line	:	Seam lines running from shoulder or armhole to the hem with no waist seam.
Pucker	:	To draw up into folds and wrinkles.
Puff sleeves	:	Short sleeves having fullness gathered into the armhole, and into a band or binding at the lower edge.
Raglan	:	A style in which the armhole seams run upto the neckline giving a loose and comfortable fit.
Ravel	:	Yarns drawn out along the edge of the fabric.
Redingote	:	Double breasted semi-fitted coat.
Reinforce	:	To add strength to corners and areas of great stress by adding rows of stitching or a patch of fabric.
Rever	:	That part of the bodice which folds back onto the front of the garment in open-necked styles.
Ribbon	:	An attractive woven fabric with a lustrous appearance, used for trimming and adornment.
Ric rac	:	A flat, woven braid made in zigzag form.
Ring collar	:	A band collar standing well away from the neck.
Rip	:	To open a seam by pulling out or cutting the stitching.
Roll collar	:	A collar which rises up the neck and then curves down again without a sharp crease.
Rolled hem	:	A kind of hem used on sheer fabrics. The edge is rolled tightly between the thumb and forefingers of the left hand and hemming is done to hold the roll in place.
Rosette	:	A form of ribbon decoration in the shape of a rose.
Ruffle	:	A band of fabric that is gathered or pleated and applied to an edge as a trimming.
Sag	:	The stretch that occurs in the bias grain of a garment after hanging or as the effect of strain on any part of a garment.
Sash	:	An ornamental band or belt worn around the waist.
Scallop	:	An edge finish made up of a series of semicircles.

Seam	:	The means by which two pieces of fabric or parts of a garment are joined together.
Seam allowance	:	Extra fabric allowed along the seams.
Seam finish	:	Finish applied to a raw edge to control ravel and fraying.
Seamline	:	The stitching line used for joining seams.
Semi-fitted	:	Partly conforming to the figure.
Selvedge	:	The finished ends of woven fabric.
Shank	:	The stem between the button and the fabric to which it is sewn. Can be made with thread as the button is sewn on.
Shawl collar	:	Collar cut in one piece with the front bodice and ending at the centre back, thus forming a shawl over the shoulders.
Sheath gown	:	A straight, close-fitting gown.
Shirring	:	Several rows of stitched gathers.
Shirt dress	:	A dress which is based on a long version of man's shirt.
Shirt sleeve	:	A straight sleeve with a neatened slash on its lower edge, attached to a buttoned cuff.
Shrink or Shrinkage	:	The reduction in length or width of a fibre yarn or fabric. It may be induced by setting or steaming.
Silhouette	:	The outline of a dress.
Size	:	The measurement classification within a figure type which allows for variation in body measurements such as bust, waist and hip. Each figure type has a range of sizes.
Skew	:	A cloth condition in which the warp and weft yarns, although straight, are not at right angles to each other. This effect is due to the cloth's structure.
Skimmer	:	Description of garment which follows the lines of the figure, being neither tight or loose.
Slash	:	A fairly long cut made to a point or a corner.
Slot seam	:	A seam which has an underlay of fabric and resembles an inverted pleat.

Smock	:	A straight garment with a gathered or smocked yoke.
Stand	:	The part of a collar which extends upwards from the base of the neck and determines the height of the collar.
Stay	:	A reinforcement in fabric or tape, to hold a part of a garment securely in position.
Stay binding	:	A narrow, woven fabric generally used for the covering of seams and the strengthening of garments.
Stay stitching	:	A row of stitching worked just inside the seam allowance and close to the stitching line in order to prevent areas on the bias or curve from stretching.
Straight of goods	:	A term used to designate the length-wise grain in a fabric.
Sunburst pleats	:	Pleats that are wider at the bottom than at the top.
Tabard	:	A loose top, often with a small cap sleeve and a straight neckline.
Tack	:	To fasten two fabric surfaces together loosely by running stitches.
Tailored sleeve	:	Two-piece sleeve with no darts but shaped within two seams.
Tailor's tack	:	A stitch used to transfer pattern markings to the fabric.
Taper	:	To decrease width gradually and bring to a point.
Tent	:	A loose, unwaisted dress, wide at the hemline.
Thread count	:	The number of threads in a square inch of fabric.
Tiers	:	Bands of flounced or pleated fabric placed one above another, often at graduated widths, to make a skirt or dress.
Toggle	:	An oblong shaped button with a groove in the centre used usually with a frog fastener.
Top stitching	:	A line of stitching along the seam line on the right side of a garment, to add strength or design.
Trapunta	:	Quilting in which only the design part is padded.
Trim	:	To cut off ragged edges or a part of a seam allowance to prevent it from being bulky and to give the seam a neat edge.
Trimming	:	An ornamental addition used on garments.

Trumpet sleeve	:	Medium length flaring sleeve.
Tubing	:	A hollow cylinder of fabric used for button loops and decorative trim.
Tucks	:	Straight folds of fullness, evenly stitched.
Turtleneck	:	A high, rolled collar worn well away from the neck.
Underlap	:	A part of a garment that extends or laps under another part.
Underlay	:	An additional piece of fabric placed under a section for the purpose of joining, as in a pleat or slot seam.
Underlining	:	A suitable fabric used to back a section or an entire garment. It is used to give body and shape and to prevent sagging and sretching of outer fabric.
Understitching	:	A row of stitching along the edge of a faced seam, holding the seam allowance to the facing. The purpose is to hold the facing in place and sharpen the seam edge.
Unit construction	:	Organization of the sewing procedure so that an entire garment section is completed before it is joined to another.
Vent	:	A lapped, finished opening on the hem edge of a sleeve, jacket or skirt.
Virago sleeves	:	Very full sleeves tied in intervals to form puffs.
Wadding	:	Synthetic or cotton-pressed layers used for quilting and for shoulder pads.
Weave	:	The pattern of interlacing of warp and weft yarns in a woven fabric.
Wrap	:	The upper part of an opening which overlaps the under layer.
Yardage	:	The amount of fabric needed to make a particular garment.
Yoke	:	Separately made shoulder piece of bodice or the top of a skirt.

CHAPTER 3

DRESSMAKING EQUIPMENT

Every craft requires tools and proper selection is essential to obtain good results.

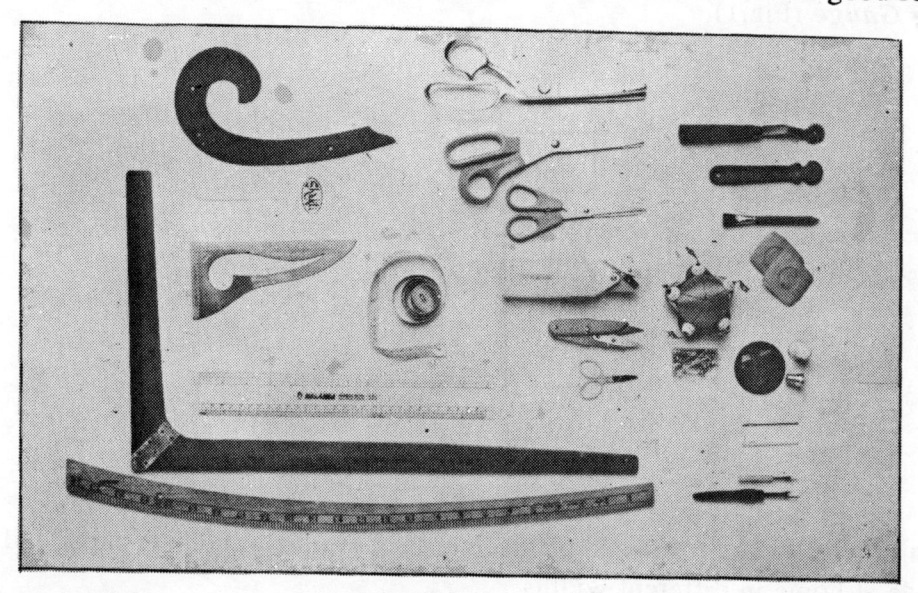

Sewing Machine

An electric sewing machine is ideal, being less strenuous and quicker to use, in leaving the hands free to manipulate the fabric. If you are interested in fancy sewing, you may select the new models with decorative stitching attachments. A zigzag attachment is very essential as it is the quickest and easiest method of finishing the seam edges.

A beginner will find the foot or treadle machine easier to handle.

Measure Tape

Those marked on both sides and which can be used from either end are the most useful. There are also those that have both the inch measure and centimetre measure on the same side. This is useful for people who still think in inches.

Rulers

Foot ruler

'L' shaped ruler to mark the horizontal lines at right angles to the vertical lines.

Curved ruler used for drawing the side seam curve of a skirt or trouser.

The tailoring triangle is available in chart paper or plastic. This is used to draw drafts to scale.

Measuring Gauge (Fig.1)

Used to mark even widths for hems, pleats, etc. It is available in chart paper and can also be made at home in different widths.

Tracing Wheel

Used to mark perforations in the fabric to indicate seams, darts, the position of pockets, necklines, pleat widths, etc. By using a carbon paper, these can be used to transfer markings on both sides of the fabric. The tracing wheel should be made of steel and have sharp edges.

The Art of Sewing

Dressmaker's Carbon

These are available in various colours.

Tailor's Chalk

These are also available in various colours. Use those which have a fine edge for accuracy in marking. Tailor's chalk rubs off easily and can be used especially to mark on the right side of the fabric.

Dressmaker's Pencils

If these are not available, ordinary coloured pencils may be used. Pencils have the advantage of having sharp points which are better for marking darts. These are especially good to mark fine lines on dark fabrics.

Pins

The pins should be of stainless steel and have fine, sharp points so that they do not spoil the fabric. Attractive dressmakers' pins with pearl heads are available.

Pin Cushions

Attractive pin cushions can be made at home by using soft fabric and filling it with hair instead of cotton wool as it will be easier to push the pins through.

Shears

Shears are available in many sizes; for normal home sewing the blades should be 7"-8" long so that they are light and easy to handle. To keep shears in good condition, wipe the lint after use and oil the rivet once in a while.

Scissors or Clippers

These are usually 3"-6" in length and are used for clipping threads and for making notches or slashes on the fabric.

Pinking Shears

These have zigzag edges and are used for cutting fabrics that fray easily.

Electric and Battery-Operated Scissors

These are useful for people who sew frequently. The battery-operated scissors are small and easy to carry. They have short blades and are ideal only for smooth fabrics. They cannot be used for handloom and furnishing fabrics which have an irregular weave.

Seam Rippers
They are very handy for picking seams and are also used to cut buttonholes.

Thimble
The thimble is worn on the middle finger and is used to protect the finger while pushing the needle through thick fabrics. Metal thimbles are ideal.

Machine Needles
These are available in various sizes. The size of the needle is selected according to the type of fabric.

Size of Needle	Fabric
No. 9	Flimsy fabrics such as net, chiffon and silk.
No. 11	Sheer fabrics such as tafetta, silk, satin and synthetics.
No. 14	This size of needle is most commonly used because it is suitable for light-weight cotton fabrics such as cambric, rubia, lawn and poplin.
No. 16	Heavy materials such as gabardine, heavy suitings, denim, corduroy and light-weight furnishing fabrics.
No. 18	Heavy fabrics such as towelling and thick furnishing fabrics.

Special needles with a slightly rounded tip are available for knitted fabrics.

Machine Threads
Most threads are made of cotton because it is suitable for many different kinds of fabric. Cotton threads are merceried and available in sizes ranging from No. 20, which is coarse, to No. 80 which is fine. The weight of the fabric determines the size of the thread to be used. The supersheen variety of thread is fine, strong and colour-fast and is recommended for most sewing.

For terrycotton and other synthetic fabrics, spun polyester thread may be used. While working with synthetic thread, the upper and lower tension of the sewing machine should be kept slightly loose. When a perfect match of thread is not available, a darker shade should be used.

Hand Sewing Needles

There are many varieties, each having a different use.

Crewels are embroidery needles.

Sharps are shorter than embroidery needles and are used for normal hand sewing.

Betweens and Blunts are shorter than sharps and used by tailors to do fine work on heavy fabrics.

Straws or Milliners are longer than sharps and are used for darning or basting.

Tapestry Needles are thick, with large eyes and rounded tips and are used to embroider with wool.

Chenile is the same as the tapestry needle except that the tip is pointed. This is used for doing heavy embroidery work on closely woven fabric.

Bodkins are large needles with large eyes and are used for threading elastic or ribbon through casings. The rounded tip is used for pushing out the stitched corners of collars.

An ideal needle size for hand sewing is Pony-Crewel No. 9 because of its length and fineness. It has a large eye for easy threading.

Stiletto

This is a pointed metal with a wooden handle and is used to make eyelet holes or openings.

French Curves

These are used to draw curves while drafting designs. They are made of plastic and are available in different shapes and sizes.

Iron and Ironing Board

A good light-weight steam iron is essential. Use the iron to press and flatten seams, hems and darts. Pressing during sewing ensures a neat finished garment.

Tailor's Cushion or Tailor's Ham

It is an oval, rounded cushion, about 8" long. It can be made at home and filled with cotton or rags. It is used to press curved seams, darts and the top of sleeves which require shaping to give a rounded appearance.

Chapter 4

The Sewing Machine: Its Use and Care

The Sewing machine is the most expensive item in the equipment required for tailoring and it is important to know how it works and how to care for it. Before use, read the Instruction Manual provided with the machine carefully.

The Sewing Machine and Its Parts (Fig. 2)

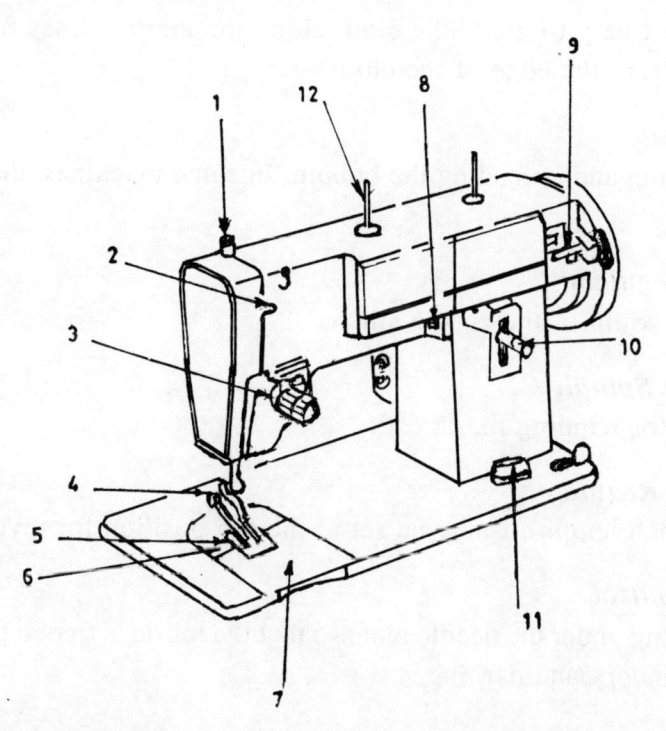

FIG. 2 SEWING MACHINE AND ITS PARTS

1. *Pressure Regulating Screw*
The screw should be tightened while working with finer fabrics like organdie, chiffon and lace and loosened to accommodate thick furnishing fabrics, denim and extra layers of fabric.

2. *Take-Up Lever*
It controls the flow and movement of the spool thread.

3. *Spool Thread Tension Dial*
It can be turned to the right to increase and to the left to decrease the tension of the spool thread.

4. *Needle Clamp*
It holds the needle in position.

5. *Presser Foot*
It holds the fabric in place, ready to be sewn. Under the presser foot is the feed dog which feeds the fabric during the sewing process.

6. *Needle Plate*
It has markings that help to guide the cloth along the marked lines for working at the required distance from the edge of the cloth.

7. *Hinged Bed Plate*
It flips up for loading and unloading the bobbin. In some machines, the bed plate slides out.

8. *Stitch Width Regulator*
This regulates the width of the zigzag stitch.

9. *Bobbin Winder Spindle*
Holds the bobbin for winding the thread.

10. *Stitch Length Regulator*
It regulates the stitch length. It may be set at the top position for reverse stitching.

11. *Drop Feed Control*
It lowers the feed dog under the needle plate so that the fabric is free to be moved by hand for machine embroidery and darning.

The Art of Sewing

MACHINE FAULTS AND HOW TO RECTIFY THEM

Often the fault is very small and can be corrected easily.

The machine does not stitch
This happens when the thread is entangled around the bobbin. Move the balance wheel back and forth to release the threads. Lift the throat plate and remove the entangled thread. Brush off all the lint and replace the bobbin and make sure that the thread slides out through the bobbin clamp.

The spool thread breaks
The spool thread breaks if the tension is too tight or if the thread is inferior. If the spool thread breaks at the eye of the needle, it must have been threaded from the wrong side of the needle or the needle fixed incorrectly.

The stitch length is not consistent
The stitch length varies when the fabric is pulled intermittently. It is important to guide the cloth with a light hand.

The fabric puckers and the threads get pulled
The needle is blunt and needs to be changed.

The needle bends or breaks
The fabric may have been pulled with the needle in it causing it to bend. The bent needle strikes the metal plate around it and breaks. Remember to lift the needle above the surface of the cloth by turning the hand wheel before pulling out the fabric.

The needle skips stitches
This happens if the needle has been placed too high or too low in the needle bar. Check the needle position. The newer models of the sewing machine do not have this problem since the slot in which the needle is inserted is of a fixed size.

In case the fault is difficult to handle, it is advisable to consult a competent mechanic.

CARE OF THE SEWING MACHINE

A sewing machine will run smoothly if it is cleaned and oiled regularly. Use a good machine brush to clean all dirt, lint and loose threads. A good brand of machine oil should be used for oiling each of the points indicated. If the machine is used regularly, it needs to be oiled once a week.

Wipe all surplus oil and place a folded piece of fabric under the presser foot to absorb any excess oil. Clean again before re-using the machine to prevent the fabric from getting soiled.

When the machine is not used regularly, the oil will dry up, thereby making the machine hard to run. Put a drop of liquid paraffin into each of the oiled parts and run the machine without fabric. After a few hours, clean and oil once more and the machine is ready for use.

Chapter 5

Sewing Construction Details

Basic Sewing Techniques

Basting

Basting is also known as tacking. Basting is a row of running stitches made by hand or machine to hold two pieces of fabric together, before being fitted or machined. Some seams and hems can be held in place with pins but for seams that need accuracy, hand basting is very essential. Basting should not be considered a waste of time because it ensures a neatly finished garment and may also avoid the bother of re-doing or ripping seams. Ripping open seams also causes the fabric to stretch, making it even more difficult to sew on again.

A single strand of thread is used for most hand sewing. The ideal length of the thread to enable quick basting and to prevent entanglement, should be about 12". The colour used should be different from that of the fabric, so that the thread is clearly visible while being machined and is easy to pull out later. When the basting is not to be removed, for enclosed seams in plackets, cuffs and waistbands, a matching thread should be used.

A double strand of thread may be used for basting while fitting a dress or when basting heavy fabrics to give strength and to ensure that the thread does not break easily.

Even basting is done when close, firm stitches are required for attaching yokes, collars, sleeves, plackets and gathers. While working on the later, always hold the gathers on top so that they can be distributed evenly and also to make sure that they do not slip during basting or while being machined.

Even basting is also done while attaching piping, gathered lace and to hold together fabrics that slip easily. (Fig.3)

— — — — — — — — — — — — FIG 3

UNEVEN BASTING is a larger stitch and the size of the stitch and the space between each is not equal. It is used for side seams, hems, lace that is not gathered and while attaching firmly, woven fabrics that do not slip easily. Position lines on the garment such as the centre front, centre back and grain lines are marked by uneven basting. It is also used to hold pleats in position and while attaching the lining and the garment section.

Since uneven basting is long and therefore loose, it is necessary to take a back stitch after every 4.0 centimetres and especially at corners so that if the basting gets pulled it will not come out altogether. (Fig. 4)

— — — — — — — FIG 4

SLIP BASTING is tacking through a fold of cloth and it is used to match checks and stripes on garment pieces, to prevent them from shifting while machining. One seam is lapped onto the other and they are tacked together, slipping the needle through the fold. The garment is then turned to the wrong side and machined as an ordinary seam. (Fig. 5)

Slip basting is also useful while taking in seams from the outside during the fitting of a garment.

FIG. 5   MATCHING STRIPES

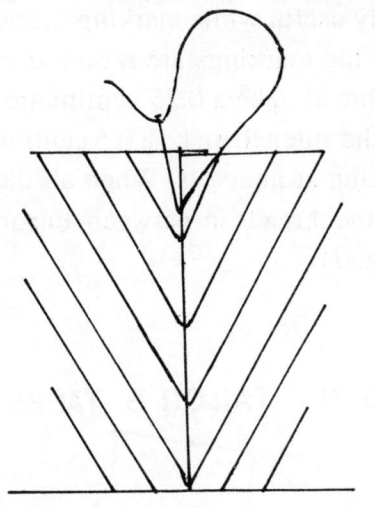

GATHERING is a row or rows of even running stitches. The first row may be taken 0.5 centimetre above the seamline and the second row, along the seamline. The threads are pulled to either side, forming gathers. Wind the thread around a pin to hold it in place. (Fig. 6)

FIG. 6   GATHERING

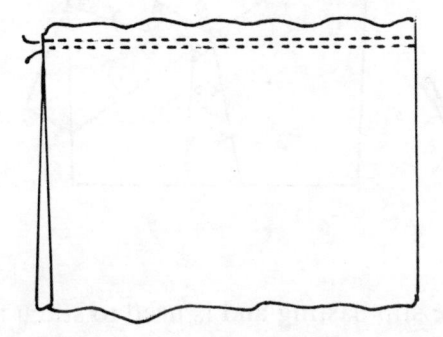

SHIRRING is rows of gathering given to create design at the waistline or at the wrist of long sleeves. Elastic in thread form is loosely wound on the bobbin. It is not passed through the clasp on the bobbin case as the flow would be restricted. The spool thread tension is kept a little looser than usual. Machine as usual and the elastic in the bobbin will draw up the fabric, giving a gathering or shirring effect. There should be three rows of gathering for a proper shirring effect. The number of rows is dependent on the width of the area to be covered. The distance between each row should be 0.1 centimetres. If the fine bobbin elastic is not available, work a row of gathers, draw it up and machine onto a band of fabric or a folded bias strip cut to the required width.

Tailor's tacks are large, looped tacks given to mark darts and seams on two or more layers of fabric. It is specially useful while marking fabrics like brocade and wool which do not mark easily or when the markings are required on the right side of the fabric.

Use a double length of thread, take a 0.25 centimetre stitch through all the layers of fabric to be marked. Repeat the stitch to make a 0.5 centimetre loop and cut off the thread. Repeat in this manner, marking at intervals. When all the points have been marked, lift the layers of fabric and clip the threads in-between, ensuring that you leave the marking on each layer of fabric. (Fig. 7)

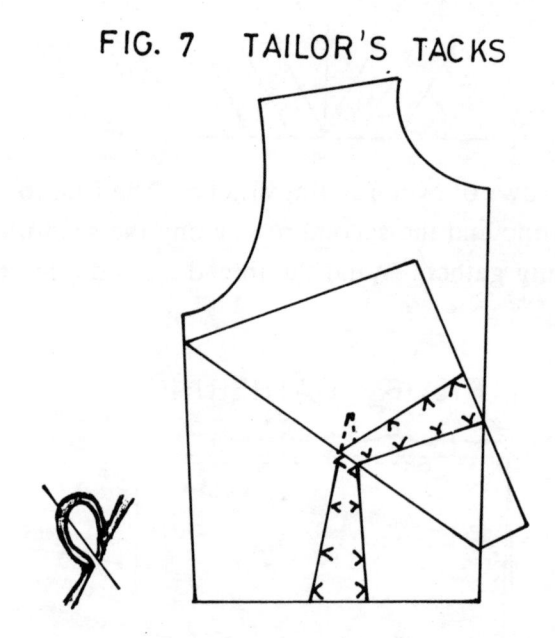

FIG. 7 TAILOR'S TACKS

French tacking is like slip basting and is used to stitch the lining to the garment at the hem.

Back Stitch

Back stitch is a firm stitch and is used instead of machine stitching in areas which the sewing machine cannot reach easily — such as gusset corners and ends of zippers. A back stitch is made by bringing the needle through the fabric from below, then taking a short stitch backward, bringing the needle through to the right side again, a little ahead of the first stitch. (Fig. 8)

The Art of Sewing   29

BACK STITCH

FIG.-8

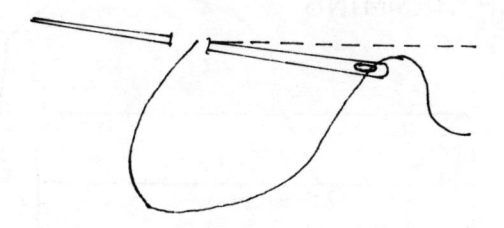

Hemming

Hemming is an essential hand stitch. A hem stitch which is large and visible or where the thread is mismatched or faded, can mar the appearance of the garment. The stitches should be close and neatly finished, but at the same time, without too many perforations visible on the right side of the garment. The hem stitch should not be too large so as to get pulled; it should be firm, neither loose or too tight and about 0.5 centimetre in length. (Fig. 9)

FIG.- 9 HEMMING

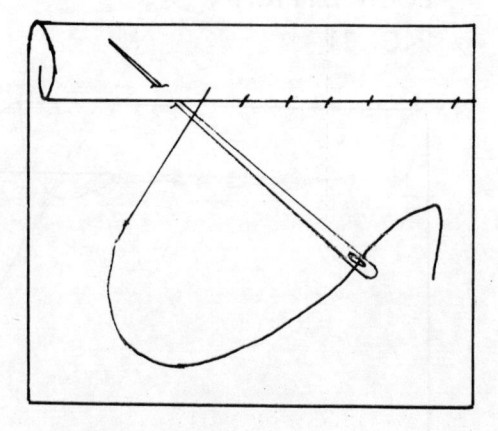

Slip hemming is the same as hemming except that the thread is slipped through the fold of fabric between each stitch. It is invisible from the wrong side and gives a neat appearance but it is not firm and long lasting. (Fig. 10)

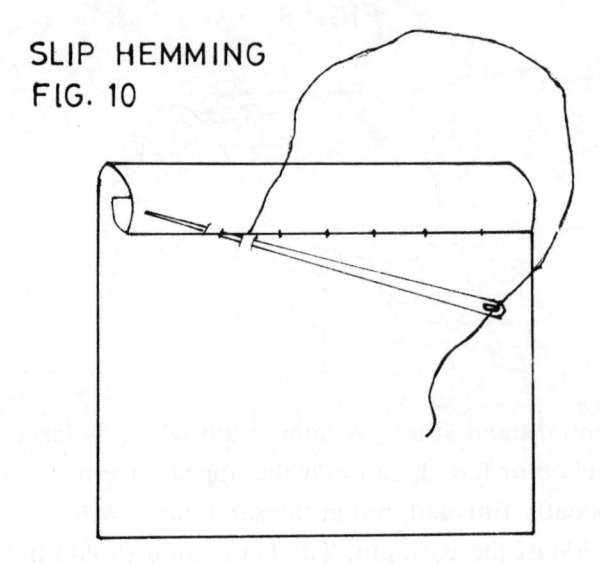

SLIP HEMMING
FIG. 10

Lock stitch is made by passing the thread back through the loop of the hem stitch. Since each stitch is locked, this hem stitch has added strength and is especially good for children's garments that are washed frequently. (Fig. 11)

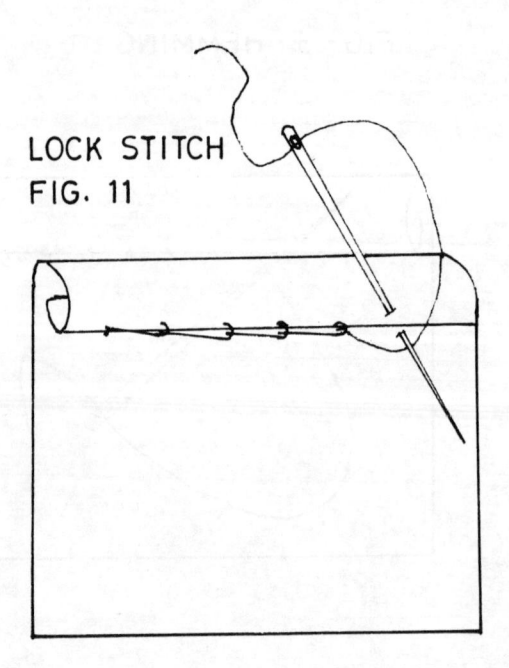

LOCK STITCH
FIG. 11

CATCH STITCH HEMMING is like a loose herringbone stitch and is ideal for knitted fabrics. Since the stitch is loose, it allows the fabric to stretch without causing the stitches to break. (Fig. 12)

FIG. 12 CATCH STITCH HEMMING

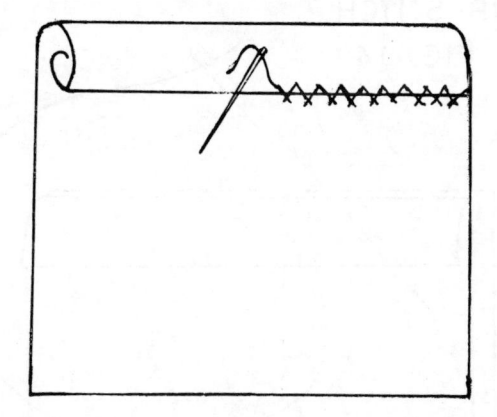

INVISIBLE HEMMING is taken about a centimetre below the edge of the hem, so that the hem stitch is not visible from the wrong side. This hem is suitable for knitted fabrics where the edge has been finished with zig zag stitching. (Fig. 13)

FIG.-13 INVISIBLE HEMMING

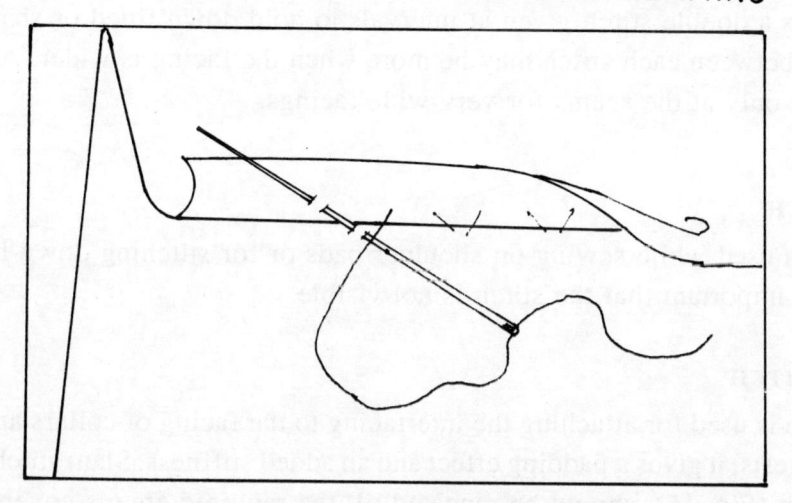

Whip Stitch or Over Sewing (Fig. 14)

Whip stitch is a small, slant stitch taken over a single folded or rolled edge. It is also used to hold two edges together as a seam finish.

A picot edging is formed when a second row of whip stitching crosses over the first. This stitch is also used to join seams of hand-knitted sweaters.

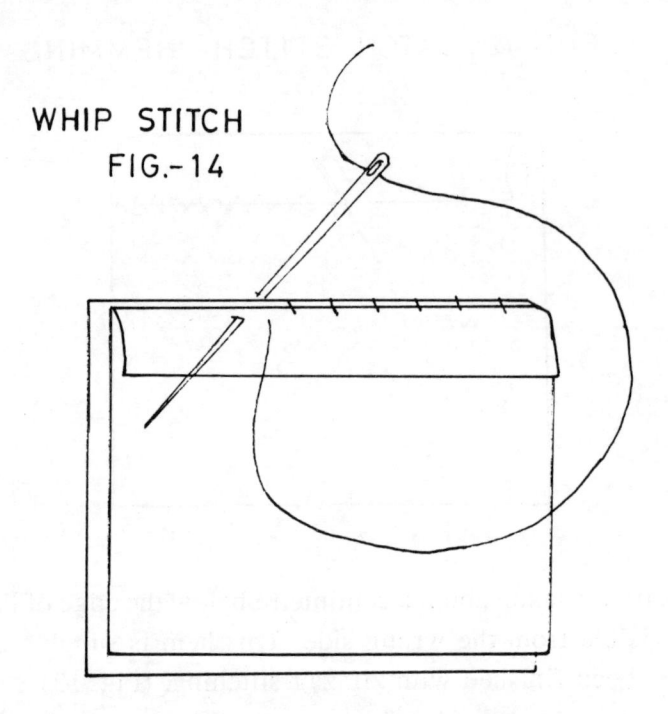

WHIP STITCH
FIG.-14

Catch Stitch

Catch stitch is a double stitch given at intervals to hold down fitted or shaped facings. The distance between each stitch may be more when the facing is wider. A catch stitch may be given only at the seams for very wide facings.

Blind Stitch

Blind stitch is used while sewing on shoulder pads or for stitching down fly seams on trousers. It is important that the stitch is not visible.

Padding Stitch

Padding stitch is used for attaching the interfacing to the facing of collars and lapels. As the name suggests, it gives a padding effect and an added stiffness. Slant stitches as shown in the diagram (Fig. 15), should be repeated till the required area is covered.

FIG. 15   PADDING STITCH

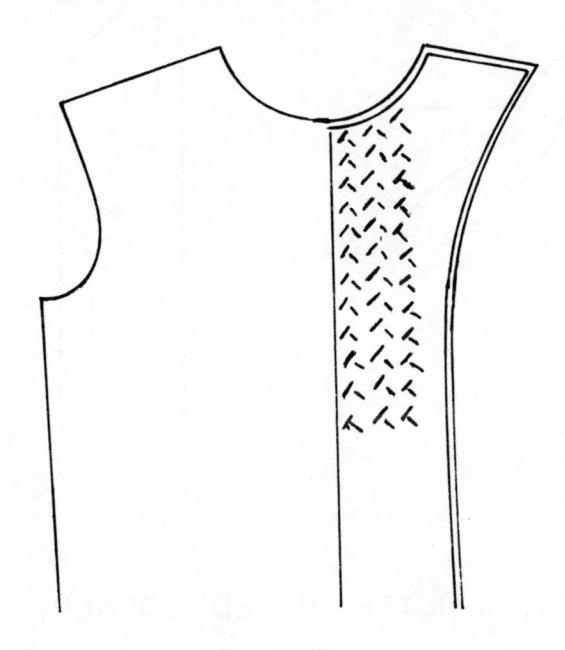

Mitring

Bound corners have excess fabric which has to be mitered with a diagonal seam at the corner and taking up the excess fabric in the seam. This method is used while joining borders for blankets or attaching borders, braid or lace around saris, table cloth etc. The folded portion may be cut off to avoid bulk. A different method is used when the border extends beyond the cloth and has to be folded back onto the seam line. Two darts are taken, both tapering to the fold line. (Figs. 16a, 16b)

Bar-tacks

Bar-tacks are decorative thread reinforcements used on the right side of the garment at the ends of pockets and pleats. (Fig. 17)

Tacking Arrowheads

Also called **Sprattshead** is an embroidered triangle worked in tacking stitch and shaped like an arrowhead. These are used as an ornamental finish at the ends of pockets or at the

INNER MITRED CORNER
FIG.- 16a

OUTER MITRED CORNER
FIG.- 16b

WRONG SIDE

RIGHT SIDE

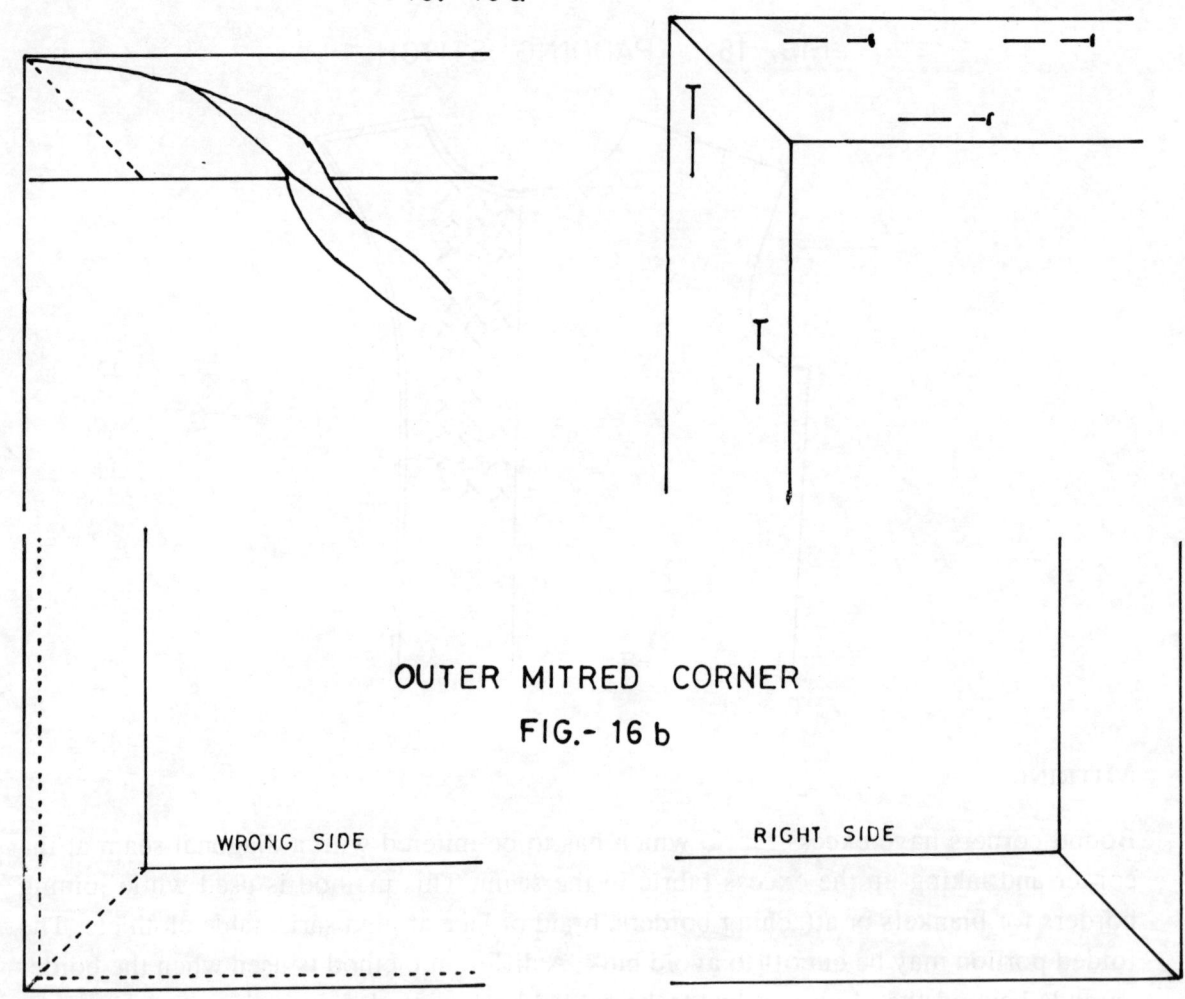

FIG. 17 BARTACKS

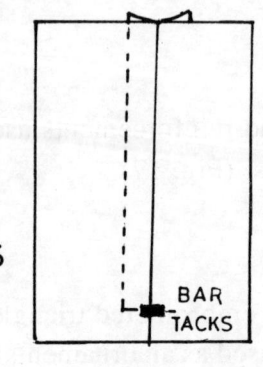

BAR TACKS

points where the pleat ceases to be stitched down. It is worked by marking a triangle 1.5 centimetres high. Starting at the lower left hand corner, the thread is brought through from below at that point. Take a small stitch across the top tip of the triangle with the needle pointed to the left. Carry the thread diagonally down to the lower right hand corner and from there, take a long stitch back to the starting point. Repeat working in the same way inside the previous stitch and continue till the triangle is filled up. (Fig. 18)

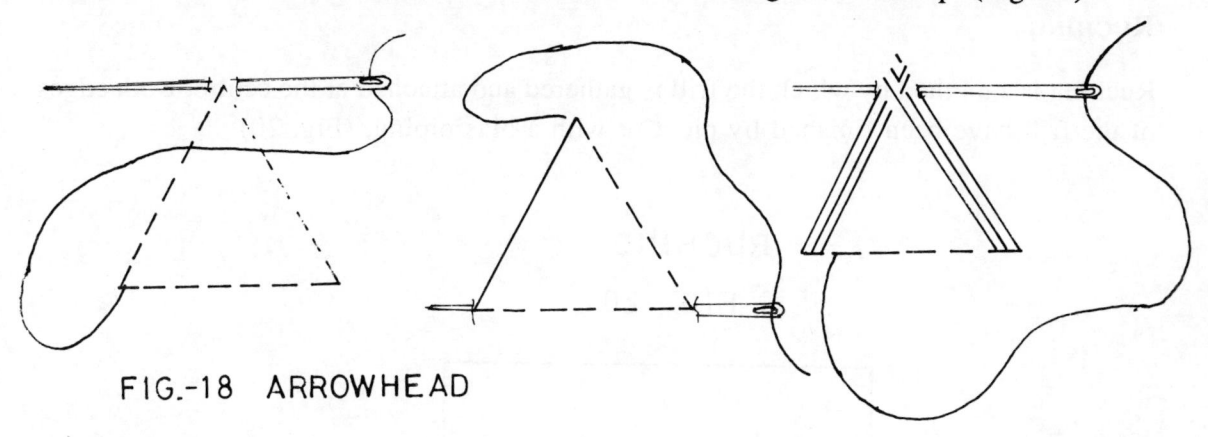

FIG.-18 ARROWHEAD

Belt Carriers

Belt carriers hold the belt across at the required position. The carrier is made by taking the threads across the required length three times and then working in buttonhole stitch from one end to the other. Use double thread for thickness. (Fig. 19a)

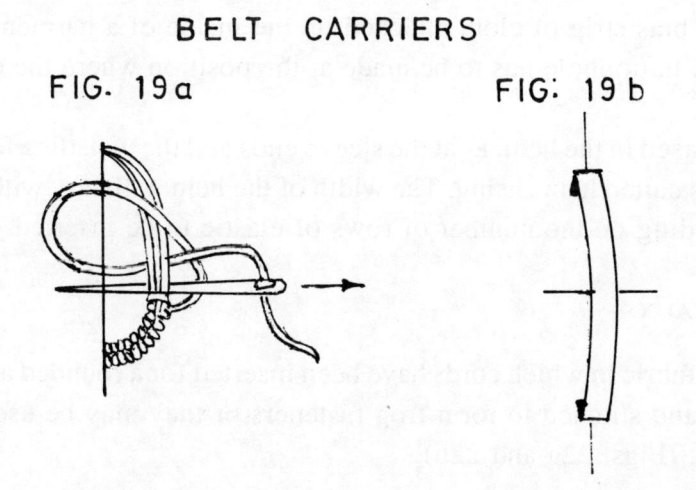

BELT CARRIERS

FIG. 19a   FIG. 19b

Belt carriers can also be made with the same fabric as that of the garment. Cut a strip of cloth three centimetres wide, take a seam on the 0.5 marking and turn the strip inside out. The finished width of the belt carrier will be 1.0 centimetre. The length of the carrier should be 1.0 centimetre more than the width of the belt for ease in sliding the belt through. (Fig. 19b)

Ruching

Ruching is a method by which the frill is gathered and attached at the centre. Both edges of the frill have been finished by picot or with a bias piping. (Fig. 20)

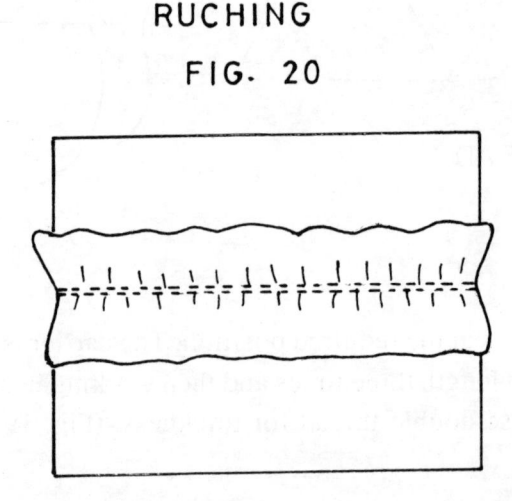

RUCHING

FIG. 20

Casing

Casing is a straight or bias strip of cloth attached on the inside of a garment to encase tape, cord or elastic. A buttonhole has to be made at the position where the cord has to be drawn out and tied.

When elastic is encased in the hem, as at the sleeve ends and the waistline for trousers, skirts and pyjamas, it is called hem casing. The width of the hem will vary with the width of the elastic or depending on the number of rows of elastic to be inserted. (Fig. 21)

Rouleau or Rouleaux

These are fine tubes of fabric in which cords have been inserted for a rounded appearance. These may be shaped and stitched to form frog fasteners or they may be used as cords that are laced and tied. (Figs. 22a and 22b)

The Art of Sewing

FIG. 21   CASING

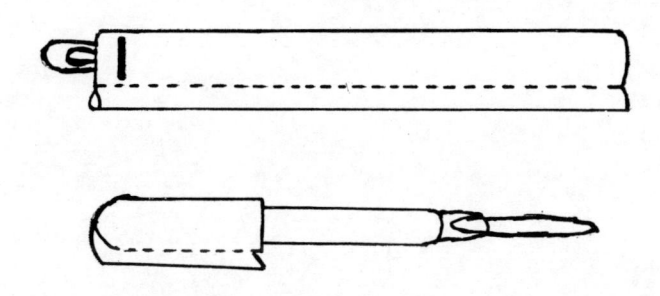

FIG. 22   ROULEAU

(a) FROG   (b) TIE STRING

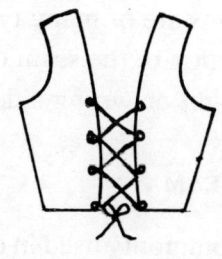

Seams and Seam Finishes

A seam is a line of stitching given to join two or more pieces of fabric or sections of a garment. It is used to give strength to a garment and also as a form of decoration. The width of the seam allowance is dependant on the type of fabric and the type of seam to be constructed. The width should be sufficient to avoid fraying and yet not too wide as to appear bulky.

There are two types of basic seams : enclosed and structural seams. Enclosed seams are not visible since they are enclosed between two layers of fabric. For example, the inside seams of collars and cuffs. Structural seams join the main garment sections together such as the side seams, attachment of sleeves to the bodice and bodice to the skirt. Structural seams are of many types and may be selected to suit the fabric, the kind of garment, the position of the seam on the garment and depending on whether the seam is stitched on the right or wrong side of the garment.

Flat or Plain Seam

This seam is most commonly used in dressmaking. The seam allowance is turned to either side and pressed flat. The seam edges may be cut with pinking shears or finished by overcasting or zig zag edge stitching to prevent ravelling. The seams at the armsyce and waistline are turned in one direction and hence both edges may be finished together. (Fig. 23)

FIG.-23 FLAT OR PLAIN SEAM

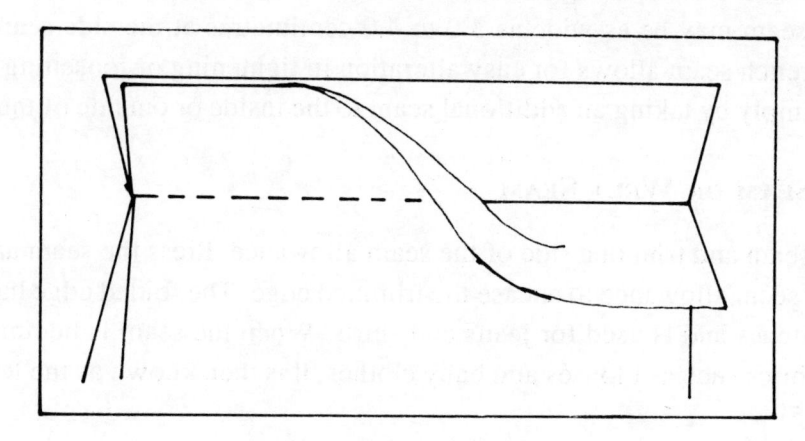

FRENCH SEAM

Make a plain seam on the right side of the fabric at a distance of 0.5 centimetres from the edge of the fabric. The seam is then pressed to one side, turned over to the wrong side of the fabric and then machined at a distance of 1.0 centimetre or at the actual seam line. The first seam is thus enclosed by the second seam line. (Fig. 24)

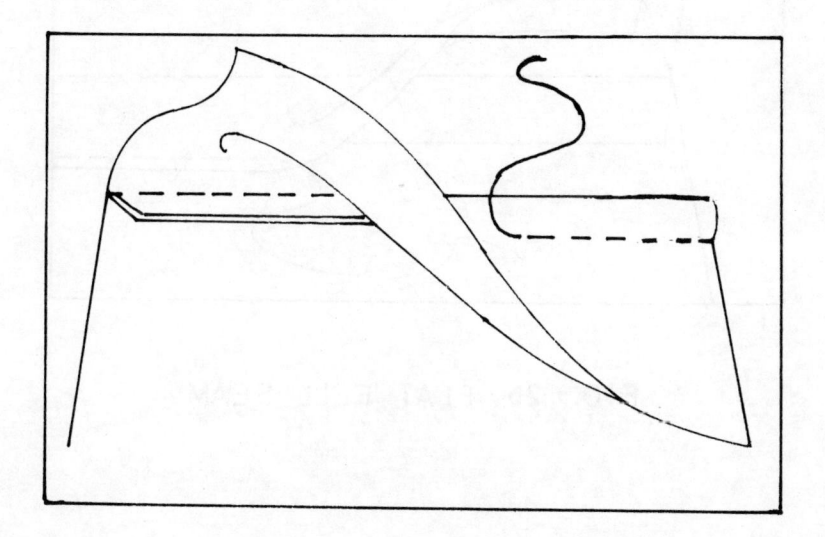

FIG.-24 FRENCH SEAM

A French seam can be narrow and used as a finish for children's clothes and also for sheer fabrics such as voiles and organdie. French seams which are to be pressed flat are turned towards the back of the garment.

A French seam may be as wide as 3.0 to 4.0 centimetres at the side seam for a sari blouse. The French seam allows for easy alteration in tightening or loosening a garment. This is done simply by taking an additional seam to the inside or outside of the seam line.

FLAT FELL SEAM OR WELT SEAM

Make a plain seam and trim one side of the seam allowance. Press the seam and turn and fold the larger seam allowance to encase the trimmed edge. The folded edge has two rows of machine stitches and is used for jeans and shirts. When the seam is hemmed in place for delicate fabrics such as blouses and baby clothes, it is then known as the Run and Fell Seam. (Fig. 25)

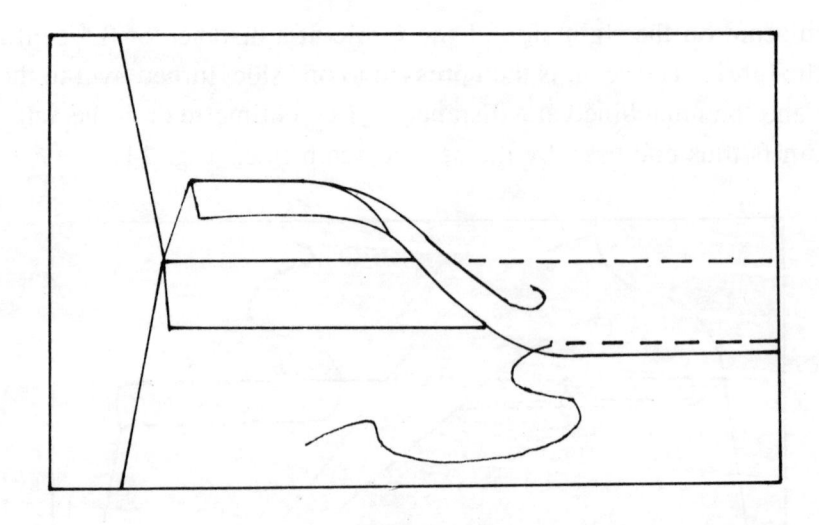

FIG.- 25 FLAT FELL SEAM

When the fabric is very thick and does not ravel, the seam allowance is not folded but simply pressed to one side and machined at a distance of 0.5 or 1.0 centimetre from the seamline. This seam is known as the single channel seam.

Double Channel Seam

It is used to attach lace or a strip of fabric in between the skirt, either as a design feature or to add length to the garment. This lace is known as insertion lace and has fabric on both edges onto which the garment sections are folded and attached. The strip of fabric to be inserted may be of a contrasting colour, printed, or decorated with embroidery or pin tucks. (Fig. 26)

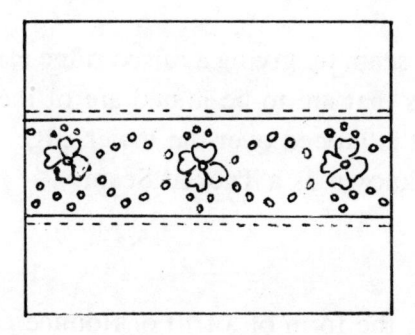

FIG. 26 DOUBLE CHANNEL SEAM

Shaped Seam

It is used while attaching shaped or decorative facings onto the right side of the garment. The seam allowances are trimmed and tapered at the centre of points and at corners. Baste the facing or yoke onto the garment and machine at the edge, taking care to stitch the points and corners neatly. (Fig. 27)

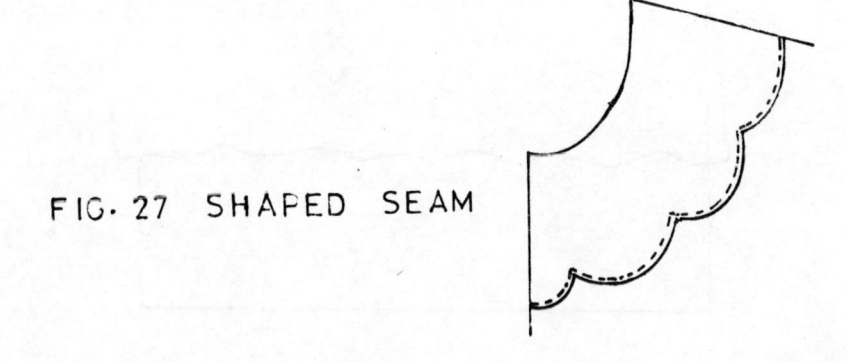

FIG. 27 SHAPED SEAM

When the shaped or decorative yoke is attached to a gathered portion of the garment, it is machined from the wrong side. The yoke should be lined when it is not heavy enough to hold the weight of the gathered section. While joining the lining, all three layers of fabric may be machined together, enclosing the gathered seam in between. If the yoke is attached to the lining at the neck edge, the lining is then hemmed down at the seam that joins the yoke to the gathers.

Lapped Seam

This adds emphasis to the seam by giving a raised ridge effect, useful when the yoke and dress, or any two sections that are to be joined are of the same colour and fabric. The upper part of the garment is lapped over the lower edge. When the lap is wide, giving the effect of a tuck, it is known as a Tucked Seam.

Mantua Seam

It is used to attach lace in the form of a frill or flounce on sheer fabrics. Fold the hem of the dress or the sleeve edge onto the gathered edge of the lace, baste and machine along the edge of the fold. The raw edges of the lace and hem may be finished with a bias binding or bias facing (Fig. 28)

FIG. 28   MANTUA SEAM

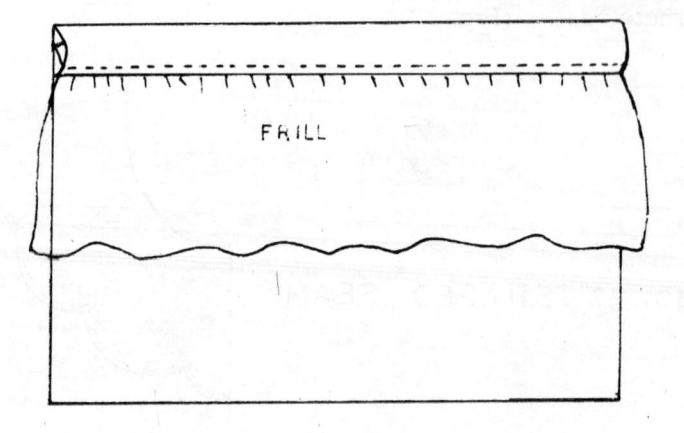

Bound Seam

The seam edges are bound by a bias strip of a thinner fabric to keep the seam from fraying without adding bulk. This is used on heavy garments which are not lined and on the seams of cushions or sofa covers.

Crossed or Intersecting Seam

When two seams intersect at a point it is known as an Intersecting Seam. The seam that joins and front the back of a trouser, salwar or pyjamas at the crotch is an example of such a seam. If the two seams are French seams, care must be taken to match the seam widths.

Piped or Corded Seam

Piped or corded seams are those where a narrow fold of bias binding is inserted in a seam to give emphasis. A cord may be passed in between the binding to give a rounded appearance.

Faggot Seam

Here two finished edges are joined by a bar stitch or herringbone stitch. The edges are tacked onto a piece of paper to keep them at an equal distance. The paper may be pulled away after the seams have been joined by the decorative stitch. This seam is used when an extra width of fabric is added onto bed-covers or table clothes; it is also used as a form of decoration on sleeves and between panels on skirts etc. (Fig. 29)

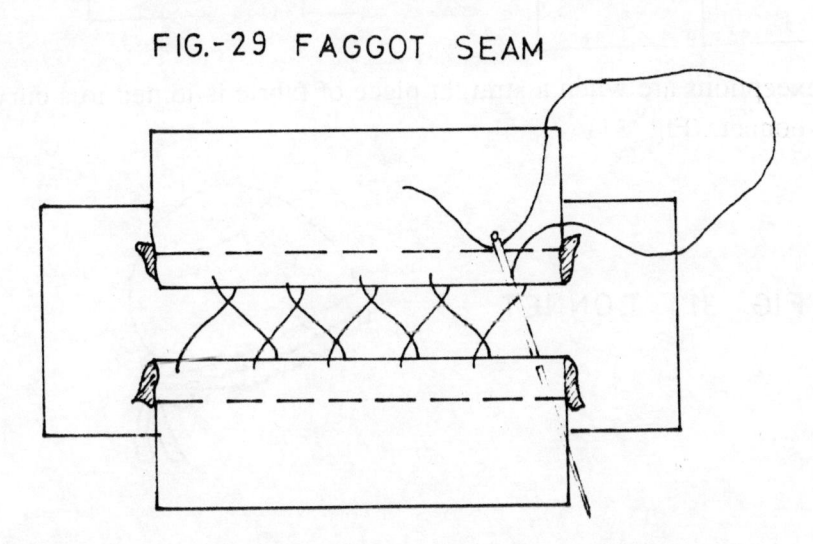

FIG.-29 FAGGOT SEAM

Rolled Seam

This seam is used for garments made of transparent materials where an ordinary seam would look clumsy when seen through. Make a plain seam, trim one side of the seam allowance, then with the thumb and first finger roll the wider seam allowance over the trimmed one almost to the sewing line. This may be then finished with top sewing.

Slot Seam

This is decorative seam and may be used while adding extra length to a garment. It is similar to a Channel Seam but the stitch is taken a little away from the edge.

Seams are usually of equal length and shape. (Fig. 30)

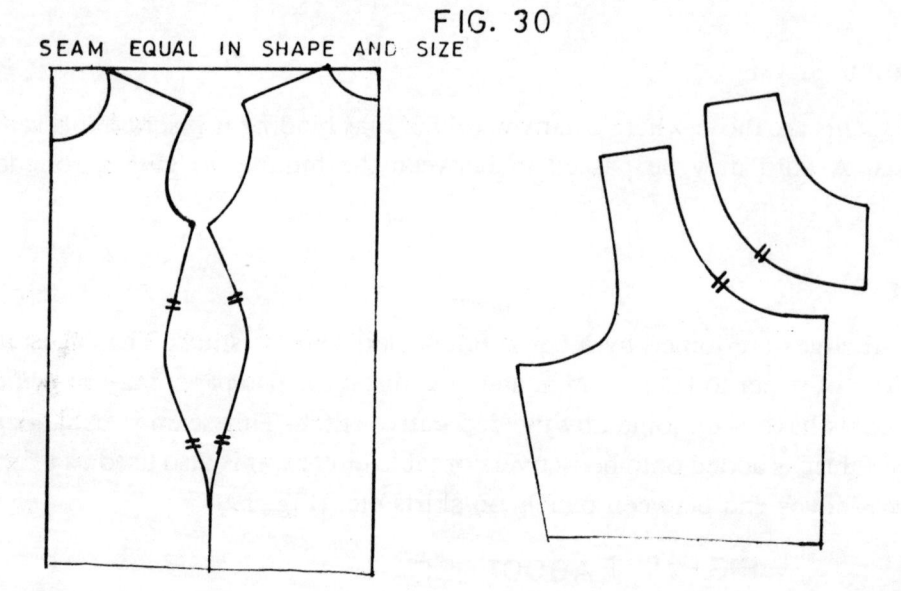

FIG. 30
SEAM EQUAL IN SHAPE AND SIZE

The exceptions are when a straight piece of fabric is joined to a curved piece as for a baby's bonnet. (Fig. 31)

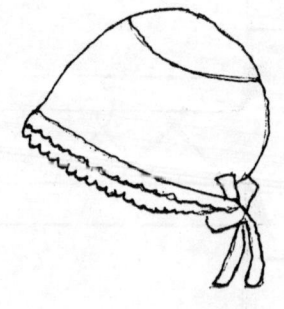

FIG. 31 BONNET

The Art of Sewing

When seams are not of equal length they have to be eased, gathered or pleated. (Figs. 31a, 31b)

FIG. 31 a GATHERED TO FIT INTO A PIPING, BAND OR A SECTION OF THE GARMENT

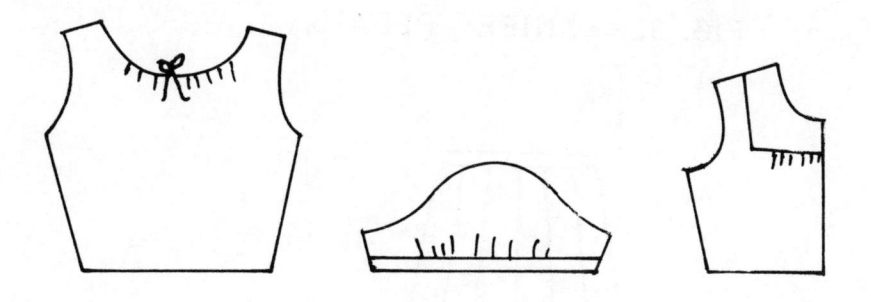

FIG. 31 b SLEEVE EASED INTO SMALLER ARMHOLE

Eased: A plain sleeve is always cut two to three centimetres larger than the bodice armsyce. The sleeve then has to be eased to fit into the smaller curve.

Gathered: A piece that has to be gathered to fit another section of the garment may be three times wider as in the case of skirts or only a few centimetres wider for yokes or a gathered neckline. The gathers have to be pulled to match the section to which it is to be attached.

Pleated: Pleats are folds taken in the fabric to control fullness. The amount of fabric required is calculated according to the type of pleats, the number of pleats, the depth of each pleat, the distance between each pleat and the width of the garment section within which the pleats are to be attachd. **Knife Pleats or Accordion Pleats** are folds of cloth, faced in one direction and with an equal distance between each pleat. The amount of fabric taken into the fold gives the depth of the pleat. If the width of the pleat is 4.0 centimetres, the amount taken in the fold should be 8.0 centimetres. Thus the total amount of fabric required for one knife pleat would be 12.0 centimetres. The distance between the pleats and the amount allowed for each fold can be adjusted according to the amount of fabric available. (Fig. 32)

Sunburst pleats are similar to knife pleats but are narrow at the waist and wider at the hem

FIG. 32   KNIFE PLEATS

The Box Pleat is folded back at both sides to meet at the centre line of the pleat on the under side. If the width of the box pleat is 4.0 centimetres, the amount folded is 4.0 centimetres on either side, making the total amount 12.0 centimetres of a single box pleat. (Fig. 33)

FIG. 33   BOX PLEAT

The Inverted Pleat is the reverse of the Box Pleat and requires the same amount of fabric. To form an Inverted Pleat mark a point and fold two Knife Pleats on either side, turning the folded edge towards the marked point. (Fig. 34)

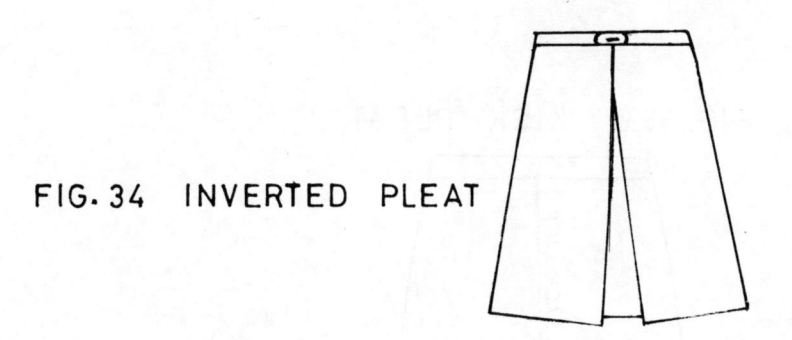

FIG. 34 INVERTED PLEAT

All pleats may be stitched down to a point to give emphasis. Pleats are often combined for interesting design variation. (Fig. 35)

FIG. 35 COMBINATION OF PLEATS

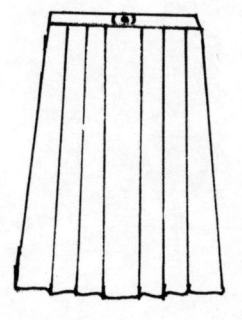

The Kick Pleat is often used on tight skirts, at the centre back seam to allow for freedom of movement - thus its name. A Kick Pleat is about 20.0 centimetres in length and is cut as an extension of the centre back seamline. The allowance for the pleat should be about 16.0 centimetres. (Fig. 35a)

FIG. 35a KICK PLEAT

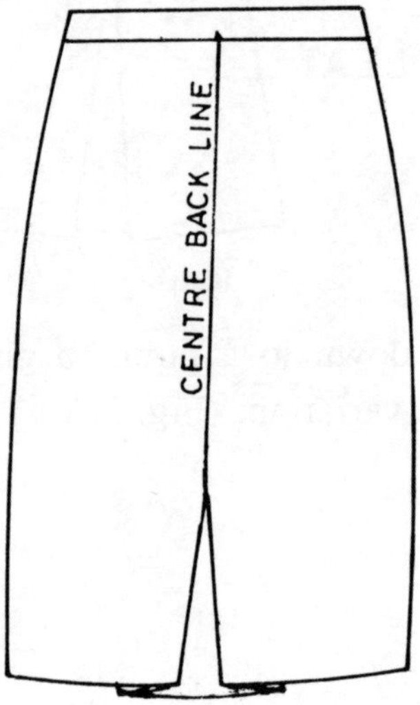

NECKLINE FINISHES

The neckline finish is of vital importance for the final appearance of the garment. Neckline are generally curved and hence tend to stretch during handling. A stretched neckline can spoil the appearance of the garment and should therefore be avoided, taking the utmost care. Work a row of stay — stitching at a distance of 0.5 centimetre from the edge of the neckline to prevent stretching (Fig. 36).

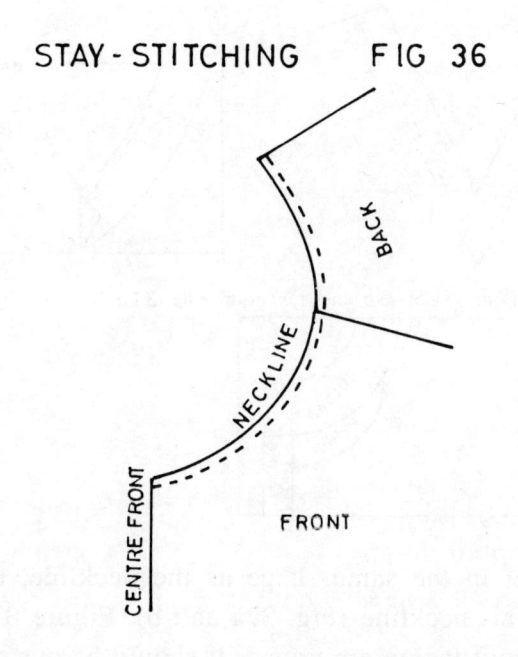

STAY-STITCHING   FIG 36

A neckline may be finished with a facing, a binding a frill or a collar.

FACINGS

The Fitted or Shaped Facing (Fig. 37)

NECKLINE SHOWING SHAPED FACING
FIG 37

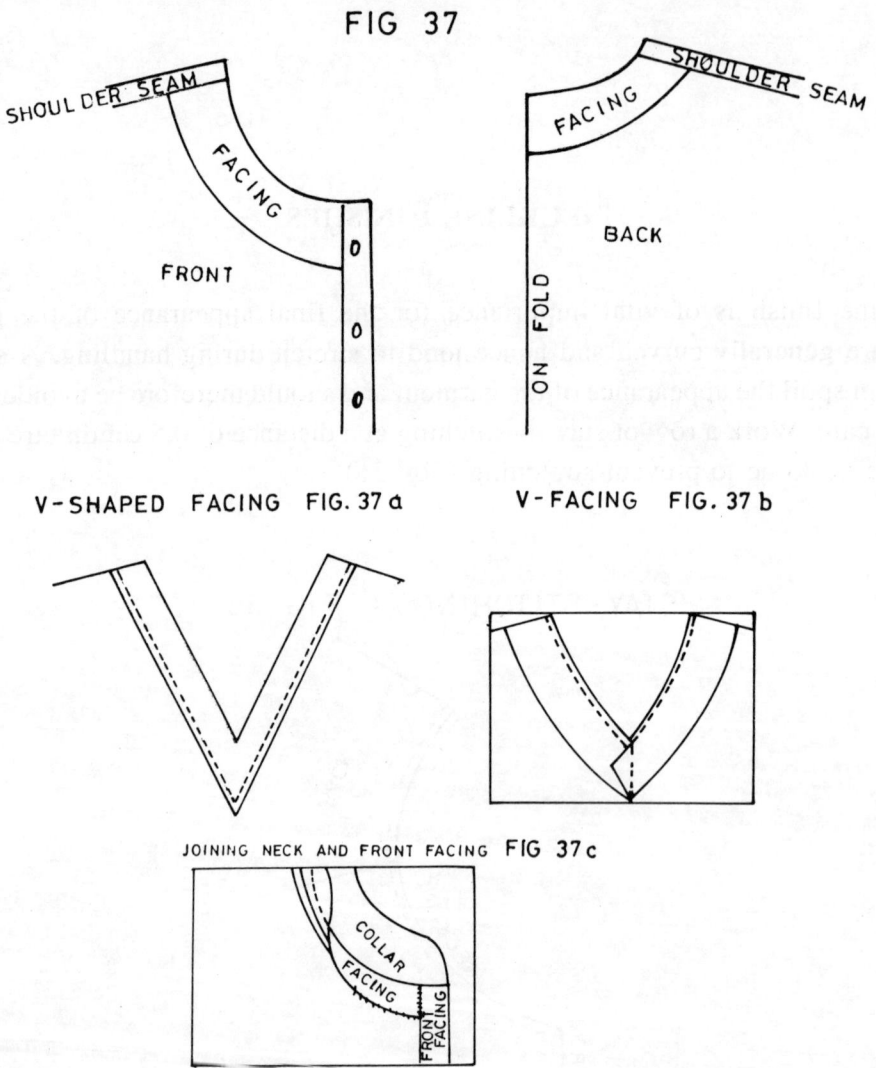

(SHOULDER SEAM — FACING — FRONT)
(FACING — SHOULDER SEAM — BACK — ON FOLD)

V-SHAPED FACING FIG. 37 a   **V-FACING FIG. 37 b**

JOINING NECK AND FRONT FACING FIG 37 c

(COLLAR FACING / FRONT FACING)

The fitted facing is cut in the same shape as the neckline, be it square, V-shaped, Scalloped or a sweetheart neckline (Fig. 37a and b). Figure 37c shows how the neck facing and the centre front facing are joined. It should be cut on the same grain as the edge to be faced to enable it to lie smoothly. A fitted facing is usually about 4 to 5 centimetres wide and is cut evenly all around.

The seam allowance should be the same for the garment and the facing. Join the seams of the facing and also that of the garment sections separately. Pin both the garment and facing, keeping right sides together, matching them at the shoulder seam, centre front and centre back. After pinning into position, baste and then machine along the seamline. Make notches on the neck edge, cut a V-shaped notch at the corners, almost upto the seam, taking care not to clip the machine stitches. Turn the facing to the wrong side of the garment, press well and baste, making sure that the seam line is not visible from the right side of the garment. While working with light-weight fabrics the fitted facing may be hemmed.

For medium-weight fabrics the edge of the facing is folded and machined. The facing is then held in place with catch stitches. Very wide facings are caught down only at the seams. For heavy fabrics, the edge of the facing should be finished with zig zag stitches to avoid bulk. These are then attached at the seams with catch stitches. The facing for heavy fabrics may be cut from a light-weight fabric of the same colour. A shaped facing can also be used at armholes and for shaped hemlines. The neckline and armholes may be faced with a combined facing (Fig. 38).

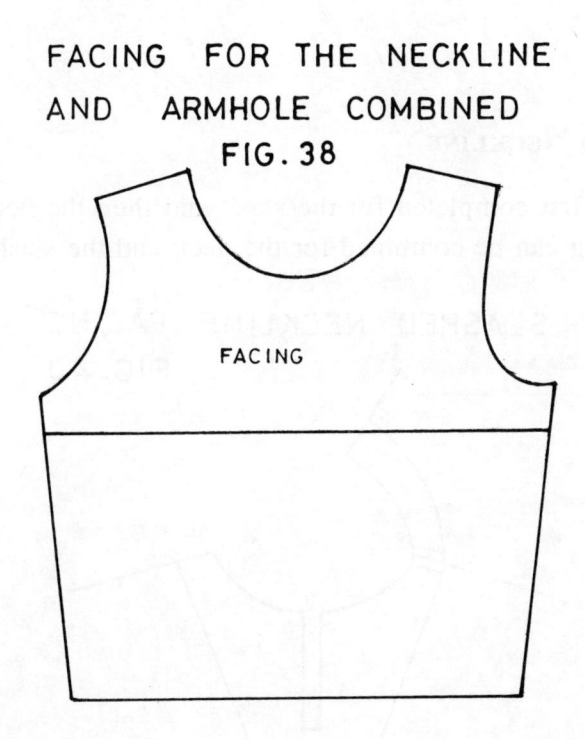

FACING FOR THE NECKLINE AND ARMHOLE COMBINED
FIG. 38

All-in-one Facing

This is cut as an extension of the garment and used for both the shawl collar and the convertible collar.

The centre front line of the garment is extended by 2.0 centimetres. Place on a fold of fabric, mark the shape of the neck and half the shoulder line. Shape the facing from the shoulder to the waistline as shown. The facing is joined to the shoulder seam, or attached to the back neck facing. (Figs. 39a, 39b)

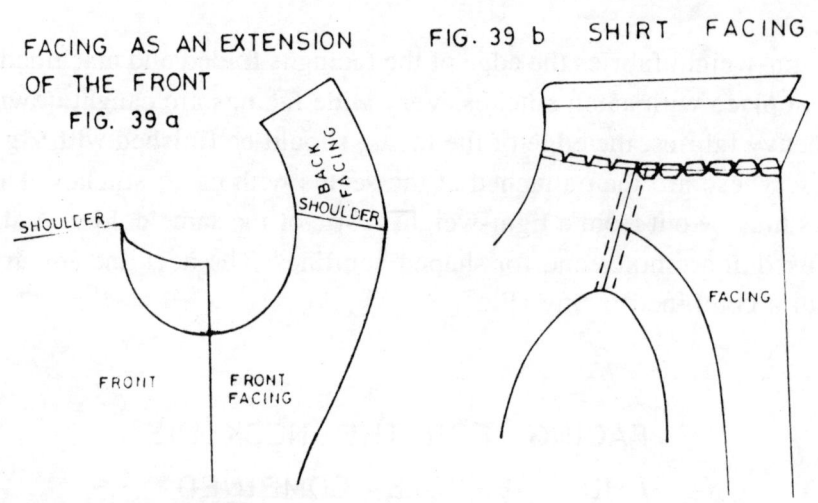

FACING AS AN EXTENSION OF THE FRONT
FIG. 39 a

FIG. 39 b   SHIRT FACING

FACING A SLASHED NECKLINE

The facing may be first completed for the slash and then the neckline facing may be attached or the facing can be combined for the neck and the slash. (Fig. 40)

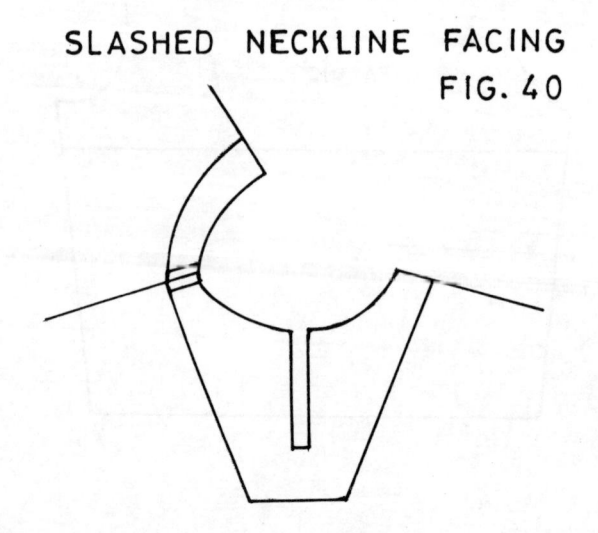

SLASHED NECKLINE FACING
FIG. 40

The Art of Sewing

Bias

A true bias falls on a diagonal line halfway between two grain lines at an angle of 45°. Fold a piece of fabric such that the lengthwise threads when folded fall in the direction of the crosswise threads. This fold line will be a true bias. Mark an even width of bias on either side of the fold line and cut out the bias strips. The ends of each bias strip have to be cut along the grain line. To do this, pull out a thread at each end and cut along the line from which the thread was pulled out to ensure that each strip is a true bias. It is very essential that the width of the bias strips are even all through its length, otherwise joining the strips would not only be difficult but would not result in a smooth, straight strip. Never try to make the width equal after the strips have been cut as it will continue to be irregular. (Figs. 41, 41a)

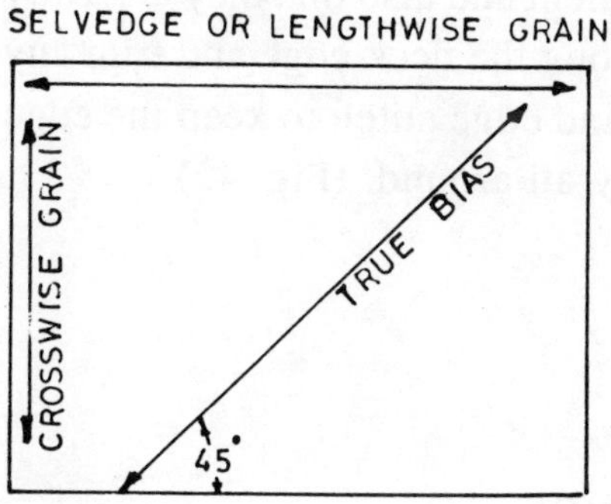

SELVEDGE OR LENGTHWISE GRAIN   FIG 41

FIG 41 b

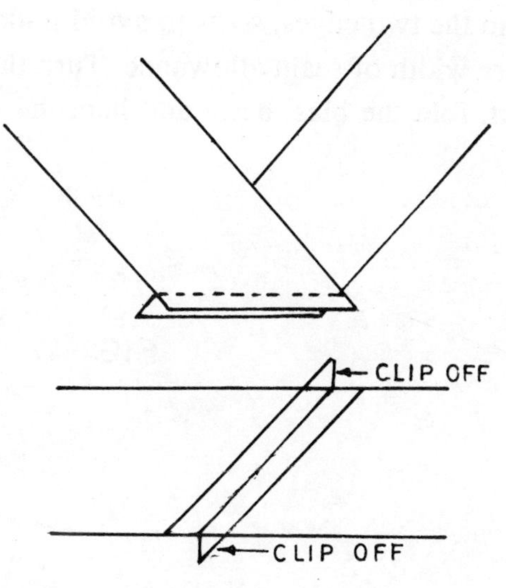

FIG 41 a

PULL THREAD AND CUT ALONG THE LINE

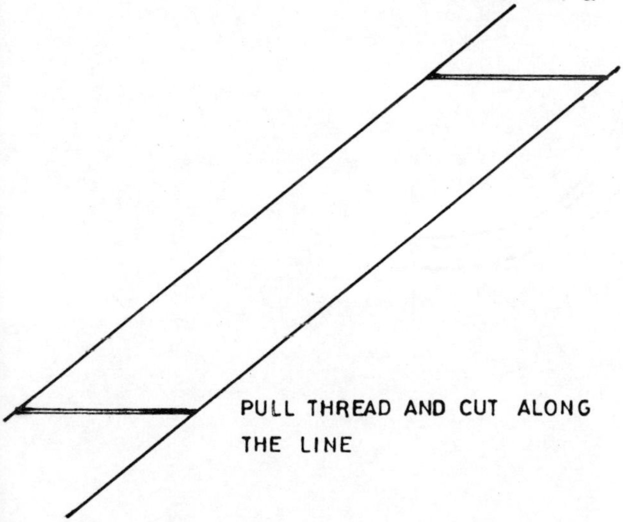

FIG. 41 c

JOINING ENDS OF BIAS FACING OR PIPING

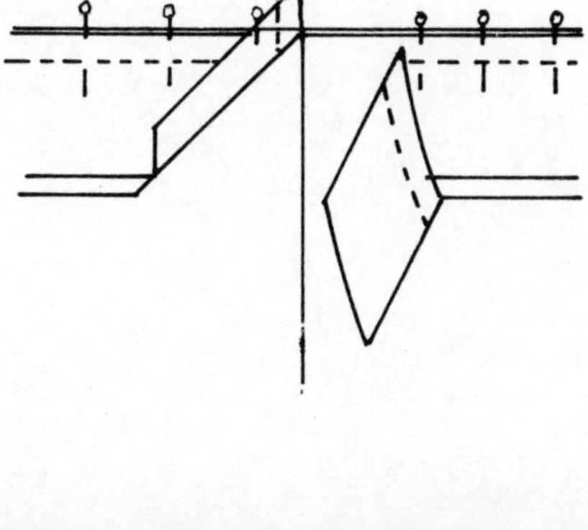

Place two strips of bias as shown in the diagram (Fig. 41b). The triangles that extend at both ends should be of equal size. Baste from one corner to the other and then machine along the same line. The machine threads are then tied together at the two ends. Press open the seams, clip off extra threads and the triangular ends. The bias binding is then ready for use.

Fig. 41c shows how the two ends of a bias facing or piping are joined after it has been attached onto the garment.

The Bias Facing: The bias strip is turned in completely as a facing. A bias facing is narrower than the shaped facing and is usually not more than 2.0 centimetres wide.

The narrower the width of a bias, the better it can take the shape of the neckline curve. While attaching the bias facing, make sure to ease the bias onto the neck edge because the bias has to rest flat onto a wider curve when folded back. Take care that the seams of the bias strip do not coincide with the seams on the garment and also that they are away from the two edges, so as to avoid bulk. Make slashes along the neck edge and trim any extra width of seam allowance. Turn the bias out, press and edge stitch to keep the edge neat, fold the bias, baste and hem the bias facing evenly all around. (Fig. 42)

FIG. 42 BIAS FACING

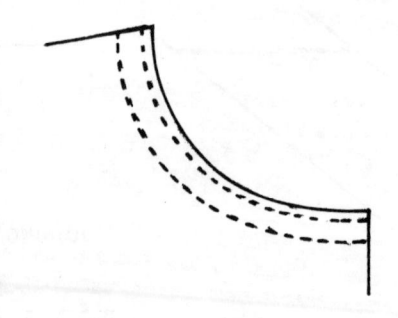

The Bias Binding: The bias binding extends beyond the neckline. While attaching the bias strip for a binding, pull the bias slightly at the edge to be attached. The piping has to be eased slightly while attaching it to an outside curve such as a flared hem. It is advisable to first baste the bias before machining. The finished width of a bias binding is normally less than 0.5 centimetre but it may be wider to give emphasis when a contrasting colour or print is used. For narrow bindings, cut the bias strip 2.5 centimetres wide and trim off 0.5 after machining. Then fold the bias into half and then to a quarter for the width to give a narrow, rounded look. A French binding is cut twice the width of an ordinary bias, then folded into half and pressed. This is then attached so that both the raw edges are at the neck edge, ensuring evenness all through. Since the raw edges have been taken care of, this bias binding can be folded over a little beyond the seam line and machined from the right side of the garment at a point just below the seam line. A cord may be inserted to give the piping a rounded finish. (Fig. 43)

FIG. 43   BIAS   BINDING

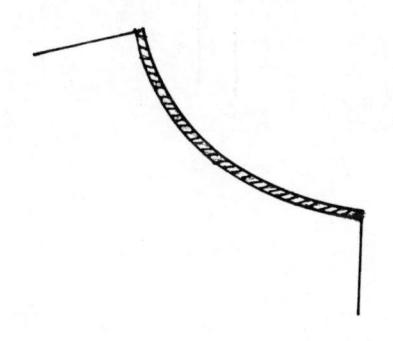

Fitting Bias Binding At Right Angle Corners: When fitting a bias binding at a square or right angle corner, the bias is attached upto the corner, the presser foot is then lifted leaving the needle in the fabric. The fabric is turned and an allowance for an extra fold of the bias is made at the corner (as shown in the previous chapter under "Mitre" in Fig. 44) before machining along the second side.

FIG. 44   MITRE   BINDING

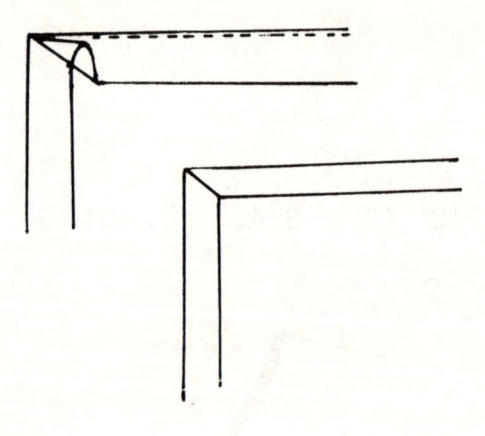

LININGS AND INTERFACINGS

LINING

This is the fabric attached on the inside of the garment. Lining is applied on transparent fabric to give it thickness. It may be applied on fabrics like silk or brocade to give strength at the seams and on wool and organdie which are uncomfortable when in direct contact with the skin. Lining fabrics are generally of mulmul, voile, cambric, satin and taffeta. All lining fabrics should be pre-shrunk and tested for colour fastness. Mulmul is generally used for lining and is available in 45" width. Cambric may be used to line silk and brocade. Satin and taffeta are used to line coats; and skirts are lined with cambric or taffeta.

Lining for skirts, coats and jackets: The outer garment is made up separately and so also the lining sections. These are then put together with the wrong sides facing, so that raw edges and seams are not visible. The coat or jacket may be attached to the lining at the neckline, with the collar inserted into the seam. The jacket hem and the fold of the sleeves are turned up and hemmed onto the lining.

The skirt sections and lining sections are made up separately. These are then turned with the wrong sides facing and then attached together at the waist by a waistband. The hemline of the lining should be about 2.0 centimetres shorter than that of the skirt. (Fig. 45)

FIG. 45 LINING SKIRTS

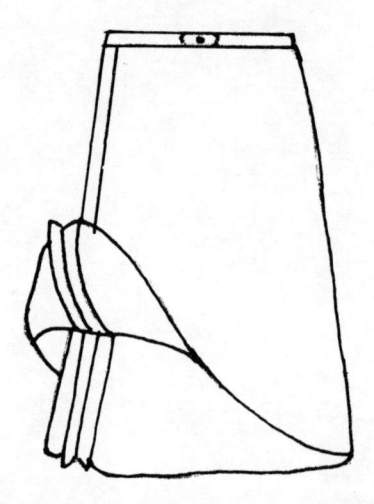

Lining for dresses and sari blouses: Cut out all the garment sections, and baste these onto the pre-shrunk lining. All markings, such as the darts and seam lines, should be marked on the lining fabric. Tack along the dart markings so that the lining does not move when the darts are folded and stitched. Cut out the lining along the same lines as the garment sections. The two layers are then considered as one and made up in the usual manner. (Fig. 46)

FIG. 46 LINING OF BLOUSE

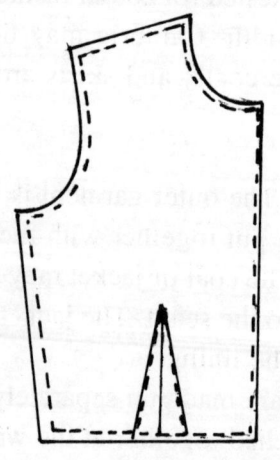

INTERFACINGS

An interfacing is an extra piece of fabric attached between the garment and the lining or the facings. Interfacings are applied to give strength, shape and stiffness to collars, cuffs, plackets, belts, pocket flaps and the salwar "pauncha". An interfacing may be cut on the bias when used on parts of the garment that need to stretch. Interfacings are cut without seam allowance because it is not pliable and will add to the bulk of the seam. The interfacing is basted onto the facing or lining and held in place by the top stitching after it has been turned back. (Fig. 47)

FIG. 47 ATTACHING AN INTERFACING

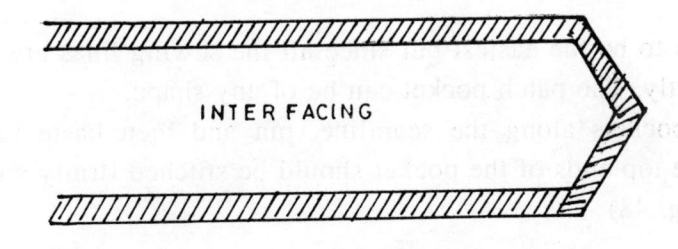

Buckram is the most commonly used interfacing. It should be closely woven so that it does not shrink on wash. Apart from buckram, the interfacings available are:

Non-woven interfacings used for soft collars.

Fusible interfacings which are ironed on and are easy to handle.

Hair canvas which is heavy cotton with hair added in the weave.

Organdie can be used as interfacing for light-weight fabrics such as net and lace.

Nylon net is washable and retains most of its crispness, useful for children's clothes. It may be attached only inside the hem-fold to hold out the flare in the skirt.

POCKETS

Pockets are useful as well as decorative, especially on children's clothing. Pockets should be finished before the garment is made up, except for the patch pocket, which may be pinned on to check its position. Children love large decorative pockets but they should be in proportion to the size of the dress and, of course, the child. Placement of the pocket on the garment depends on whether the pocket is functional or decorative.

PATCH POCKET

This may seem to be the easiest but since all the sewing lines are visible it has to be attached perfectly. The patch pocket can be of any shape.

Press the pockets along the seamline, pin and then baste into position before machining. The top ends of the pocket should be stitched firmly with a double row of machining. (Fig. 48)

FIG.48 POCKET REINFORCE

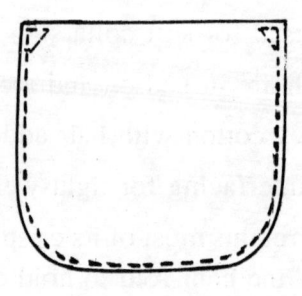

The Art of Sewing

WELT OR SLASH POCKET

This is cut in a straight or slant line at any angle as per the design. It may be finished with a wide or narrow band, a flap or a binding.

Mark the pocket line and place a fabric around it on the right side of the garment. Tack the fabric in position and machine at a distance of 0.25 centimetre all around the marked line. Slit along the pocket line and make slashes at the two corners almost upto the seam line. Now turn the pocket fabric inside press the ends of the pocket neatly and machine along the edge. The edge of the pocket opening can be finished with a bias binding or a welt or a flap. The flap is attached to the upper seam of the pocket opening.

The welt is attached to the lower seam of the pocket. It can be about 2.0 to 3.0 centimetres wide and should extend slightly beyond both ends of the pocket opening. The two ends of the welt are turned in and machined onto the garment. (Fig. 49, 49a)

FIG. 49 ONE PIECE WELT POCKET

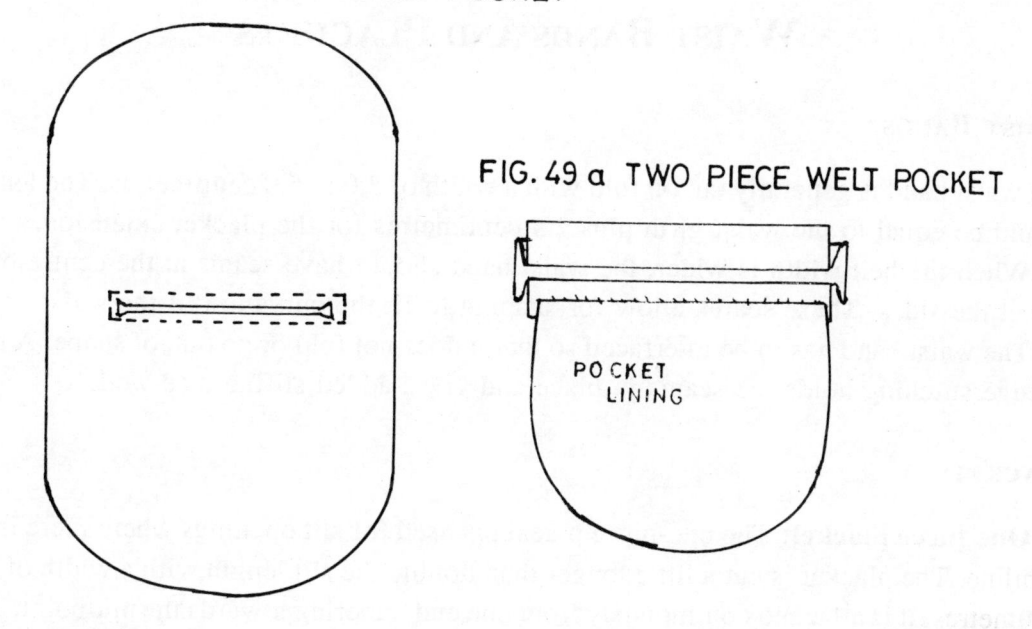

FIG. 49 a TWO PIECE WELT POCKET

POCKET LINING

SEAM POCKET

The seam pocket is attached along the seamline. A side seam pocket is used on kurtas, trousers and skirts. It is generally fixed about 5.0 centimetres below the waist band or at a distance that is convenient for the hand to reach. Lining fabric is used for the pocket. The pocket is cut in two pieces and one is attached to the front and the other to the back of the garment. The two pieces are then stitched together at the outer edge. The pocket has to be reinforced at the seam of the garment as it tends to rip open. (Fig. 50)

FIG. 50 SIDE SEAM POCKET

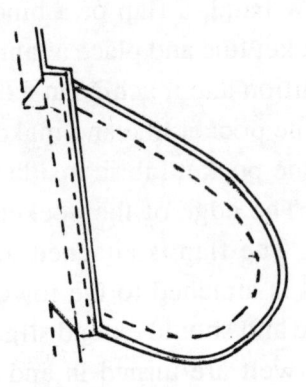

WAIST BANDS AND PLACKETS

WAIST BANDS

The waist band is generally cut on fold with a width of 3.0 to 5.0 centimetres. The length should be equal to the waist girth plus 2.5 centimetres for the placket extension.

When the belt width is wider, the waist band should have seams at the centre-back and at the sides. These seams allow for shaping to fit the curvature of the waist.

The waist band has to be interfaced so that it does not fold or go out of shape. A row of edge stitching holds the seams in place and gives added stiffness as well.

PLACKETS

One-piece placket: The one-piece placket is used for slit openings where there is no seamline. The placket is cut a little longer than double the slit length with a width of 6.0 centimetres. It is attached continouusly from one end, tapering towards the midpoint. The fabric is then turned by leaving the needle in the fabric and then machined to the other end. The placket piece is turned in fully on the side that overlaps and the underlap is folded back half its width keeping an extension of 2.5 centimetres. (Fig. 51)

Kurta or Blouse placket: The centre front line is slit to form the opening and may be 20.0 to 25.0 centimetres in length. The placket is cut in two pieces. The lower side placket piece is 6.0 centimetres wide and the top one about 8.0 or 9.0 centimetres wide,

The Art of Sewing

inclusive of seam allowances. The wider piece is attached on the right and the other on the left; both these are then folded into half and machined. The larger placket is then flattened to extend equally on either side of the seam line. The lower edge of the placket is folded into a V-shape and edge-machined. (Fig. 52a and b)

FIG. 51 WAIST BAND WITH ONE PIECE PLACKET

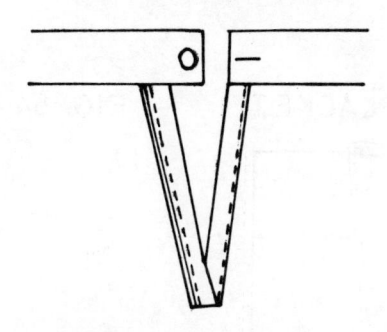

REAR SIDE VIEW

FIG. 52 a KURTA PLACKET RIGHT SIDE

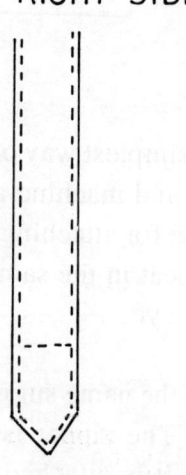

FIG. 52 b KURTA PLACKET WRONG SIDE

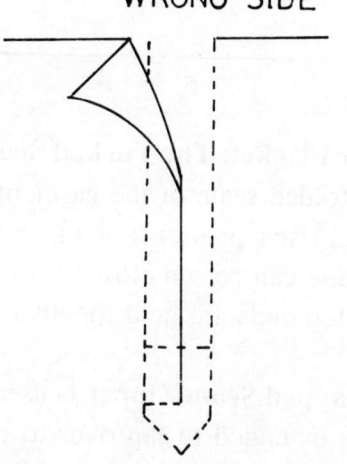

Two-piece placket: The two-piece placket is attached at the seam line. The right side placket piece is about 3.0 centimetres wide and is turned back fully and either machined or hemmed. The left side placket is 6.0 centimetres wide and is folded back half, letting it extend about 2.5 centimetres. The placket is then held in position by a double row of machining at the lower edge.

Placket for the shirt cuff: This placket is stitched with the right and left side plackets extended and overlapped. The top placket is held in place and machined, as shown in the diagram. (Fig. 53)

FIG. 53 TWO PIECE PLACKET

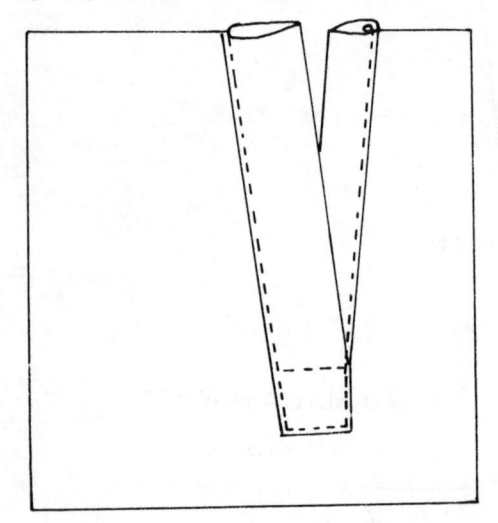

FIG. 54 ZIPPER PLACKET

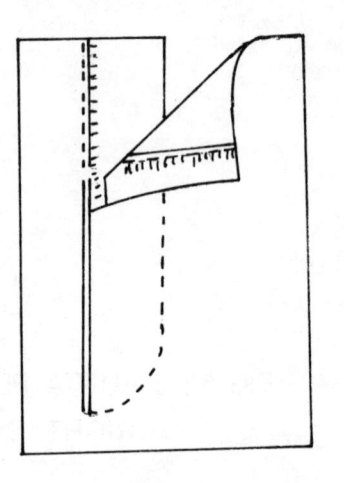

Zipper Placket: The Tucked Seam Zipper is the simplest way of attaching a zipper. Place the folded seam of the garment onto the zipper and machine as close to the edge as possible. Use a presser foot which is especially made for attaching zippers; it has only one edge and can be run close to the zipper edge. Repeat in the same way for the other side. The top ends are held together with a hook and eye.

The Lapped Seam Zipper is used for trousers. As the name suggests, one side of the opening is extended to lap over to cover the zipper. The zipper is attached about 2.0 centimetres away from the edge. On the lower side, it is attached at the seamline by simply folding the centre front onto the zipper edge. A zip guard is a fold of fabric which is attached on the underside so that the zipper does not come in contact with the body. (Fig. 54)

PREPARATION OF FABRIC BEFORE CUTTING

SHRINKING AND STRAIGHTENING OF FABRIC

Shrinking is necessary for all fabrics that do not have the Sanforized label. Soak the fabric overnight in a basin of water. Then squeeze the fabric and rinse in fresh water. Allow the water to drip and when almost dry, press along the lengthwise grain of the fabric.

    To straighten the fabric (Fig. 55) First clip at the selvedge and pull a weft thread which runs along the width of the fabric from selvedge to selvedge. Then cut along this line. Repeat for the other end of the fabric in the same way. Hold the short corners and pull the fabric diagonally. Hold the fabric in the stretched position for a few seconds. Repeat until the fabric is straight. (Fig. 55a)

CUTTING ALONG THE GRAINLINE **FIG. 55**

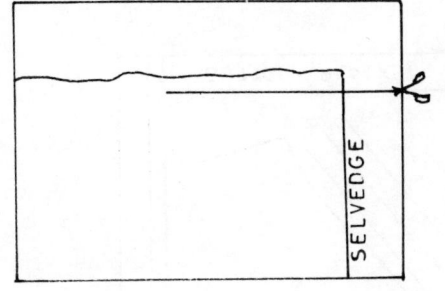

SNIP AT SELVEDGE AND PULL A THREAD, CUT ALONG THIS LINE TO ENSURE A STRAIGHT CUTTING LINE. REPEAT AT BOTH EDGES. THEN PULL THE SHORT ENDS AS SHOWN.

STRAIGHTENING THE FABRIC

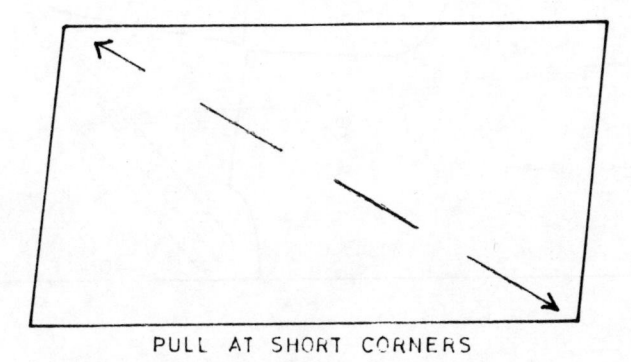

FIG. 55a

PULL AT SHORT CORNERS

The fabric grain is considered to be straight when the widthwise grainline is perpendicular to the selvedge. Fabrics with woven stripes or checks can be cut along the straight line without drawing the thread.

Placement, Marking and Cutting of Patterns

Begin by folding the fabric along the lengthwise grain, selvedge to selvedge, with the right sides of the fabric on the inside. This will ensure that fabric is marked on the wrong side.

Place the fabric onto the cutting table. Cutting tables are generally fitted with felt or flannel. When a cutting table is not available, use newspapers to pad the work surface so that the pins can be pushed in without having to worry about the table top.

FIGURE SHOWING PLACEMENT OF THE SARI BLOUSE

FIG. 56 a

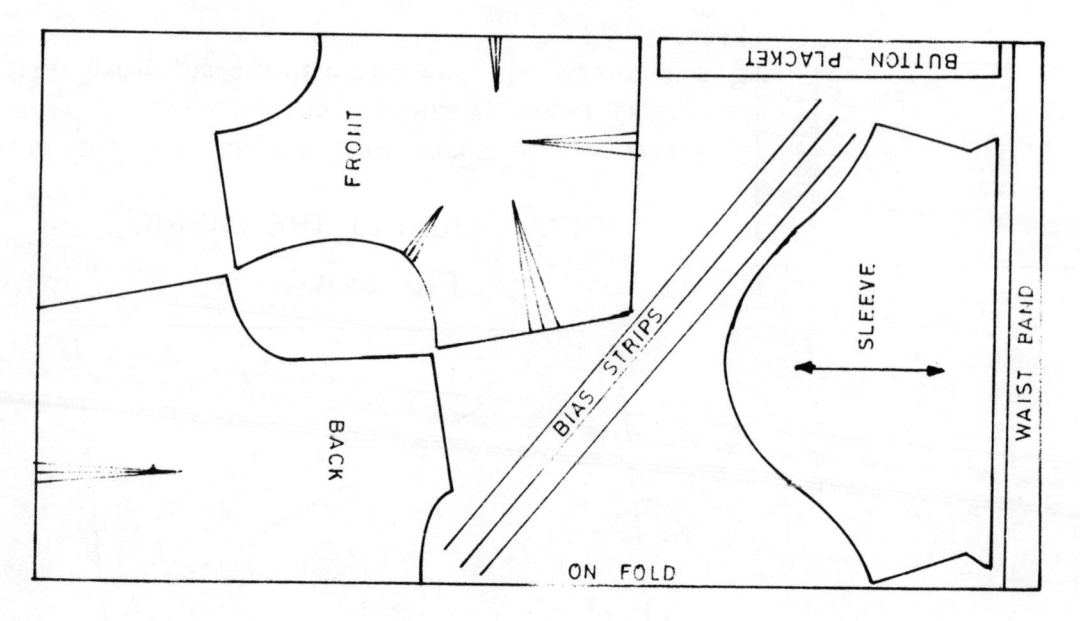

All the pattern pieces should be placed along the lengthwise grain of the fabric, parallel to the selvedge, as shown. (Fig. 56a and b). The pattern pieces that are to be cut on fold should be placed along the fold line of the fabric. If the fabric is insufficient, then the collar, cuffs and waistband sections may be placed on the widthwise grain of the fabric. Checks and stripes may be cut crosswise or diagonally in order to obtain variation in design.

When all the pattern pieces have been arranged to fit along the length of fabric, pin them in position. All markings should be transferred onto the fabric with the help of a tracing wheel and carbon paper. While marking on dark coloured fabric, a tailor's chalk or marking pencil of any pastel colour should be used. These markings rub off easily. Tailor's tack may be used on thick fabrics like wool, which cannot be easily marked. It may also be used for expensive fabrics like brocade, which too cannot be easily marked, and which should not be marred by the markings of the tracing wheel. Whereas an experienced seamstress can differentiate between the front and back of a sleeve, it is advisable for the beginner to mark every detail such as the centre-front line, placket lines, seam lines and the centre of the neck-line, etc. Accurate markings will enable ease and accuracy in sewing.

Once the markings are completed, the fabric is cut along the pattern outlines. Be sure to cut notches to mark fold lines, pleat widths, centre points on sleeves and of the neckline as well as points to match one garment section to another.

PLACEMENT OF CHILD'S DRESS FIG. 56 b

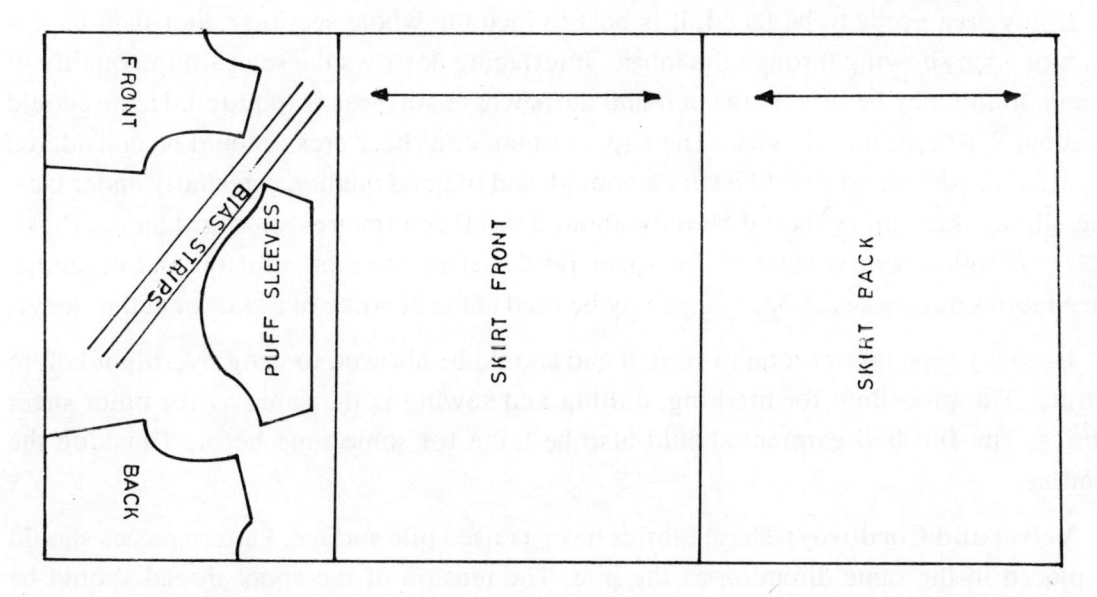

Precautions To Be Taken While Working With Different Kinds of Fabrics

There are certain fabrics that require special care while cutting, sewing and pressing.

Sheers and Lace: Sheer fabrics do not stay in place easily and should be either pinned or stuck with cellotape onto the cutting table. Tissue paper should be placed under the fabric to add weight to enable proper sewing. This also prevents the fabric surface from getting caught in the feed. The seams should be narrow so that they do not show through. A French seam may be used to give a neat finish. The dart width should be trimmed and finished with zig zag edge stitching.

If any area needs to be faced, it is best to face the whole section rather than have a seam or edge showing through the fabric. Interfacing destroys the see-through quality of sheers, lining may be used at the belt and cuffs where stiffness is required. Hems should be about 8-10 centimetres wide. The slip worn under a sheer dress should be considered as part of the dress and should be thick enough and of good quality, especially under lace. The slip or skirt lining should be only about 2.0-3.0 centimetres shorter than the dress.

A rolled hem is suitable for sheer fabrics such as crepe, chiffon and organdie. Lace fabrics having a scalloped edge may be used at the hemline of a skirt or at the sleeve.

Crepe: Crepe fabrics tend to stretch and should be allowed to hang overnight before cutting. The procedure for marking, cutting and sewing is the same as for other sheer fabrics. The finished garment should also be hung for some time before finishing the hemline.

Velvet and Corduroy: These fabrics have a raised pile surface. Pattern pieces should be placed in the same direction as the pile. The tension of the spool thread should be slightly loose to avoid puckering. While ironing, use light movements so that the pile does not get flattened.

Wool: Woollen fabrics should be straightened and pre-shrunk. If the wool is thick, it may need to be cut on a single layer. Since wool-stretches easily on curved lines, it should be stay-stitched as soon as it has been cut. All seams should be interlocked after cutting.

Whilst machining, use light pressure of the presser foot. Wool should also be pressed lightly and carefully; too much heat can destroy its natural resilience. When ironing, use a damp muslin cloth on the surface to be ironed.

Silk: Silks are expensive and difficult to handle. Silks should be worked with fine pins and needles so that the surface is not marred. Silks which are light in weight have to be lined. Interfacings may also be used to give stiffness and body to the garment. Silk fabric ravels easily and requires zigzag edge finishing or French seams. A steam iron should be used to prevent water spotting.

Knitted fabrics: Knitted fabrics should be hung on a rod for a few days before cutting. Avoid combining knitted fabrics with other fabrics as they tend to pull the knitted fabric out of shape and also because they drape or hang differently. Knitted fabrics should be sewn with a synthetic thread. The tension of the thread should be kept looser than usual. The seams should be stretched slightly while sewing to prevent the stitches from breaking during wear. Knitted garments should have a single fold at the hem, the edge of which is finished by lock stitching.

Plaids, Stripes and Figure Prints: Always buy an evenly woven plaid. The plaids and stripes have to be matched at all seams. They may be cut in different directions for variation in design.

While buying printed fabrics, note the direction of the motifs. If they are in all directions then there is no problem. But if the figures are in one direction only, care should be taken to cut all pieces of the garment accordingly.

Chapter 6

Fabric Selection

Fabric is an integral part of dressmaking and its proper selection is of the utmost importance. It has to be selected to suit the personality of the wearer, the style of the dress, the occasion for which it is to be worn and for its fit and drape.

The quality of the fabric is dependent on the type of fibre, its inherent characteristics, its thickness, the number of twists, the fabric construction and the finishes applied. Fibres can be natural such as cotton, linen, wool and silk or man-made such as rayon, nylon and terylene.

Fabric is either woven, knitted or felted. Knitted fabrics are made with yarns looped together. These fabrics stretch more, do not crease easily and are ideally suited for sports and casual wear. Knits are made of cotton, man-made fibres or their blends.

Felted fabrics are generally made of wool. These are made by pressing loose fibres together with heat and moisture.

The fabrics most commonly used are those that are woven. The fibres are first converted into yarns. These yarns may be fine or coarse, tightly or loosely twisted, smooth or rough. The warp or lengthwise yarns are stronger and are held taut on the loom. The weft or crosswise yarns are then used to interlace or weave into fabric. The warp yarns are closer together at the two edges and as the weft yarns turn at the edge they add additional firmness. This is known as the selvedge. The closer the weave of the warp and weft yarns, the higher the count, the finer the fabric. Loosely woven fabric is coarse and has less number of yarns per square inch.

The warp yarns and the selvedges are parallel to each other and the crosswise yarns are at right angles to the warp yarns. A proper right angle ensures that the grain of the fabric is perfect. A perfect grain is essential for good sewing as it affects the fall or drape of the garment.

Fabrics are woven in different ways to create various textures. It is texture that affects both the visual and tactile quality of fabrics. The visual quality of the fabric, such as its roughness or smoothness, its shine or dullness, depends on the amount of light that is reflected. Smooth fabrics will reflect more light than coarse fabrics.

When we say that fabric is soft or rough to the touch, we are referring to its tactile quality. It could be stiff or silky, warm or cool. While selecting fabrics, people usually drape them across the shoulder or feel them between their fingers. To most people the tactile quality of fabric is more important than the visual.

We select cotton for summer because it is light and absorbent. Silk and wool are ideal for winter as these have a natural insulating property. Synthetic fabrics are suitable for the monsoon because these generally have low water absorption and do not go limp in damp weather. Moreover, they dry very quickly.

Fabrics can have a psychological effect on the wearer. People feel delicate and feminine in chiffons, fresh in organdie or in crisp cottons, dignified in silk and rustic in handlooms.

After the cloth has been woven, it is dyed, printed and treated chemically, to give different finishes that improve its feel, texture, colour and performance. Some of the common finishes are mercerization to give lustre, sanforization to pre-shrink and wash-n-wear finish to make the fabric crease-resistant.

Some fabrics are made up of two or more types of fibres and are known as blends. Fabrics are blended to improve quality and sometimes to reduce the cost.

Tericotton is a blend of polyester and cotton. It has the moisture-absorption quality of cotton as well as the crease-resistant quality of polyester, thus making it more comfortable to wear and easy to care for.

Cotton and silk are blended to make fabric stronger and less expensive than pure silk. This blend has the lustre of silk and is both attractive and durable.

With so many new varieties of fabric in the market it is important to know and understand their properties and characteristics in order to make a correct choice. For those with less experience in judging quality, it is best to look for the details on the labels.

While buying blends it is important to know the proportion in which the two fibres have been blended to be able to understand how the fabric will behave. Tericotton fabrics that have a higher percentage of cotton will be easier to handle, being less slippery but will form wrinkles more easily. They will be less expensive and more comfortable to wear than those that have a higher percentage of polyester fibres.

SELECTING FABRIC TO SUIT THE PERSON

Fabric should be selected to suit the type of person and also the figure. Soft fabrics such as voile, silk, chiffon, and crepe drape into gentle folds and are ideal for the woman who likes to appear feminine and delicate.

Firmly woven fabrics feel crisp and smooth. They flatter a heavy figure, giving a smooth line without adding bulk. Firm fabrics include cottons such as denim and man-made fibres such as tericotton, terene and finer corduroy.

Heavy fabrics such as tweed, velvet, corduroy and brushed cotton add bulk to the body.

Shiny and lustrous fabrics reflect light and emphasize body contours. These should be worn only by the slim figure with the right body proportions. Dull textures absorb light and as a result do not enlarge the body size.

SELECTION OF FABRIC TO SUIT DRESS STYLES

It is important to understand fabrics and the way they behave to be able to make the right selection for a particular style. Fabric is suitable for a style if it takes the shape or silhouette required of the style. Garment design details call for varying degrees of fabric manipulation. Fabric to be eased in the case of set-in sleeves requires compression of the sleeve cap yarns to enable it to fit smoothly into the armsyce. Firmly woven and crease resistent fabrics resist compression and stretching, making eased construction difficult.

If the style is of an A-line dress which is required to stand away from the body, the fabric texture should be firm, stiff and should have weight. If the style calls for gathers or frills, the fabric should be soft and pliable so that the gathers form and fall well. The fall of the fabric can be tested by holding it in folds.

A soft, knitted fabric clings to the body but is comfortable as it allows movement. Jersey and knitted garments need careful handling as they stretch. So the design of the garment should be simple, having minimum seams and should be cut with enough ease added to avoid cling.

Crisp and stiff fabrics are less flexible and do not cling to the body. Thus, they have the ability to hide figure irregularities. Fabric chosen for pleated styles should be firm in order to hold the crease well.

Pure silk is the finest and most luxurious of fabrics. There is a certain amount of resilience in the yarn which lends itself to a perfect fit.

Fabrics that are of a plain weave can have elaborate styles and trimmings, whereas those that are elaborately woven should be used for plain styles that enhance the beauty of the weave.

SELECTION OF FABRIC TO SUIT THE OCCASION

The basic rule for dress is that darker colours and shiny fabrics are for evening and night-wear. Lighter colours and dull textures are appropriate for day-wear. Knitted fabrics are ideal for sports-wear and casual-wear.

Garments that are to be worn for long periods of time should be made from fabric that is comfortable. Garments that are to be worn for a shorter period of time may be of fabric that is in fashion.

Chapter 7

Colour

The most striking aspect of clothes is their colour. Colour is the one factor that makes one instantly like or dislike a garment. Appreciation of fabric, style, trimmings etc. are secondary.

Hue is the word used to distinguish one colour from another.

Value is the degree of lightness or darkness of the colour. White is added for tints and black for shades.

Intensity is the brightness or dullness of a colour. All greyed colours are called 'tones'.

Colours are divided into warm and cool. The red end of the spectrum is warmer than the blue end because light colours reflect and dark colours absorb heat from the sun. White and tints not only look cooler but also feel cooler than black and other dark colours.

Because of this effect of warmth and coolness, we select white and pastel colours for the summer months and the brilliant warm colours and purple, navy blue and black for the winter months. Colour also conveys an effect of weight; dark colours give a feeling of weight and so we use the darker shades for the lower garments such as skirts and trousers and lighter hues for blouses and shirts.

Different fabrics absorb dyes differently and that is why the same colour looks different in different fabrics. Black looks attractive in chiffons but appears drab in fabrics of dull texture such as poplin. Light also affects the appearance of colour. If the fabric is shiny, the colour appears bright and if the fabric is rough or coarse it makes the colour appear dull.

Colour affects a person psychologically and holds different meanings for different people. A particular colour may be a favourite because you were complimented while wearing that colour or because it brought you good luck or simply because you feel good in it without knowing why. Psychologists say that your favourite colour and your order of preference of colours reflect the type of person you really are. There are many colour tests that show there is more to colour than meets the eye.

Colours can affect one's mood and then mood may effect your choice of colour. A person may feel pretty and feminine in pink, elegant in white, sophisticated in black, cool in greens, bright and cheerful in yellows and royal in blue and purple. Without knowing why, you realize that for days together you've been wearing one particular colour, showing that your mood affected the colour choice or that you feel depressed the whole day and suddenly you are aware that the colour you are wearing is what makes you feel that way. It is more important that you are psychologically happy in a particular colour rather than whether it suits your skin colouring. There are different opinions about the colours suitable for a particular skin colouring and even about what shade of skin can be termed dark, brown or fair. Generally the extrovert will select colours that are warm, bright and gay such as red, yellow and orange, whereas the introvert would choose cool pastels, blue and green.

Colours are also classified as advancing or receding. Yellow, orange and red are advancing colours whereas green, violet, blue and black are receding colours. And advancing colours give a feeling of warmth and are known to be stimulating in nature. The receding colours, on the other hand, give a feeling of coolness and are generally regarded as being restful colours. In addition, advancing colours have the effect of increasing apparent size, whereas receding colours do the opposite.

Colour can create a centre of interest, it can emphasize a design, cover a figure fault and add to height or weight. It is therefore necessary to understand the various colours so that you can use them to your advantage.

Red is a favourite colour for many. It has the warmth of fire. In India, red is the sign of a married woman. Red is also the colour of courage, sacrifice, vitality and gaiety.

Orange is a very warm colour and should be used discreetly. It expresses energy, spirit, hope, courage and cordiality. Neutralized forms of orange such as Peach and Rust, radiate cheer.

Yellow is associated with light, wisdom and wealth. It is the colour of the sun and has an effect of cheerfulness and gaiety. However, duller shades of yellow give a depressing feeling.

Green is the colour of nature. It is cool and soothing and symbolizes fertility and prosperity. Psychological tests have proved it to be a tranquil colour, neither exciting nor subduing. Green soothes the eyes as well as the nerves.

Blue is the colour of water and the sky and is cool and transparent in quality. After green, it is the most soothing colour and suits most people. Light shades are ideal for young people and darker shades for older people.

Violet and purple are considered to be high frequency colours. Purple was, in the early days, a costly colour to manufacture and so was reserved for royalty. These colours are considered refined, aesthetic and dignified.

Brown is traditionally associated with humility and gentleness. Brown is the colour of the earth and of dry leaves and its vibrations are too low for most people. In its tints and shades brown is attractive. *Coffee brown* is slimming and attractive for the older woman. *Beige* or *Tan* is popular with all ages and combine well with almost every bright colour.

Black is a fashionable colour but cannot be worn by all. It is a colour of dignity and formality.

White is a symbol of purity and innocence. It is worn by brides in some parts of the world as a symbol of chastity. Most people look elegant in white because of the simplicity associated with it.

Grey is a mix of black and white and therefore seems to have no particular character of its own. Light tints of grey are gentle and serene and dark shades, dignified.

Colour preference change with the age of the wearer. Pastel shades are generally associated with babies. Bright colours such as red, yellow, blue and green are associated with children and teenagers, and grey, black, brown, maroon and white, with older women.

Colours are seldom used in their full intensity in an outfit. Intense colours are combined with neutral shades or used in small areas.

People who are thin or slim should wear white and warm colours such as rust, cream and shades of yellow. Stout people should wear blue and greens. Coffee brown, maroon, midnight blue, bottle green, purple and black can make a person appear slimmer.

Not everyone is sensitive to colour. Besides, individuals vary in their perceptions and the meanings that they attach to specific hues which could be dependent on past associations and experienes with that colour. Perception is also moulded by the dictates of fashion.

Chapter 8

Understanding Your Body

The best way to understand one's body is to compare one's measurements and proportions with those of the ideal figure. Proportion is the ratio of the height to the girth of a figure. People having the same bust, waist and hip girths can appear to be quite different in size if their heights vary. Naturally the taller person appears slimmer and the shorter person, stouter.

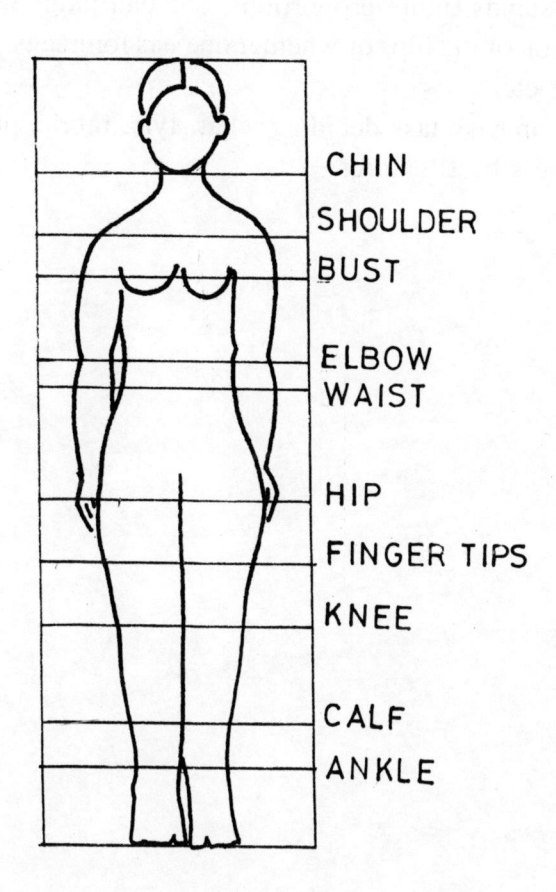

The ideal figure can be divided into 8 head lengths and the average figure into 7½ head lengths. The head length is measured from the top of the head to just below the chin with the help of a vernier caliper. The total length or height is then divided by the head length to give the number of head lengths the body is divided into. (Fig. 57)

The ideal girth difference between bust and waist and the waist and hip is 10 inches. By comparing the bust and hip girths with the waist girth, one can judge whether the bust is heavy, hips prominent or whether one has a trim waistline.

The average male and female figure can be divided into approximately 7½ head lengths. The fullest part of the hipline divides the length exactly in half. The neck is about 1/3rd the head length. Male and female proportions differ only in girth ratios. The female figure has a hipline that is visually equal to the width of the shoulders. The male figure, on the other hand, has a wider shoulder, and in comparison, the hips are narrower. Female figures also vary in their front and back measurements at the bust, waist and hip levels. The bust and waist measure more at the front and the hip measures more at the back.

Once one understands figure proportions, one can judge whether one has a high or low waist, the position of the hips or whether one has long legs and a short torso or a long torso and short legs etc.

It then becomes an easy task deciding what style, fabric, print and colour should be worn to enhance one's best features.

CHAPTER 9

HOW TO TAKE BODY MEASUREMENTS

Taking body measurements is not an easy task though accurate measurements are essential for obtaining a good fit.

EQUIPMENT REQUIRED

1) Protractor with spirit level
2) Vernier caliper
3) L-shaped ruler
4) Measure tape
5) Ribbons to mark the horizontal locations on the body
6) Eyebrow pencil.

The measurements required to be taken for the bodice block are as follows:

Vertical Measurements

1) Neck depth
2) Highest shoulder to armpit level
3) Highest shoulder to bust level
4) Highest shoulder to waist level
5) Sleeve length

Horizontal and Girth Measurements

1) Shoulder width
2) Neck width
3) Across chest front
4) Across chest back
5) Girth at armpit level
6) Girth at bust level
7) Girth at waist level
8) Round arm at armpit
9) Round arm at sleeve end

The measurements for the lower garment are as follows:

Vertical Measurements	Girth Measurements
1) Waist to abdomen level	1) Waist girth
2) Waist to hip level	2) Abdomen girth
3) Waist to crotch level	3) Hip girth
4) Waist to knee	4) Thigh girth at crotch level
5) Waist to calf	5) Mid-thigh girth
6) Waist to ankle	6) Knee girth
7) Outside leg length	7) Ankle girth
8) Inside leg length	

While the measurements are being taken, be sure to wear well-fitted foundation garments. Measurements should not be taken on loose fitted garments which do not define the body lines.

Marking Body Locations (Fig. 58)

The Art of Sewing

(1) Using a vernier caliper mark the width of the neck.

(2) Place a chain around the neck and mark the "neckline" at the position on the neck where the chain falls naturally.

(3) The highest shoulder point is marked at the point at which the mark of "neck-width" and the "neckline" cross each other.

(4) Place an L-shaped ruler at the highest shoulder pointing towards the arm; mark this as the "shoulder line."

(5) Hold a chain around the two armscyes and mark the "armhole line".

(6) The point at which the "shoulder line" meets the "armhole line" is marked as the lowest shoulder point.

(7) Tie narrow ribbons across the armpit, bust and waist levels. The ribbon should be straight at both the back and front.

(8) Tie a ribbon around the arm at the armpit level.

TAKING BODY MEASUREMENTS

Now that all the locations on the body have been marked, the actual measurements can be taken. All measurements are taken on the right side of the body.

1. The shoulder-to-shoulder measurement is taken from the right lowest shoulder point to the left lowest shoulder point across the front.

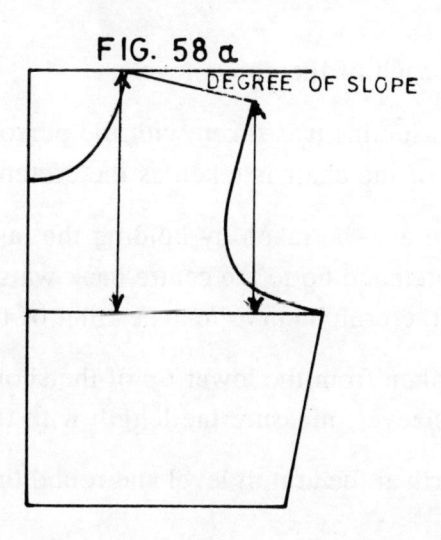

FIG. 58 a
DEGREE OF SLOPE

2. The same measurement is also taken for the back. This gives the actual width of the person and is an important measurement for any drafting. The shoulder-to-shoulder measurement for the back is more than that of the front by about 2.0 to 5.0 centimetres. This measurement is important, since it varies from person to person. It can also make a difference to the visual width of the garment.

3. (Fig. 58a) The shoulder slope may be measured by a protractor with a spirit level attached. Since this may not be available, measure the length from highest shoulder point to the armpit level and also the length from the lowest shoulder point to the armpit level. The difference between these two lengths is the slope of the shoulder. The slope may also vary from one shoulder to the other.

4. The shoulder width is measured between the highest and lowest shoulder points.

5. The distance between the two armholes at the front and back is known as the "Across Chest" measurement. It is taken at about the midpoint of the armhole. This measurement is essential, especially for tight fitted garments such as the sari blouse.

6. Holding the tape end at the highest shoulder point, measure the vertical length to the armpit, bust and waist levels.

7. While measuring the girths at armpit level, bust and waist, hold the tape neither too tight nor too loose.

8. Tie ribbons at the abdomen, hips, thigh, knee and ankle.

9. Place the tape end at the waist level and measure the length to the abdomen, hip, thigh, knee and ankle.

10. Measure the girths at each of the above levels.

11. The crotch length measurement is taken with the person seated. The measurement from the waist to the top of the chair is taken as the crotch length.

12. This measurement can also be taken by holding the tape at the centre front waist, passing it down to the crotch and up to the centre back waist. This measurement can be used as a check to see if the crotch curve matches that of the draft.

13. The sleeve length is taken from the lower tip of the shoulder to the length required. For full or three-quarter sleeves, measure the length with the elbow bent.

14. Measure the sleeve girth at the armpit level and round the arm at the required sleeve length.

The Art of Sewing

A lot of practice is needed in order to be able to take accurate body measurements and a variation of 0.5 centimetre may be overlooked. The vertical measurements are difficult to alter and therefore require more accuracy. Girth measurements are easily increased or decreased by letting out or taking in at the seams.

Chapter 10

Alterations To Fit Different Figures

A good fit is the most important aspect of a garment. A garment that is both fashionable and in a fetching colour would not merit a second look if it did not hang well on the wearer. Whereas a good fit can flatter the figure, an ill fit can completely mar a person's appearance.

There are many variables for fit, namely the figure, the fabric, the design and the occasion for which the garment is to be worn.

The figure: Body measurements vary from person to person. Two women having the same girth measurements at the bust, waist and hip, may differ in many other measurements, such as the level of the bustline, the level of the armpit and the slope of the shoulder. There are no fitting problems for the full and well-proportioned figure. But special fitting is required for those who have figure problems such as thin arms in comparison to the bust-girth, or hollow chests or prominent bones at the shoulder.

The fabric: The type of fabric, too, has a bearing on the way a garment should be fitted. Heavy fabrics require more ease than fine fabrics. Fabrics that are stiff and wrinkle easily must be loosely fitted. Garments that are to be lined also require more ease to be added to allow for the extra thickness of fabric within. Soft and stretch fabrics, such as crepes and knits, can be given a more close fit.

The design: The design or style has an influence on the fit. The style may require the shoulder line to be extended, or the armhole line to be lowered. It may require for the dress to flare out from the shoulder or for a new positioning of the waistline.

The occasion: Fit is of the utmost importance if the dress is required for a special occasion. Evening clothes are generally well fitted. For sportswear and night clothes comfort is the priority and fit comes subsequently.

While fitting a garment, always be critical. To a good seamstress it is important that the shoulder seamline is not tilted either towards the front or the back but falls exactly on top of the shoulder. To most people the shoulder line deviation may even go un-noticed. However, every minor detail is important for a good fit.

The following points should be checked to ensure a good fit:

1. The neckline should lie flat without gaping.
2. The shoulder seam should be in a straight line on top of the shoulder.
3. The armhole seam should fall along the natural curve of the arm.
4. The darts should point towards the fullest part of the bust and end 2.5 to 3.0 centimetres away from the bust point.
5. The position of the waistline.
6. The hemline.

Every garment has a certain amount of fullness or ease allowed and therefore a slight variation in the measurements will not require any alteration. The amount of ease allowed in a garment varies according to the style and the purpose for which it is to be worn. A sari blouse that seems to be tightly fitted, has a minimum ease of 8.0 centimetres at the bust level. A nightgown or a loose flowing kurta may have about 25.0 to 30.0 centimetres ease allowed and can fit various sizes without any need for alteration. Most garments have an ease of about 5.0 to 10.0 centimetres at the waist girth except for the sari blouse which has an ease of only 2.0 centimetres.

Although some amount of ease is required in the girth measurements, the length measurements should fit exactly. Girth measurements may be increased or decreased by taking in or letting out the seam allowance.

Vertical measurements are far more difficult to alter except at the hemline. Altering the armpit level, the waist level and the crotch level requires a lot of time and patience and is generally not worth the effort. It is easier to make a large garment smaller than vice versa.

Ready-made clothes are meant for the mass market. Their general attractiveness and loose flowing styles are the main draw, which makes people overlook fitting details such as the shoulder seams that hang beyond the shoulder points, unwanted creases and irregular hemlines. Those with a discerning eye, however, would not accept these shortcomings. Hence it becomes imperative to understand how to make alterations so as to be able to achieve a perfect fit. Most of the alterations are very minor and easy to carry out and can make all the difference to the appearance of the garment. The important thing to be kept in mind is that all details of fit should be taken care of before the final touches are given to the garment.

Fitting Problems

Flat cloth can be shaped to fit the curves of the figure by the use of darts. Darts generally begin at a seam and point towards the highest bust point in the upper garment and to the hip in the lower garment. Darts are wide at the seam and taper to a point. Greater fullness is created when the dart is wider and vice versa. The amount of shaping required is dependent on the differnce between the two adjoining measurements, for example, the bust girth and the waist girth. The area around the bust should fit smoothly but have enough ease to ensure comfort.

High or Low Bustline: The placement of darts is important for a good fit. The level of the bustline is taken from the highest shoulder point to the bust level. People of varying ages could have identical bust girths though there are bound to be variations in the bustline levels. Hence there is a need to alter the position of the darts accordingly (Fig. 59a and 59b)

RAISING DARTS FOR HIGH BUST FIG. 59a

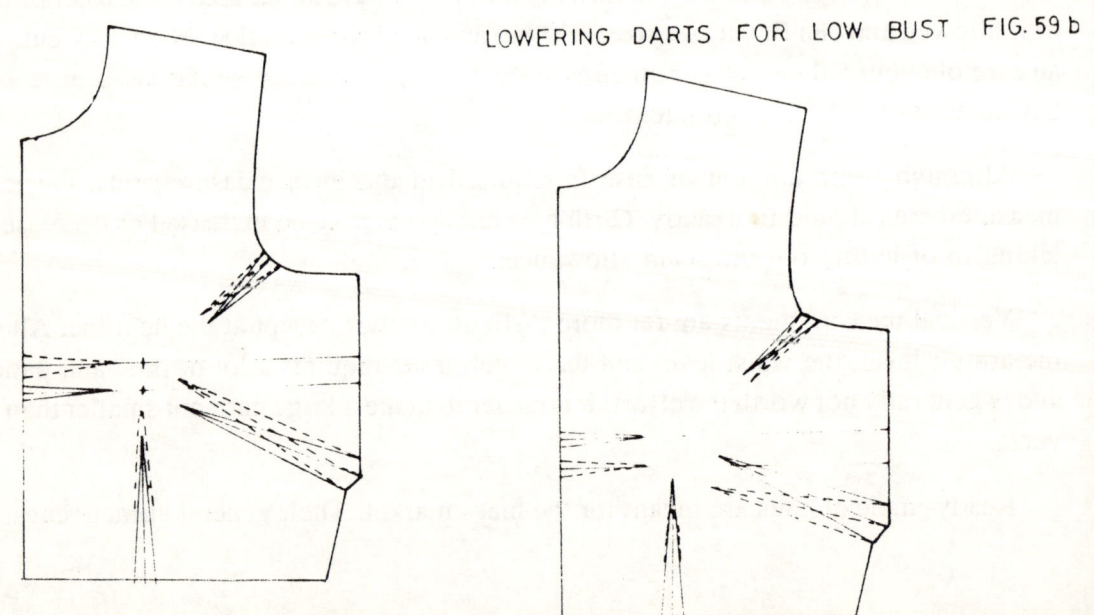

LOWERING DARTS FOR LOW BUST FIG. 59b

Neckline: The neckline should ideally fall flat and smooth on the body.

When the **neckline is too tight,** lower and widen it equally all along the line and clip around to see how far it has to be lowered (Fig. 60). For a **gaping neckline,** the extra amount has to be taken up into the shoulder seam at the neck-edge, as shown in (Fig. 61). If the **neckline is too low** and if the fabric has not yet been cut, it is easy to raise the neck as required. (Fig.62) If the fabric has already been cut low by accident, it can be raised in two ways. Attach a yoke facing of a different cloth as a design feature or attach a ruffle or lace only at the lower end of the neck. (Fig. 63)

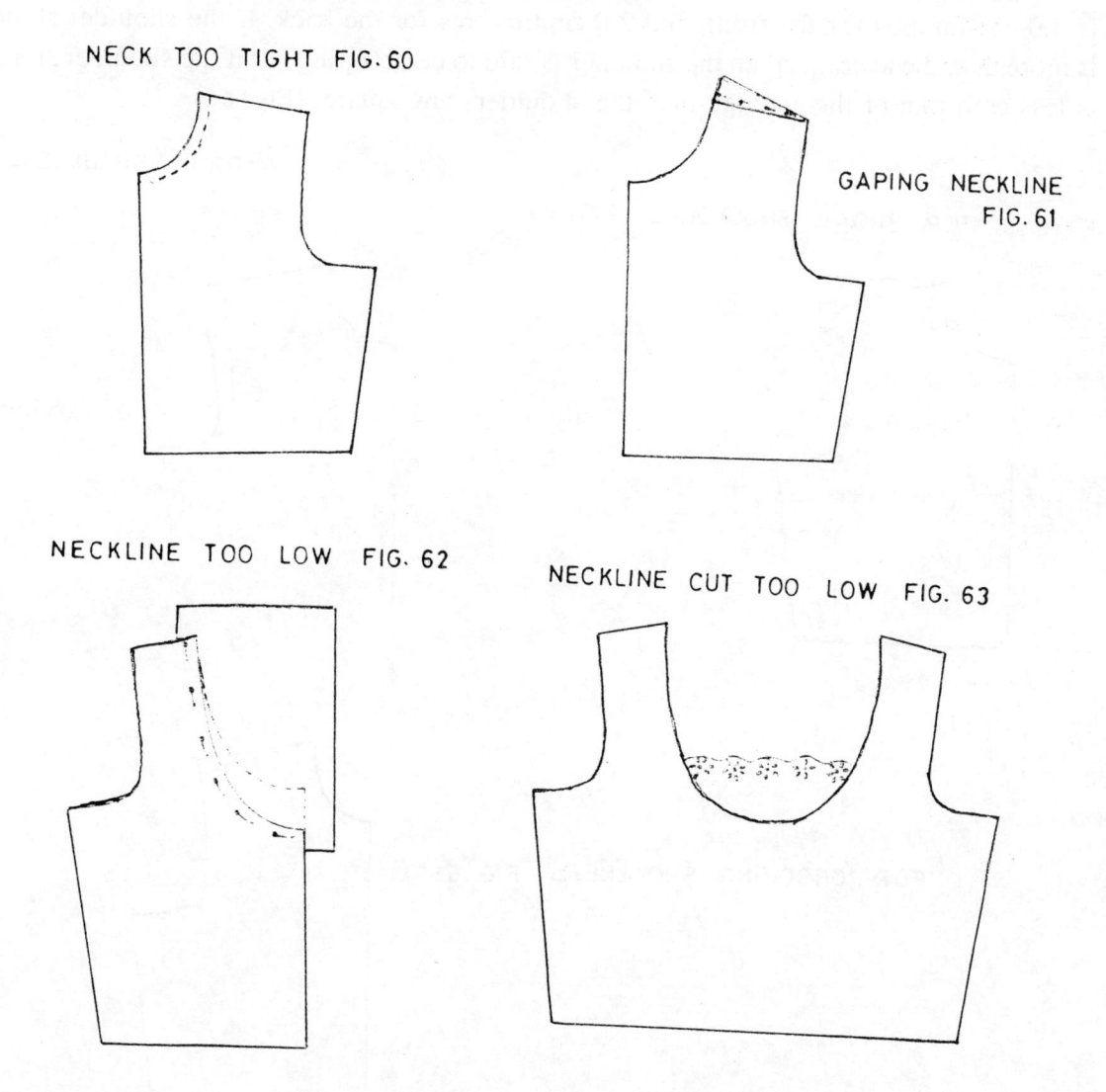

NECK TOO TIGHT FIG. 60

GAPING NECKLINE FIG. 61

NECKLINE TOO LOW FIG. 62

NECKLINE CUT TOO LOW FIG. 63

Shoulder Width: The width of the shoulder is very important. The garment will look ill-fitted if it is either too wide or too narrow. If the width of the shoulder has been widened for a particular style, it is generally fitted with shoulder pads so that it does not droop. If the garment **shoulder width is more** than the actual shoulder width, the excess width has to be taken in as shown. (Fig. 64) When the garment **shoulder width is narrower** than the actual shoulder width, the garment will be too binding and will pull across the chest. To correct this the shoulder has to be extended without changing the armhole depth. (Fig. 65) The **shoulder slope** varies from person to person and even the two shoulders of a single individual can be different, one from the other. The average shoulder slope is 3.0 centimetres for the front, and 2.0 centimetres for the back. If the shoulder slope is more than the average, then the shoulder is said to be drooping but if the shoulder slope is less than that of the average then the shoulders are square. (Fig. 66)

EXTEND FOR BROAD SHOULDERS FIG. 64

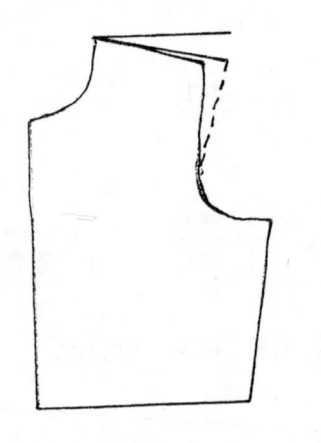

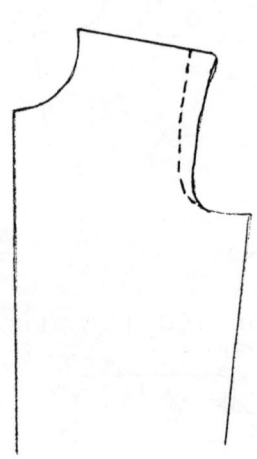

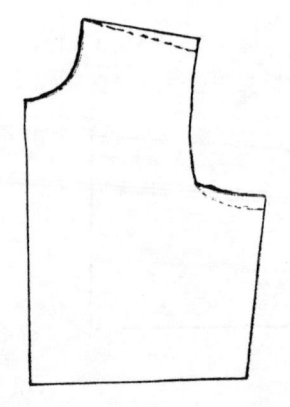

TAKE-IN FOR NARROW SHOULDERS FIG. 65

FOR DROOPING SHOULDERS FIG. 66

The Art of Sewing

After the shoulder slope has been lowered, the armhole will also have to be lowered by the same amount. (Fig. 67) The shoulder seamline may be tilted towards the front or the back at either neck or armhole edge. If the shoulder seamline tends to shift backwards, it means that only the front slope has to be decreased. If the shoulder seamline shifts towards the front, then the back shoulder slope needs to be decreased.

Bust Size: If you have a **large cup**, the chances are that the dress will pull across the front and ride up at the waist. In that case, slash along the line to be increased and spread to introduce extra fullness at the bust. (Fig. 68) If you have a **small cup,** it is likely that the front of the garment will hang in vertical folds. In order to correct this, fold along the vertical and horizontal line to reduce the amount of fullness at the bust. (Fig. 69)

FOR SQUARE SHOULDERS FIG. 67

TO INCREASE FOR LARGE CUP FIG. 68

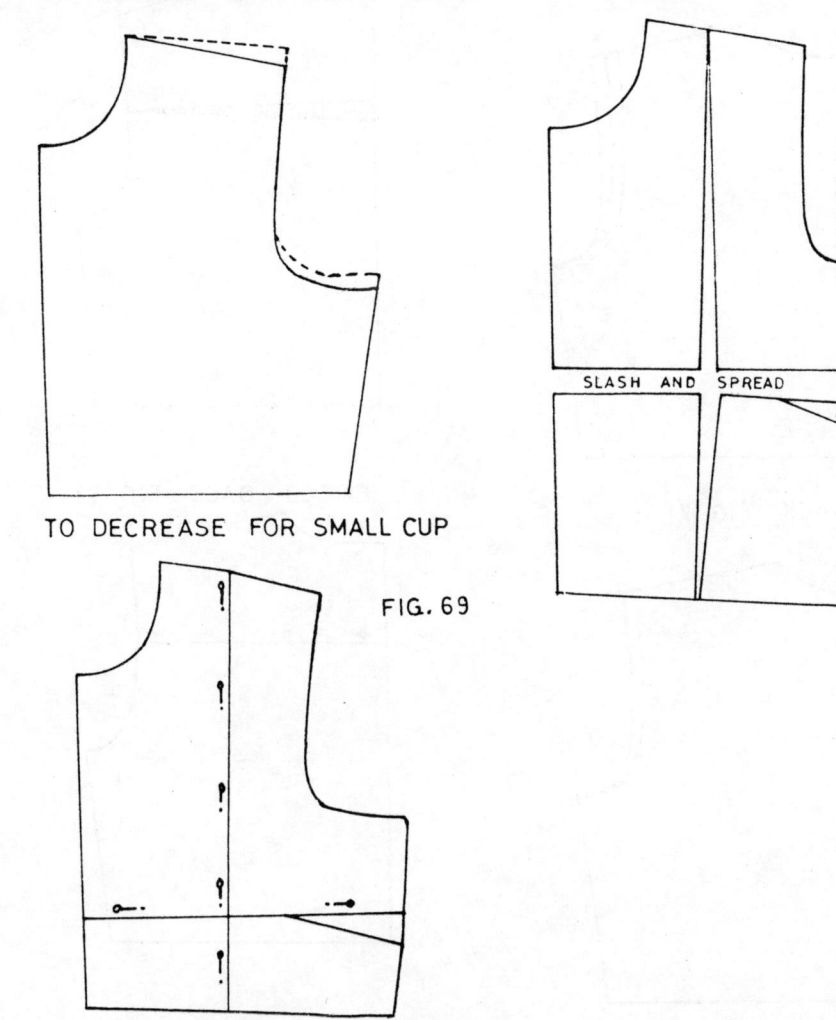

SLASH AND SPREAD

DART

TO DECREASE FOR SMALL CUP

FIG. 69

Bodice Back: If the **back is broad**, there will be horizontal creases formed due to a sideways pull. This can be eliminated by an increase at the centre back. If there is no seam at the centre back, then increase at the armsyce. (Fig. 70) If the **back is narrow,** there will be vertical folds. The excess fabric has then to be taken up into the centre back seams, the side seams and at the armsyce. (Fig. 71) To accommodate the **rounded back,** a back shoulder dart has to be given. Increase the centre back length to allow for the rounded back. (Fig. 72) For an **erect back,** it is necessary to take up the excess back length into a fold, halfway down the armsyce. The armhole should also be lowered as it will be decreased by the fold. (Fig. 73)

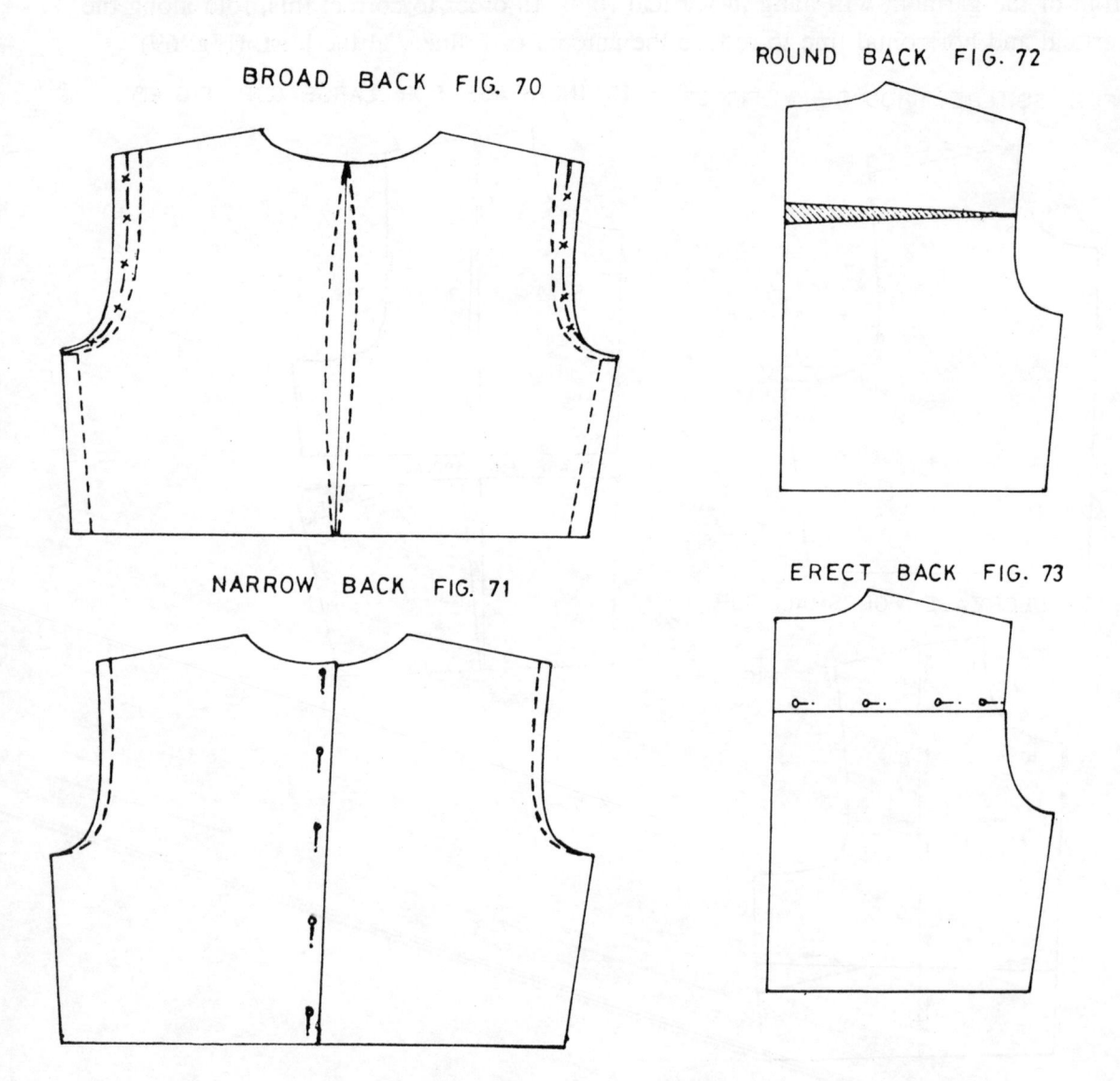

BROAD BACK FIG. 70

ROUND BACK FIG. 72

NARROW BACK FIG. 71

ERECT BACK FIG. 73

Armhole: When the **armhole is tight,** it has to be lowered both on the bodice as well as on the sleeves. (Fig. 74) When the **armhole is too loose,** it has to be raised both on the bodice as well as on the sleeves. (Fig. 75)

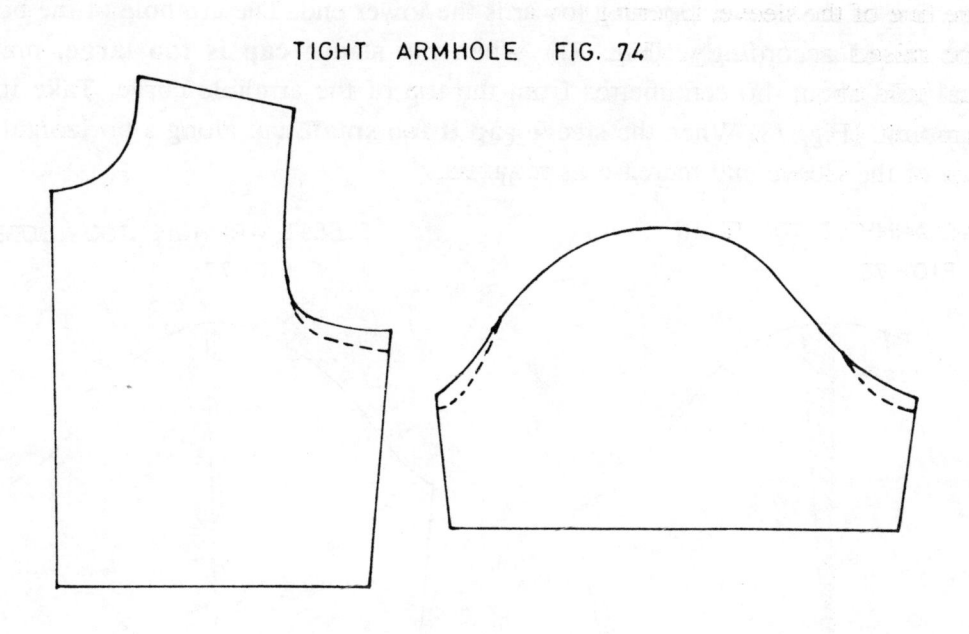

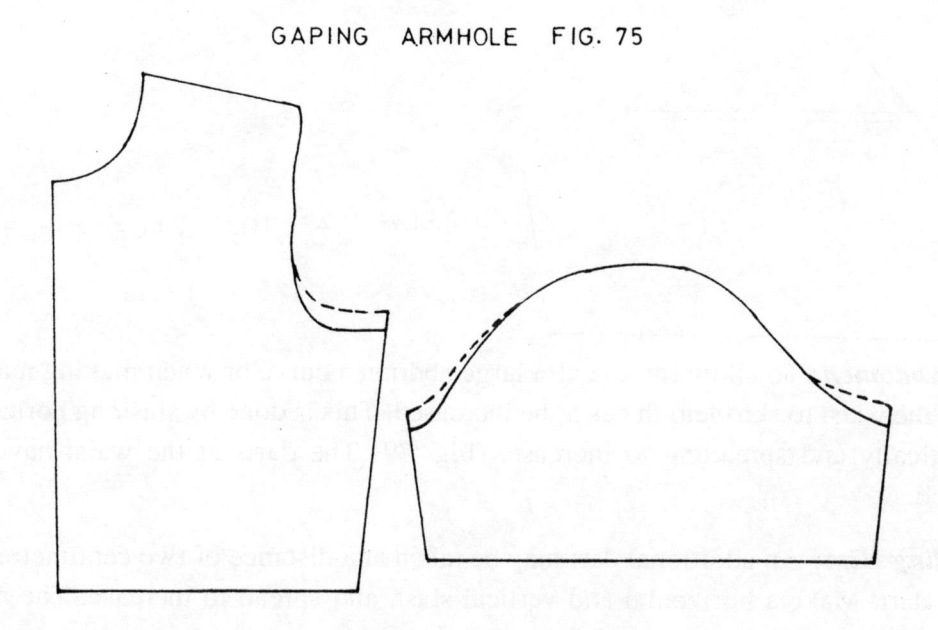

TIGHT ARMHOLE FIG. 74

GAPING ARMHOLE FIG. 75

Sleeves: When the **sleeve is too tight,** slash along the centre of the sleeve and spread as much as is required. Then draw a new curve at the top of the sleeve. The armhole of the bodice should also be lowered accordingly. (Fig. 76) If the **sleeve is too loose,** fold along the centre line of the sleeve, tapering towards the lower end. The armhole of the bodice has to be raised accordingly. (Fig. 77) When the **sleeve cap is too large,** make a horizontal fold about 4.0 centimetres from the top of the armhole curve. Take in the excess amount. (Fig. 78) When the **sleeve cap it too small,** cut along a horizontal line at the cap of the sleeve and increase as required.

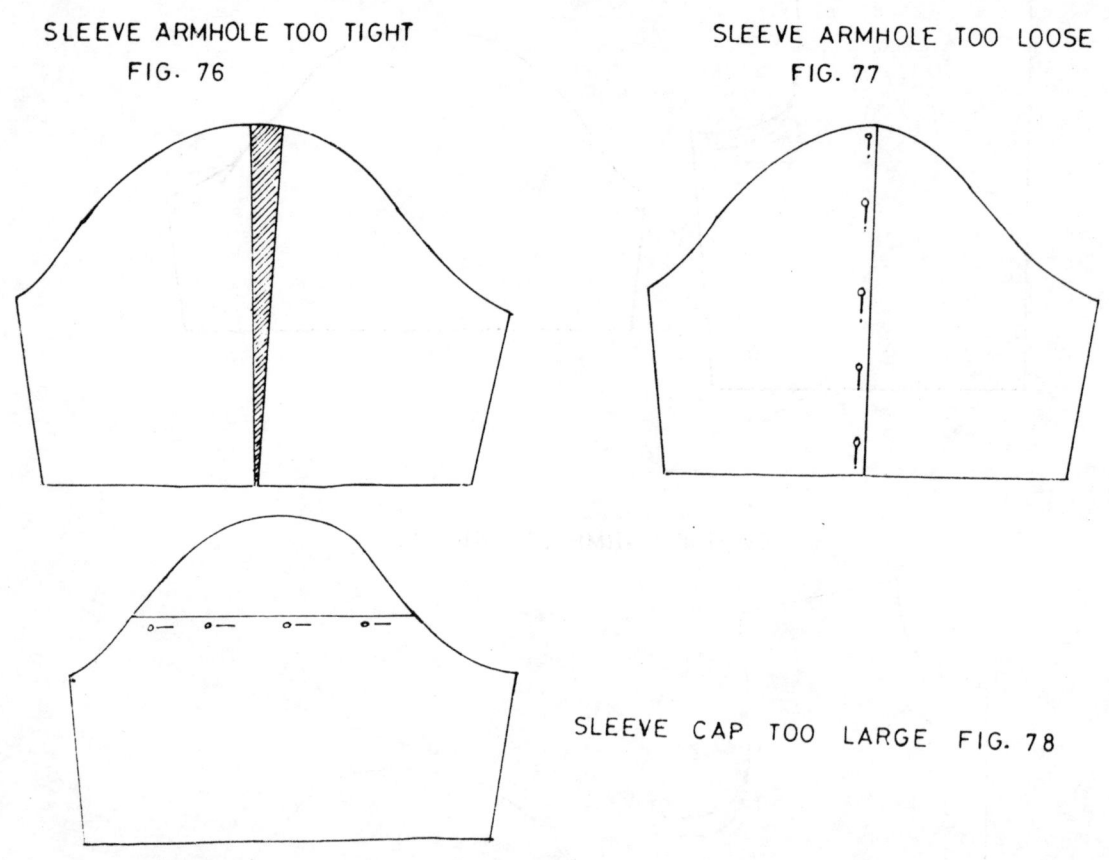

SLEEVE ARMHOLE TOO TIGHT
FIG. 76

SLEEVE ARMHOLE TOO LOOSE
FIG. 77

SLEEVE CAP TOO LARGE FIG. 78

Large Abdomen: To allow for an extra large abdomen curve or when making maternity clothes, the waist to skirt length has to be increased. This is done by slashing horizontally and vertically and spreading to increase. (Fig. 79) The darts at the waist have to be shortened.

Protruding Hips: An additional dart may be taken at a distance of two centimetres from the first dart. Make a horizontal and vertical slash and spread to increase. The method is the same as that for the large abdomen.

FOR LARGE ABDOMEN FIG. 79

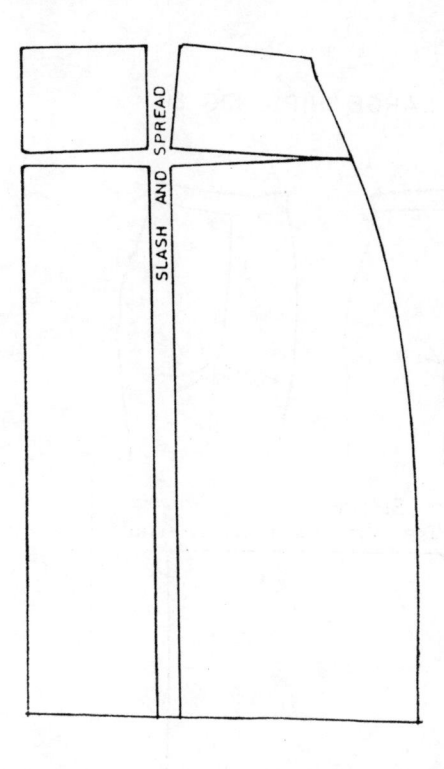

SLASH AND SPREAD

Alterations for Trousers

Fitting problems related to length alteration for the crotch should be made first. The crotch level should be at the correct position before checking other length and girth measurements.

Increasing or decreasing the length: The length can be increased by slashing and adding an extra amount or it may be decreased by folding in the extra amount. Whether the increase or decrease in length has to be made between the waist and crotch level or between the crotch level and the ankle, these are taken care of in a similar manner. Reducing or increasing the length of the trouser at the hemline is not a problem since there is no shaping involved.

Faulty crotch: The most common problem in trousers is the formation of fold lines at the crotch. These fold lines are called 'smiles' when they face upwards, and 'frowns' if they face downwards. The folds may be formed at the front or back and are caused by a faulty crotch depth or crotch curve. The folds turn upwards when the crotch is tight and downwards when it is loose.

Large Hip: Excess fabric has to be let out at the crotchline and at the side seamline to allow for large hips. (Fig. 80)

Flat Hips: Take in the excess fabric at the crotchline and at the side seams. (Fig. 81)

LARGE HIPS FIG. 80

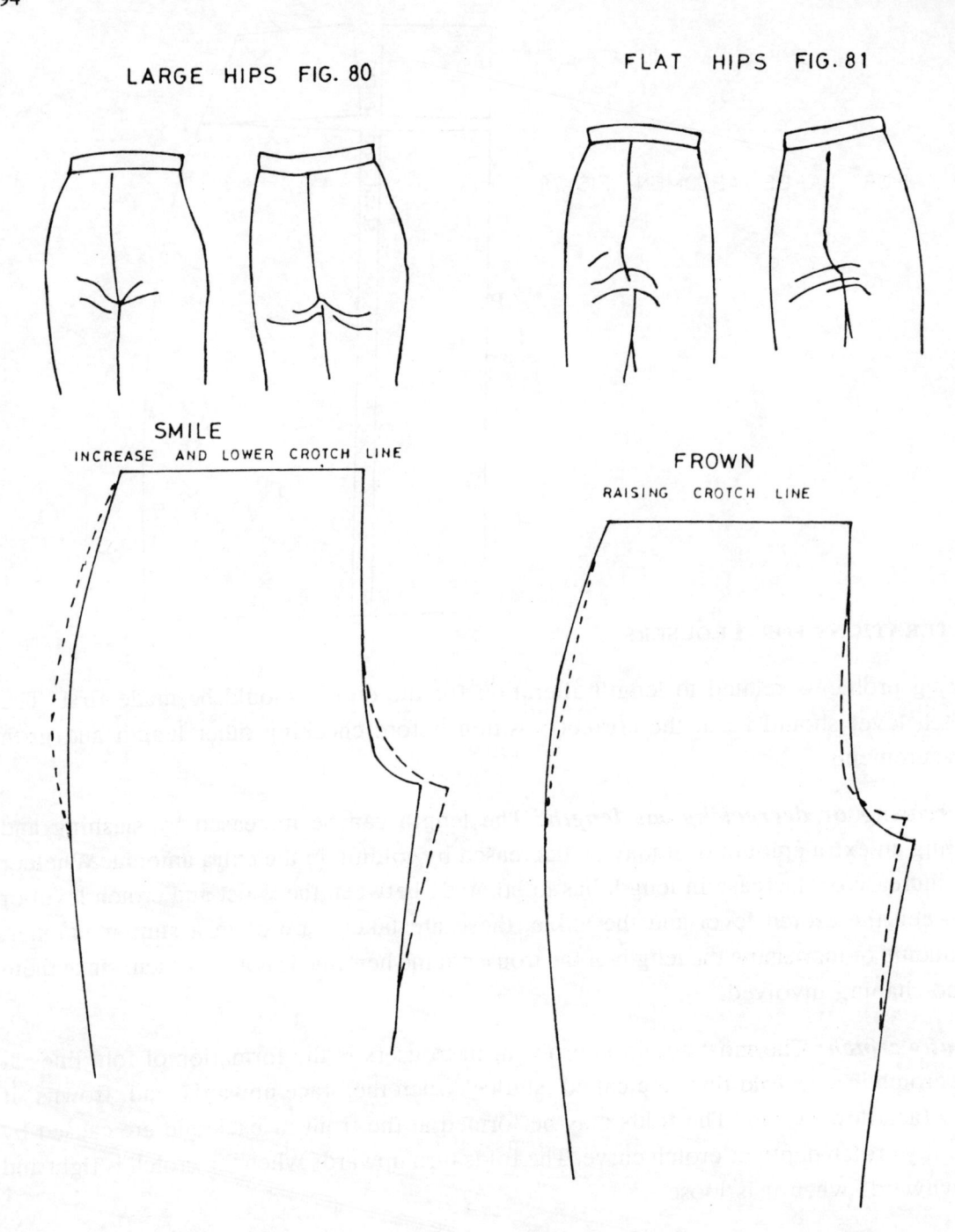

FLAT HIPS FIG. 81

SMILE
INCREASE AND LOWER CROTCH LINE

FROWN
RAISING CROTCH LINE

Tightening or loosening the legs: When the trouser legs have to be tightened or loosened, the inner leg seam is easier to handle. If, however, the amount to be increased or decreased is fairly large, then it has to be shaped at both the inner and outer seams.

Chapter 11

Design Elements

Fashion determines style and style determines the placement of the waist, the length of the skirt, the width of the shoulder, the degree of fullness and the silhouette of the garment.

A particular style looks attractive only when it is able to enhance the good proportions of the wearer. Clothing styles have the advantage of being able to hide those features that are unattractive and also to form new lines that give a graceful and pleasing appearance.

Thus, fashion style has to be adapted by the individual to suit both figure and personality. Since most individuals do not have perfect, well-proportioned figures, it becomes important to understand design elements such as line, colour, proportion, balance, rhythm and emphasis. Each of these elements should be considered and used to the best advantage of the individual. The final effect of the composition must lend to the creation of an overall state of harmony and visual stability.

Line

The most important line in a garment is the silhouette. The silhouette can be soft and figure-conforming to lend grace and feminity. It can also stand away from the body, lending a stiff and formal appearance.

Straight lines convey dignity and formality, whereas curved lines have a graceful and flowing effect. An individual can project different facets of the personality by selecting appropriate lines to suit the mood and the occasion.

Besides the general silhouette, there are lines within the dress such as the seamlines, neckline, waistline and hemline. Lines are also formed by darts, tucks, pleats, colour contrasts and buttons. These lines are generally matched to the dress silhouette. If the silhouette has straight lines, then curved lines within should be avoided. For example, for a silhouette with straight lines, a square or rectangular neckline would be more suitable than a round neckline. Similarly, the shape of the collar too, must be chosen to conform to the silhouette.

Basically, there are only vertical, horizontal and curved lines. But the visual effect of these can be varied depending on the width of each line and the distance between two adjacent lines. The visual effect that bold and wide vertical lines give is different from the effect of lines that are narrow and close together. Similarly, horizontal lines are emphasized when they are wide and with a greater space between the lines. The effect that diagonal lines provide falls somewhere between the effect of vertical and horizontal lines, depending upon the degree of slant.

Vertical Lines: Vertical lines make the eye travel in an upward and downward direction, thereby giving an appearance of length. Vertical lines are also associated with formal wear. Vertical lines can also be achieved by a row of decorative buttons or by narrow knife pleats or pin tucks or by piping inserted in a vertical seam so as to emphasize the line.

Horizontal lines: Horizontal lines make the eye travel from side to side and so give the effect of wideness.

These lines denote flexibility and informality. A horizontal effect can also be achieved by rows of tucks or lace. The effect can vary depending upon the width of the tucks or lace and also the distance between them.

Curved lines: Curved lines can be a full circle or may even appear almost straight. Curved lines are considered graceful and feminine, those in a diagonal direction are the most graceful and can be seen in the soft folds of material in a draped dress or a ruffled collar.

Colour

Colour is a vital element in garment design. Colour awareness goes a long way in the successful designing of a garment.

In order to give emphasis to design features such as draped folds, tucks or embroidery, pastel shades are most suitable. If however, the colour of the fabric is dark, this can be offset by using a white lace collar and cuffs or it can be brightened by using a vividly coloured ribbon, piping or buttons. Contrasting colours tend to reduce the apparent height of person and so should be avoided by short people but can be used to advantage by those who are tall. A colour that is unbecoming should never be worn near the face. The use of a white collar or a brightly embroidered yoke helps.

Proportion

The waistline, yokeline and the hemline comprise the main horizontal dividing lines of a garment. The placement of these lines is, therefore, of the utmost importance as it determines whether the garment is proportionate. The waistline should never divide the dress length exactly into two equal halves but should be so placed that it divides approximately, the total dress length in a manner wherein one-third of the dress is above the waistline and the remaining two-thirds below. Similarly, the yokeline should divide the bodice at about one-third of the bodice length.

The length of the dress can alter the visual height of the person. The length should thus not only be dependent on the dress style but also appear pleasingly proportionate to the person's height and to the measurement from waist to ankle.

The visual width of a person depends mainly on the shoulder width. If the shoulder width is comparatively narrow, it can be widened by padding. If, on the other hand, the shoulder width appears to be comparatively wide, it can be visually decreased by the use of raglan sleeves.

In addition to the above, the size of the collar, buttons and pockets, as also the width of the belt and cuff, can affect the appearance and therefore should be proportionate to the size of the wearer.

Balance

The distribution of elements and features on a dress contributes to its overall visual impact. When the distribution creates an equalizing impact, the dress can be considered well-balanced.

Formal balance in a dress can be achieved by evenly spaced rows of tucks and lace. The number of rows, however, should be uneven, in order to obtain optimum balance. The distribution of pockets can be done in such a way that they balance each other thereby contributing to the total effect.

Informal balance can be obtained when the two halves of a dress are not similar in size or shape but nevertheless appear balanced. This can be achieved on a double-breasted outfit by the placement of buttons to decoratively counter-balance the buttons that are meant for actual use.

Rhythm

The dress design must incorporate a harmonious sequence of regularly recurring patterns and an alternating arrangement of colours. This is known as rhythm. Rhythm confers a continuity by the regular repetition of lines, shapes and colours. For example, the colour of a collar or yoke can be repeated in the skirt in the form of a pocket, a patch design or a frill. The shape of the neck or collar can also be repeated in any other decorative feature such as flaps or pockets. This recurrence of a feature or colour in the dress arrangement gives it an acceptable, harmonious rhythm.

EMPHASIS

In any garment there should be only one area of accent or of special significance. It could be the silhouette, the colour or the fabric. When the fabric is elaborate, then the style should be simple and if the fabric is plain then the silhouette can be elaborate.

The trimmings on a dress should be restricted. Too much decoration in the form of lace, buttons and embroidery is undesirable. One simple patch design a bow or a decorative pocket would be far more striking.

CORRECTIVE STYLES FOR PROBLEM FIGURES

In designing a garment the above design elements should be considered along with the individual's figure characteristics. The average figure can carry off most styles without any difficulty. But those with figure irregularities have to adapt fashion styles to hide or make the irregularities seem less obvious.

Some of the figure problems have been listed below along with suggestions for suitable styles:

Short neck: Avoid styles with collars and ruffles at the neckline. A low-cut neckline would help to make the neck appear longer.

Long neck: High collars and standing ruffles and lace at the neck can emphasize a long neck.

Wide shoulders: Use styles that do not emphasize the shoulder width such as kimono sleeves or raglan sleeves. Shoulder pads should be avoided since they exaggerate the shoulder width.

Narrow shoulders: Dropped shoulder styles and shoulder pads can help.

Large or prominent bust: The bustline should not be emphasized. A yoke that ends just above the bustline will make it appear more prominent. Loose flowing styles from the shoulder, cut in panels or on the bias, are suitable.

Waistline: A person with a high waist or a prominent waistline should avoid styles that emphasize the waist. Loose flowing styles without seams at the waist are suitable. It would be best to avoid wearing tucked in blouses. Loose and long T-shirts or blouses, which hide the waistline, are more suitable.

If the waist is high but not prominent, then styles with a low waistline are suitable. High heels should be avoided as with the legs appearing longer, the waist would appear even higher.

For those with narrow, attractive waistlines, styles with waist emphasis such as shirring, and belts are appealing. Tucked-in blouses would look good too.

Large or prominent hips: Avoid fabrics and styles that cling to the figure. Trousers or tight skirts are best avoided. If, however, these are worn, then a long T-shirt or blouse which covers the hipline may be worn. A flared silhouette would be the most suitable.

Long legs: Trousers would look attractive as well as dresses or skirts that reach down to the calf level.

Short legs: Long dresses or skirts would only serve to emphasize the shortness of the legs. They should end at the knee level or even an inch or two above the knee, this would show more of the leg and create an illusion of length.

Tall figures: Contrasting colours and horizontal stripes are suitable. Vertical stripes, tubular skirts and long, fitted sleeves should be avoided.

Short figures: Any line or style that cuts the length of the body such as colour contrasts in yokes, horizontal lines, wide borders and belts, should be avoided. Vertical lines in the form of stripes or a row of buttons add to the apparent height.

Short and Plump figures: Avoid wide sleeves and gathered skirts. Small floral prints, plaids or spots, and fabrics that are transparent and delicate are suitable. Sleeves that are long will only make a fat arm appear fatter and shorter. A wide hem or border at the sleeve also tends to make the arm appear fatter. Plain sleeves that end 2.0 to 3.0 centimetres above the elbow, would be appropriate.

Section II

Drafts

CHAPTER 12

COLLARS

As a decorative feature, collars lend character to a garment and enhance the neckline. They may be stiff or soft and feminine and may be embellished with embroidery, with frill or lace edging.

Collars are generally cut and made up separately before attaching to the neckline of the garment, except for the shawl collar which is cut as an extension of the centre frontline and then folded back.

Basically collars are of three types:

1. The flat collar
2. The straight collar
3. The roll collar

The fall of the collar depends on the line on which it is drafted. A flat collar is cut in the same shape as the neckline curve and so lies flat against the dress. A straight collar is cut along a straight line and so it tends to stand up against the neck. A roll collar is drafted using a slight curve, the line of which lies in between the deep curve of a flat collar and the straight line of a straight collar. Hence the roll collar tends to roll and fold back onto the neckbase.

Each collar has a definite character and is selected to suit the individual, the occasion and the dress silhouette.

THE FLAT COLLAR (FIG. 82)

Draw a vertical line AB. Place the centre front line of the bodice block on AB and trace its outline. Then place the shoulder line of the back bodice block against the front shoulder line CD and trace its outline. Mark the centre back as EF. Keeping the centre back on fold, draw the collar of the required width. Shape the front edge of the collar.

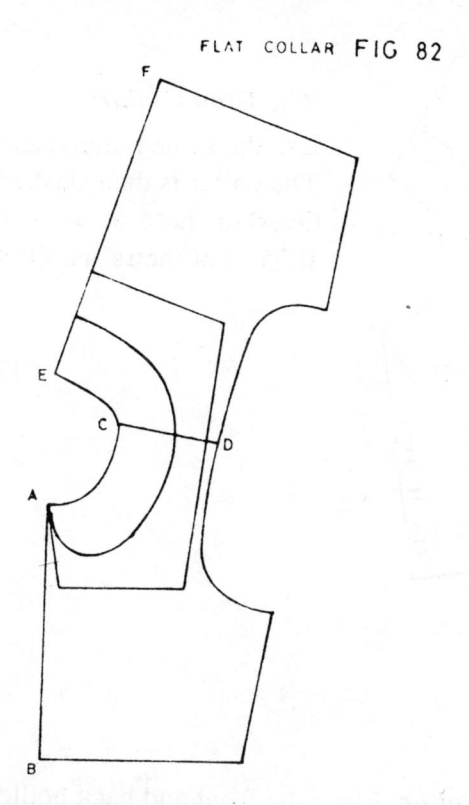

FLAT COLLAR FIG 82

Variations of the flat collar are:

The Peter Pan Collar (Fig. 83): Place the front and back bodice blocks as has been explained for the flat collar. The only difference is that the front shoulder line BC and the back shoulder line BD are overlapped at the lower shoulder point by 1.5 centimetre. Measure and mark the width of the collar. The centre front of the collar is marked G which is about 1.5 or 2.0 centimetres from the centre front line. Join AG. The point G may be rounded. When the collar has two sections, it is not kept on fold and a shape is given at both the centre back and at the centre front edges. Make sure to mark the two edges of the collar as back and front and to notch at the shoulder point.

A Peter Pan collar is only about 4.0 to 6.0 centimetres wide and is commonly used on children's garments. In case lace or frill is to be attached at the edge of the collar then remember to allow for the width of the lace at the centre front as shown in Fig. 83a.

PETER PAN COLLAR
FIG. 83

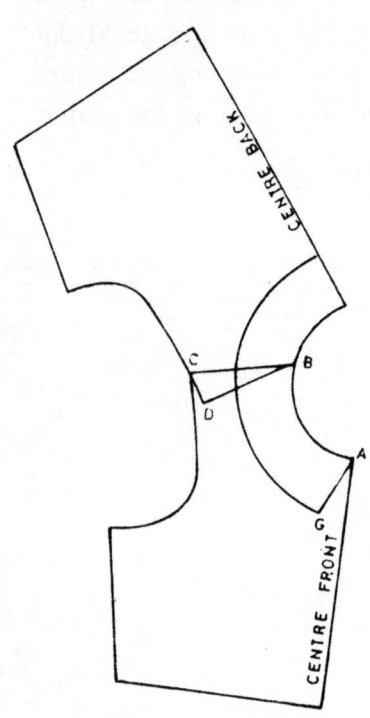

FIG. 83a

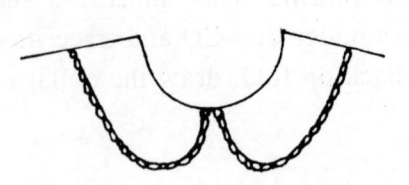

The Eton Collar:
Use the same method as for the Peter Pan collar. The collar is then slashed from the lower edge. Overlap these at the lower edge by 0.25 centimetre as illustrated in Fig. 84.

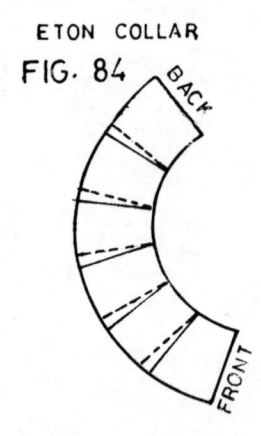

ETON COLLAR
FIG. 84

The Bertha Collar: Place the front and back bodice blocks as was done for the Peter Pan collar. The Bertha collar has a lowered neckline and it extends beyond the shoulder. The neckline is lowered both at the front and back by about 6.0 centimetre. Draw a lowered neckline all around. Then measure the width of the collar from this lowered neckline, extending it beyond the shoulder. The extension may be about 2.0 centimetres or more. Draw the shape of the collar with the front edge 1.5 centimetre away from the centre front line as shown in Fig. 85.

Other variations of the Flat Collar are the Sailor Collar (Fig. 86), the Flat Collar with Dropped Front (Fig. 87) and the Cross-Over Flat Collar (Fig. 88).

The Art of Sewing   105

SAILOR COLLAR FIG. 86   FLAT COLLAR WITH DROPPED FRONT FIG. 87

CENTRE BACK

CENTRE FRONT

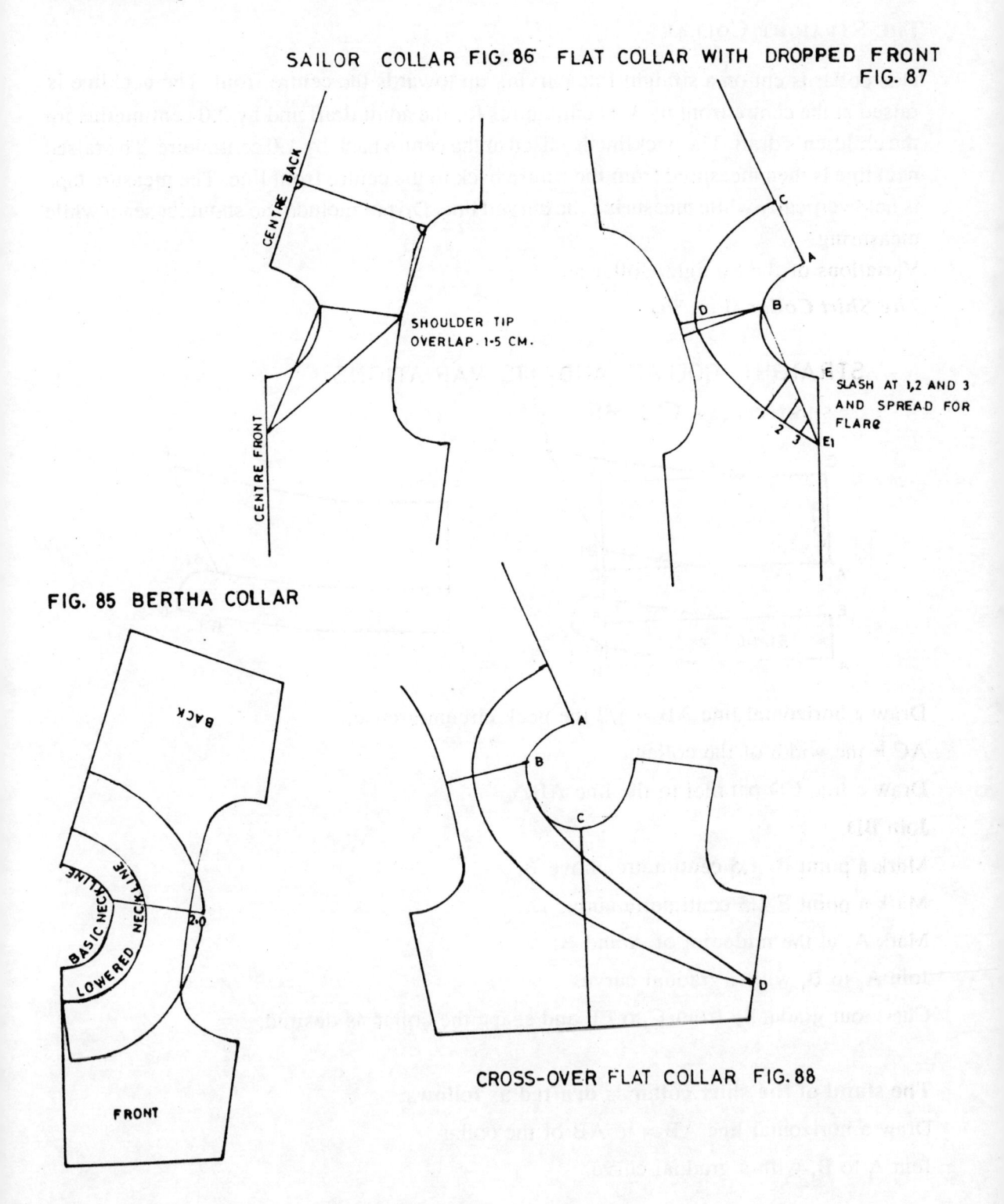

SHOULDER TIP OVERLAP 1·5 CM.

SLASH AT 1, 2 AND 3 AND SPREAD FOR FLARE

FIG. 85 BERTHA COLLAR

BACK

BASIC NECKLINE
LOWERED NECKLINE
2·0

FRONT

CROSS-OVER FLAT COLLAR FIG. 88

THE STRAIGHT COLLAR

This collar is cut on a straight line curving up towards the centre front. The neckline is raised at the centre front by 3.0 centimetres for the adult draft and by 2.0 centimetres for the children's draft. The neckline is raised at the centre back by 1.0 centimetre. The raised neckline is then measured from the centre back to the centre front line. The measure tape is held vertically while measuring the curved line. Do not include the shoulder seam while measuring.

Variations of the Straight Collar are:

The Shirt Collar (Fig. 89):

STRAIGHT COLLAR AND ITS VARIATIONS
SHIRT COLLAR FIG. 89

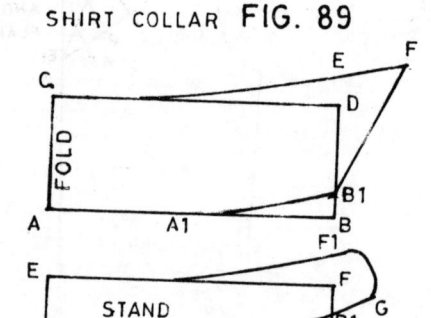

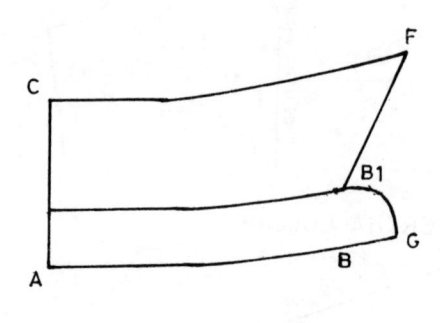

Draw a horizontal line AB = 1/2 the neck circumference.

AC = the width of the collar.

Draw a line CD parallel to the line AB.

Join BD.

Mark a point B_1 1.5 centimetre above B.

Mark a point E 1.5 centimetre above D.

Mark A_1 at the midpoint of A and B.

Join A_1 to B_1 with a gradual curve.

Curve out gradually from C to EF and shape the collar as desired.

The stand of the shirt collar is drafted as follows:

Draw a horizontal line AB = to AB of the collar.

Join A to B_1 with a gradual curve.

Extend B_1 by 2.0 centimetres to G.

Draw AE = 3.0 centimetres.

Draw a line EF parallel and equal to AB.

Join BF.

Mark F_1 1.5 centimetre above F.

Extend F_1 by 1.5 centimetre and curve out to G.

The collar and the stand of the collar are cut in one piece as illustrated.

The Chinese or Mandarin Collar (Fig. 90):

CHINESE OR MANDARIN COLLAR FIG. 90

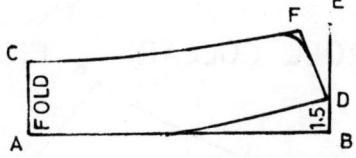

Raise the front and back neckline as mentioned under Straight Collar.

Draw a line AB = 1/2 the neck circumference.

AC = Width of the collar.

BD = 1.5 centimetre.

Curve AD as shown.

DE = AC.

EF = 2.0 centimetres.

Join DF with a straight line.

Curve out from C to F. The corner at the point F may be straight or curved as desired.

If the Mandarin collar is wide it requires shaping at the top edge for a closer fit. The top edge of the collar is slashed and overlapped 0.5 centimetre at each slash as shown in Fig. 90a.

SLASH AND OVERLAP FOR A CLOSE FIT **FIG. 90 a**

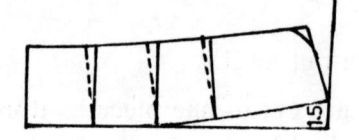

THE ROLL COLLAR

Partial Roll Collar (Fig. 91):

PARTIAL ROLL COLLAR   FIG. 91

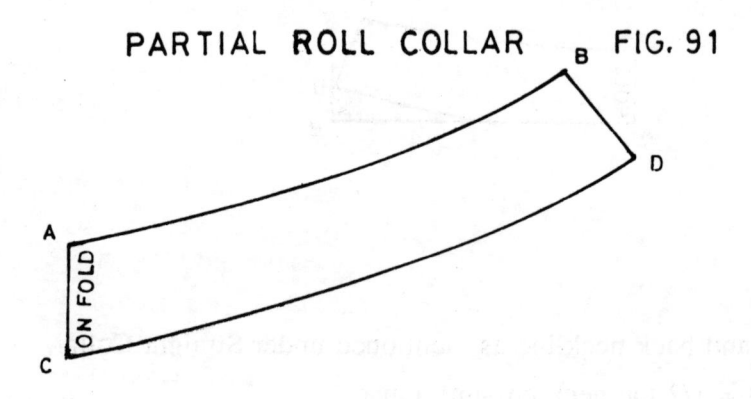

Draw a gradually curved line AB.

AB = 1/2 the neck circumference.

AC = the required width of the collar.

Draw the outer shape of the collar from C to D as illustrated.

The Shawl Collar (Fig. 92):

Draw a vertical line AB.

Plae the centre front of the bodice block on the line AB and mark the outline.

Extend the shoulder line and the centre front line and mark the point of intersection as A_1.

SHAWL COLLAR FIG. 92

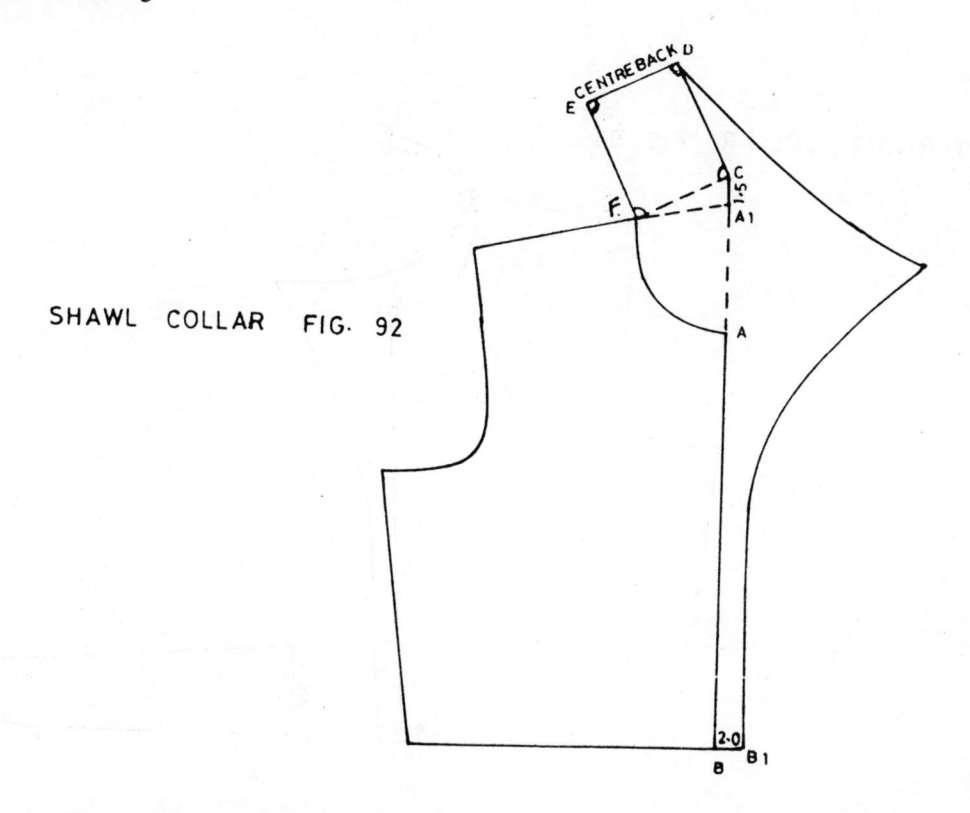

Mark a point C 1.5 centimetre above A_1.

Join C to F.

Draw a line CD at right angles to CF and equal to the length of the back neckline.

Complete the rectangle FCDE making DE = CF and CD = EF.

The line DE is the centre back of the collar.

DE is attached by a seam to the corresponding line on the second front section.

Mark a line at a distance of 2.0 centimetres, parallel to the centre front line AB.

From the point D shape out as desired and curve down to the extended centre front line as illustrated.

The Convertible Collar (Fig. 93):

This collar is open at the centre front and has a lapel.

On a vertical line place the centre front of the bodice block and mark it as AB.

Raise the front neckline at A by 2.5 centimetres and mark it as F.

Raise the back neckline by 1.0 centimetre and mark it as E.

Draw a raised new neckline joining the points ECF. Measure the neckline ECF.

CONVERTIBLE COLLAR FIG. 93

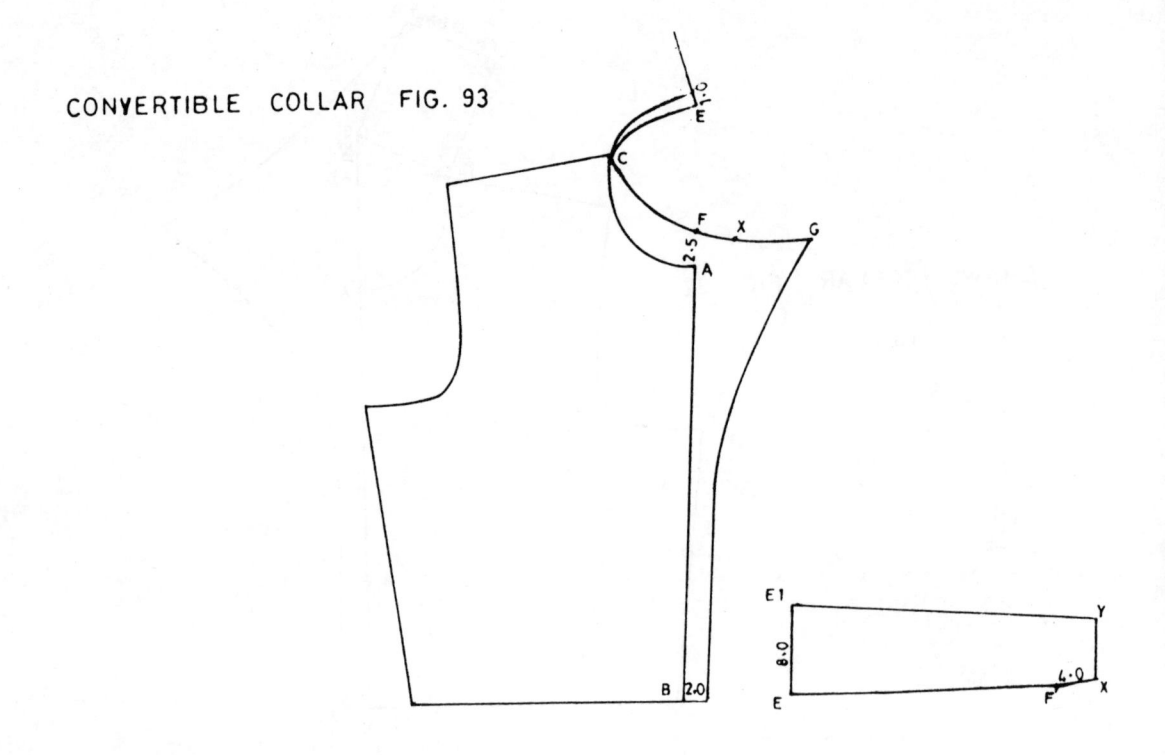

Extend F to G as shown in the diagram.

X is marked 4.0 centimetres from F.

The distance of G depends on the width required for the lapel. G is then joined to the extended centre front line of the bodice block.

The collar draft:

Draw a line EF equal to 1/2 the neck circumference.

F is slightly raised with respect to the horizontal through E.

Extend F to a point X at a distance of 4.0 centimetres.

Make XY = 5.0 centimetres.

Make E E_1 = 8.0 centimetres.

Now join E_1 to Y.

The front edge of the collar marked X is matched to the point X on the neckline.

The shawl and convertible collars both have the facing cut along the same outer line as the collar and extending upto half the shoulder width as shown in Figs. 39a and 39b. The centre back of the under collar is matched with that of the garment and attached upto the shoulder point. The top collar is then turned over the neck seam and either stitched by hand or by machine. A notch is made at the shoulder point and the front of the collar is inserted between the garment and the facing. Turn the facing over and press well. The facing is held in place along the centre front line by the buttons and buttonholes. The lower edge of the facing is machined or hemmed together with that of the garment.

CUTTING AND SEWING INSTRUCTIONS

After the collar has been drafted, cut it out onto a tracing paper and place along the neckline of the dress to check whether it fits the curve. The collar is cut on two layers of fabric. The top collar is cut 0.25 centimetre larger than the under collar. The interfacing for the collar is cut without seam allowance. Fusible interfacings are most suitable since they are easy to use and also since they maintain the shape better. The fusible interfacing is fixed onto the top collar. The interfacing may be cut on the bias to give a perfect roll. After attaching the interfacing, turn the two right sides of the collar to face inwards and then machine together from one end of the collar to the other. Take care to make sharp neat points at the corners. Clip off the extra seam allowance. Then slash or notch the seam allowance of the collar almost upto the seamline. The seam allowance at the pointed tips of the collar should be clipped diagonally to avoid bulk. Turn out the collar, press well and baste all around to ensure that the undercollar is not visible. Edge machine the collar at the distance of 0.5 centimetre from the edge. The collar is then attached to the neckline of the garment.

Chapter 13

Sleeves

By virtue of their location on a garment, the visual impact of sleeves is instant. There are a wide variety of sleeves and they are selected to conform to the dress silhouette.

A well fitted sleeve is the mark of a good seamstress. In most sleeves, the curve of the sleeve cap is cut larger than the curve of the bodice armhole. This extra fullness or ease is essential for the sleeve to fit the roundness of the top arm. The amount of ease to be added depends on the garment style and the type of fabric but it should be a minimum of 2.0 to 3.0 centimetres.

The extra fullness is then eased to fit the armhole. Using the largest size of stitch, run a row of machine stitches from point A to point B as shown in the diagram (Fig. 94). The lower machine thread is pulled to form the ease, which is then distributed evenly by moving it between the thumb and index finger, to give the sleeve cap a smooth and raised appearance. The sleeve cap and the garment armhole are matched. Pin the sleeve onto the garment armhole, matching the centre of the sleeve to the shoulder seam. The sleeve is then basted with small, even stitches to hold the ease securely until it has been machined. If the sleeve has not been eased smoothly, small folds may be formed after machining.

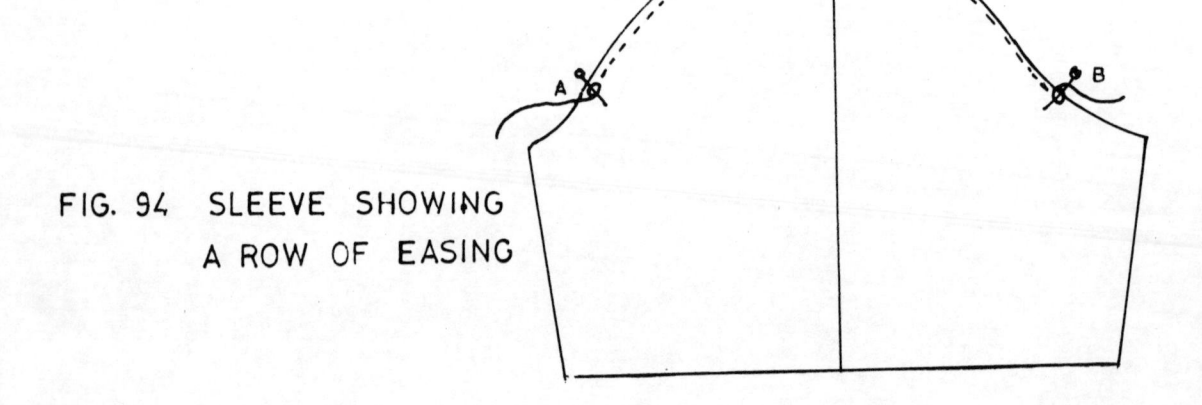

FIG. 94 SLEEVE SHOWING A ROW OF EASING

There are two ways in which sleeves are stitched. In **Set-in Sleeves,** the sleeve is set into the armhole after the side seams of the garment and that of the sleeve have been machined. In **Open Construction Sleeves**, as the name suggests, the sleeves are attached keeping the garment flat and open. They are attached before joining the side seams making it convenient to attach the sleeves. It also allows for ease in alterations at the side seams. This method is used especially when the armhole is small, as in children's garments. It is also used for garments that are finished with the flat-fell seam or the French seam.

There are three basic types of sleeves:

SET-IN SLEEVES

Puff Sleeves (Fig. 95): There are three types of puff sleeves. In the first type, the gathers are both at the top end and at the lower end.

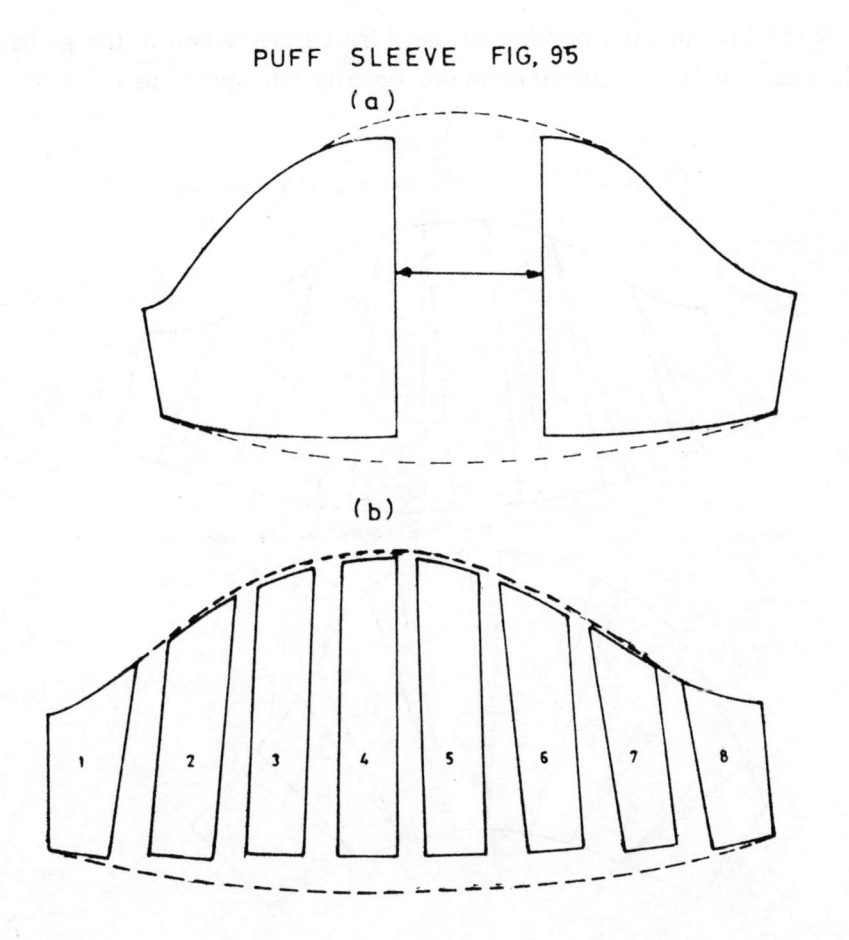

PUFF SLEEVE FIG. 95

In Fig. 95a, the basic sleeve block has been shown cut at the centre line and the two halves placed about 10.0 to 12.0 centimetres apart to allow for the gathers. The highest point of the sleeve cap is raised by 1.5 centimetre and a smooth curved line is drawn. Similarly, the lower end of the sleeve is lowered by 1.0 centimetre at the centre point and a smooth curve is drawn as shown in Fig. 95a.

Another method of drafting the puff sleeve is by cutting the basic sleeve block into a number of segments and placing them apart to allow for gathers. Draw a curved line slightly raised above the upper edge of the sleeve block. The lower end of the sleeve block is lowered 1.5 centimetre at the centre point. Join the lower extended sleeve edge by a smooth curve. (Fig. 95b)

Figure. 95c illustrates a second type of Puff Sleeves. In this, the gathers are only at the lower end. The sleeve block is slashed from the lower edge and spread to allow for the fullness.

Figure. 95d illustrates the making of the third variety wherein the gathers are at the top end. The sleeve block is slashed from the top edge and spread to allow for the fullness.

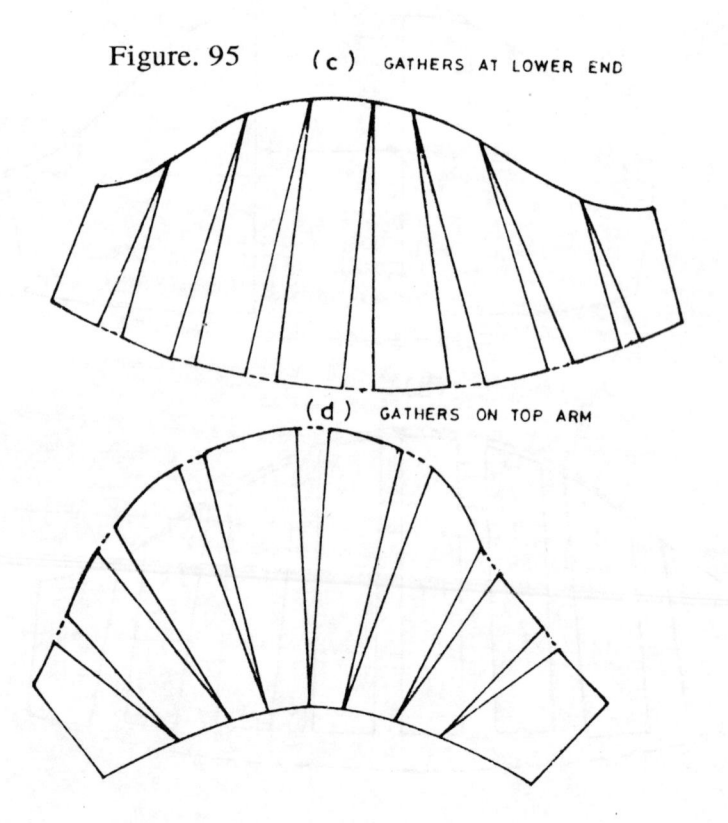

Figure. 95   (c) GATHERS AT LOWER END

(d) GATHERS ON TOP ARM

Bishops Sleeves (Fig. 96): In this, the basic sleeve block is divided vertically into six sections. Draw a vertical line AB in which AB is the actual sleeve length minus the required cuff width. The sleeve is gathered into a narrow cuff, the width being 4.0 centimetres. Slash the sleeve block into six sections and number them as shown. Place the section 3 and 4 in such a way that they are 2.0 centimetres apart from AB at B. The slashed sections are spread 8.0 centimetres between the back sections and 4.0 centimetres between the front sections. Draw a horizontal line at B. Since the slashed and spread sections of the sleeve block will present the lower end as a curved line, the slashed sections should be extended to meet the horizontal line. Now lower the point B by 10.0 centimetres to the position C. Finally draw an outward curve at the back and an inward curve at the front as shown in the diagram.

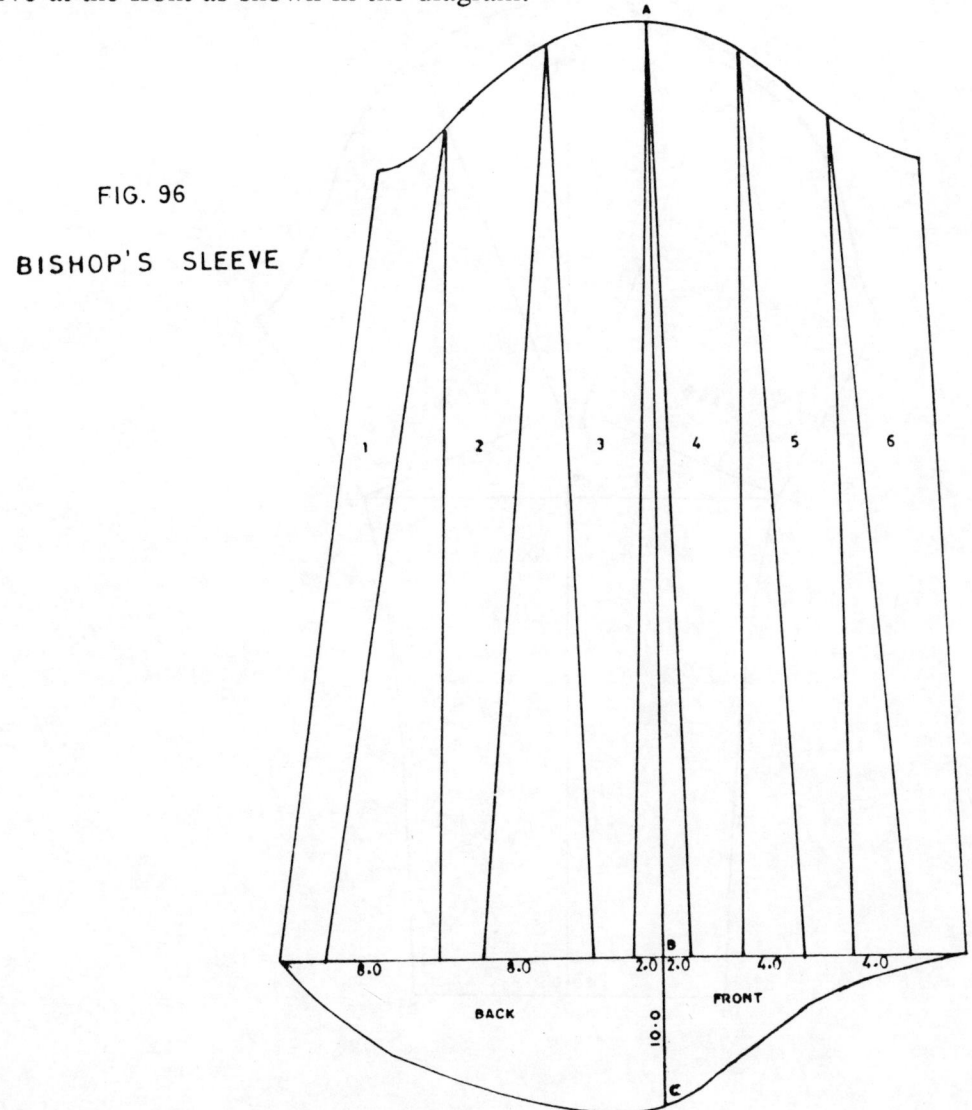

FIG. 96

BISHOP'S SLEEVE

Leg O' Mutton Sleeves (Fig. 97): Draw a horizontal line EF as shown in the figure. Place the Basic Sleeve Block on EF. Now cut along the centre line of the Sleeve Block marked as AB. Spread the two cut sections of the sleeve block as shown, raising B by 6.0 centimetres from EF. The point A_1 is the midpoint of the top of the sleeve cap. Raise A_1 by 4.0 centimetres to a point C. Now draw a vertical line from C down to D, equal to the actual sleeve length plus 10.0 centimetres. Draw a horizontal line at D and mark D_1 and D_2 such that $D_1 D_2$ is the wrist measurement plus 5.0 centimetres. Finally join E to D_1 and F to D_2 with smooth, inward curves.

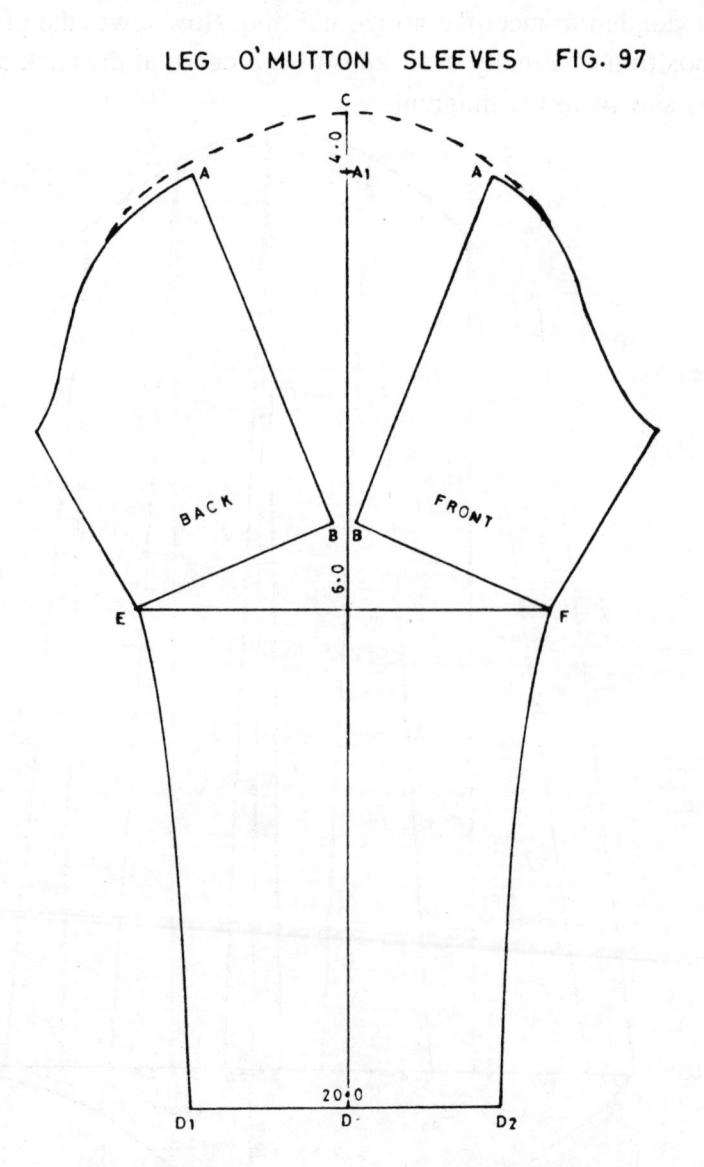

LEG O' MUTTON SLEEVES FIG. 97

Petal Sleeves (Fig. 98): Mark a point D_1 about 8.0 to 10.0 centimetres from the point D of the sleeve block as shown in the figure. Similarly mark point A_1 such that $AA_1 = DD_1$. Mark also the point X at the centre of the sleeve cap. Join BD_1 and CA_1 as shown by smooth outward curves. Now trace the petal shapes AA_1 XD_1 B and DD_1 XA_1 C separately on a paper and cut their outlines. Use these to obtain the sleeve from the fabric by placing the petals in such a way that AB and DC coincide. Thus the sleeve is obtained with AB and DC as the centre line and the curved portion of the sleeve cap on either side. The curved sections are notched at the points marked 'X' as shown in Fig. 98. The centre line AB/DC will become the underarm seam of the sleeve. Fold the two curved ends of the sleeve to overlap matching at the notches marking the centre of the sleeve cap. The sleeve is then attached in the usual manner.

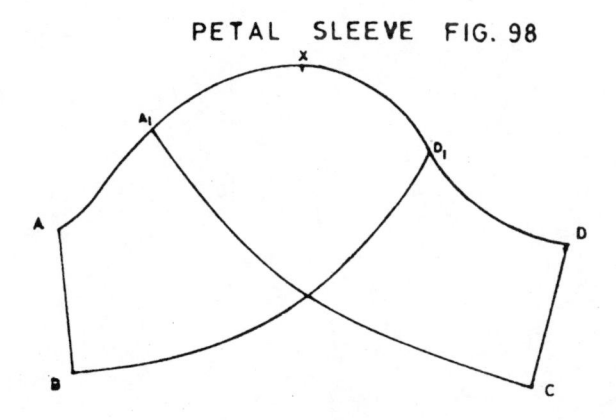

PETAL SLEEVE FIG. 98

Raglan Sleeves (Fig. 99, 99a)

This sleeve is joined to the bodice by a diagonal seam extending to the neckline. It is a good choice for shoulders that are hard to fit and also for growing children.

Place the centre front the bodice block on a vertical line and trace its outline. Place the back shoulder also along the front shoulder line and similarly trace out the back bodice block. The front and back raglan sleeve positions can now be marked. The front position begins 4.0 centimetres below the shoulder line on the front neckline and ends at the armhole which has to be lowered by 4.0 centimetres. Similarly, the back position begins 3.0 below the shoulder line on the back neckline and ends at the lowered armhole. Now the sleeve block is placed, matching the centre of the sleeve with the shoulderline. Draw the raglan sleeve line from neck to armhole as shown in the diagram. This seamline can be curved both at the front and at the back to take in the extra ease at the hollow of the chest, as shown marked by dotted lines. The lowered armhole is then joined to the sleeve block, completing the raglan sleeve. No shaping is necessary in the case of the child's raglan sleeve.

ADULT'S RAGLAN SLEEVE FIG. 99   CHILD'S RAGLAN SLEEVE FIG. 99a

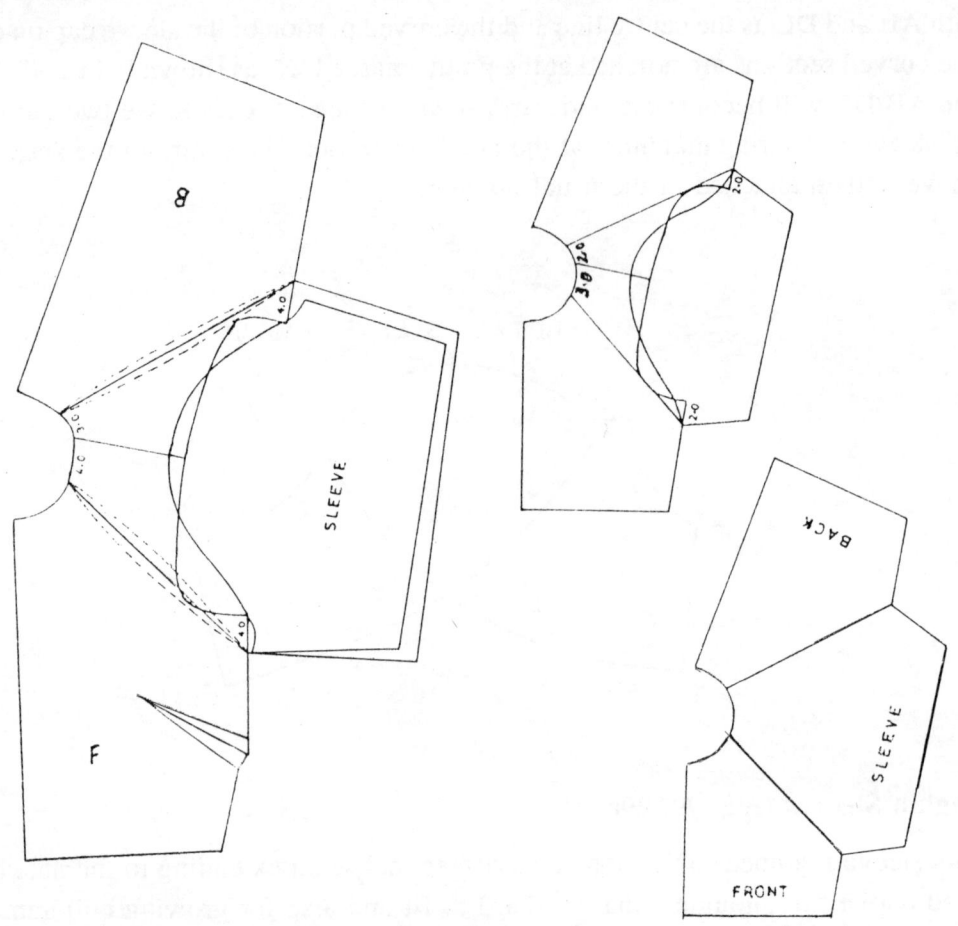

Sleeves Cut as an Extension of the Bodice

Kimono Sleeves: The sleeve is cut in one piece, with the bodice curving out from the waistline to the sleeve edge. The shoulder seam is sloped 4.0 centimetres as shown (Fig. 100).

Dolman Sleeves: This sleeve is similar to the kimono sleeve in that it appears to be an extension of the bodice. However, it is actually joined by a seam on the bodice which may be either curved or L-shaped (Fig. 101).

The Art of Sewing 119

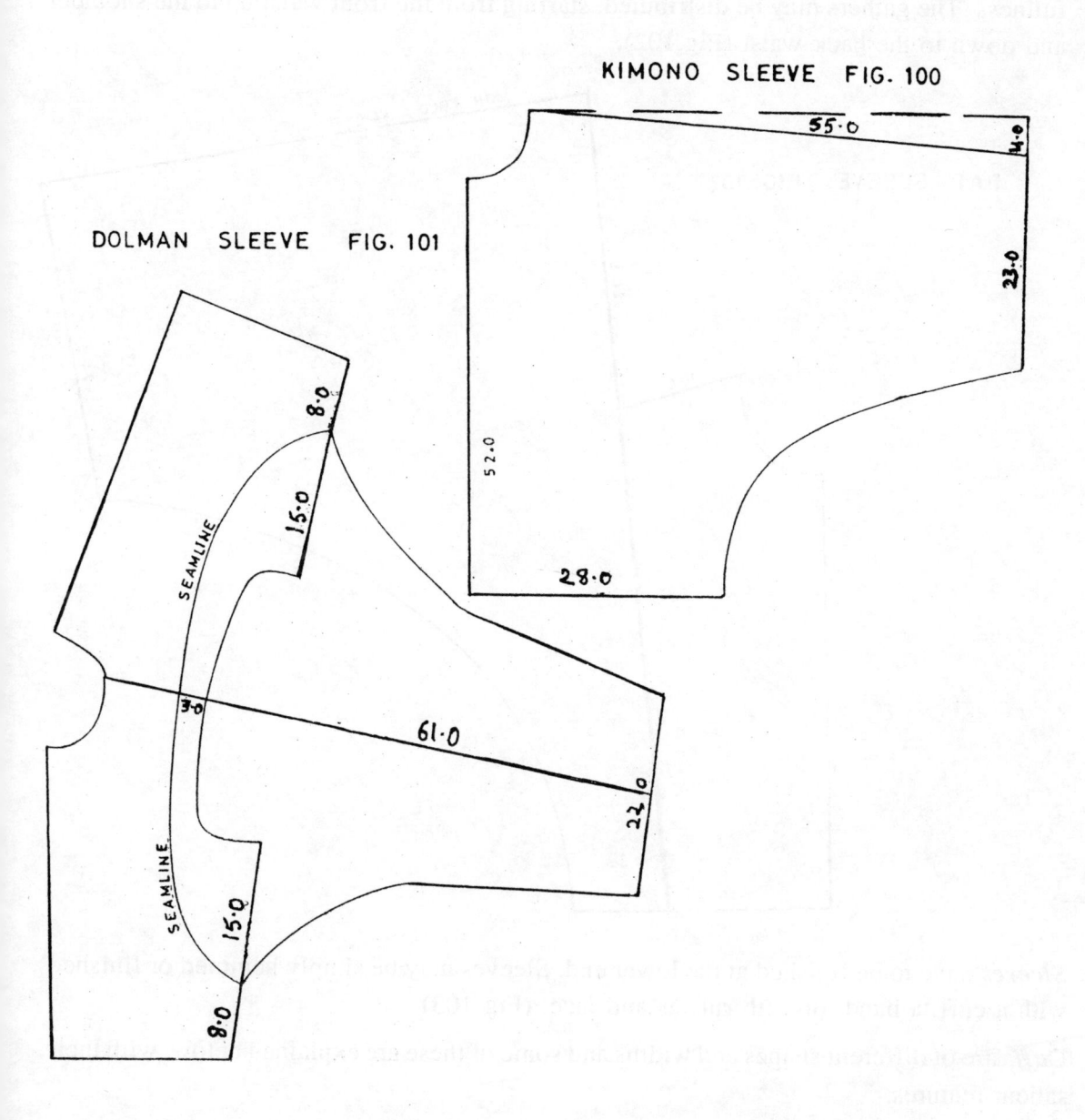

KIMONO SLEEVE FIG. 100

DOLMAN SLEEVE FIG. 101

Bat Sleeves: This sleeves is similar to the Dolman sleeve except that it has additional fullness. The gathers may be distributed, starting from the front waist up to the shoulder and down to the back waist (Fig.102).

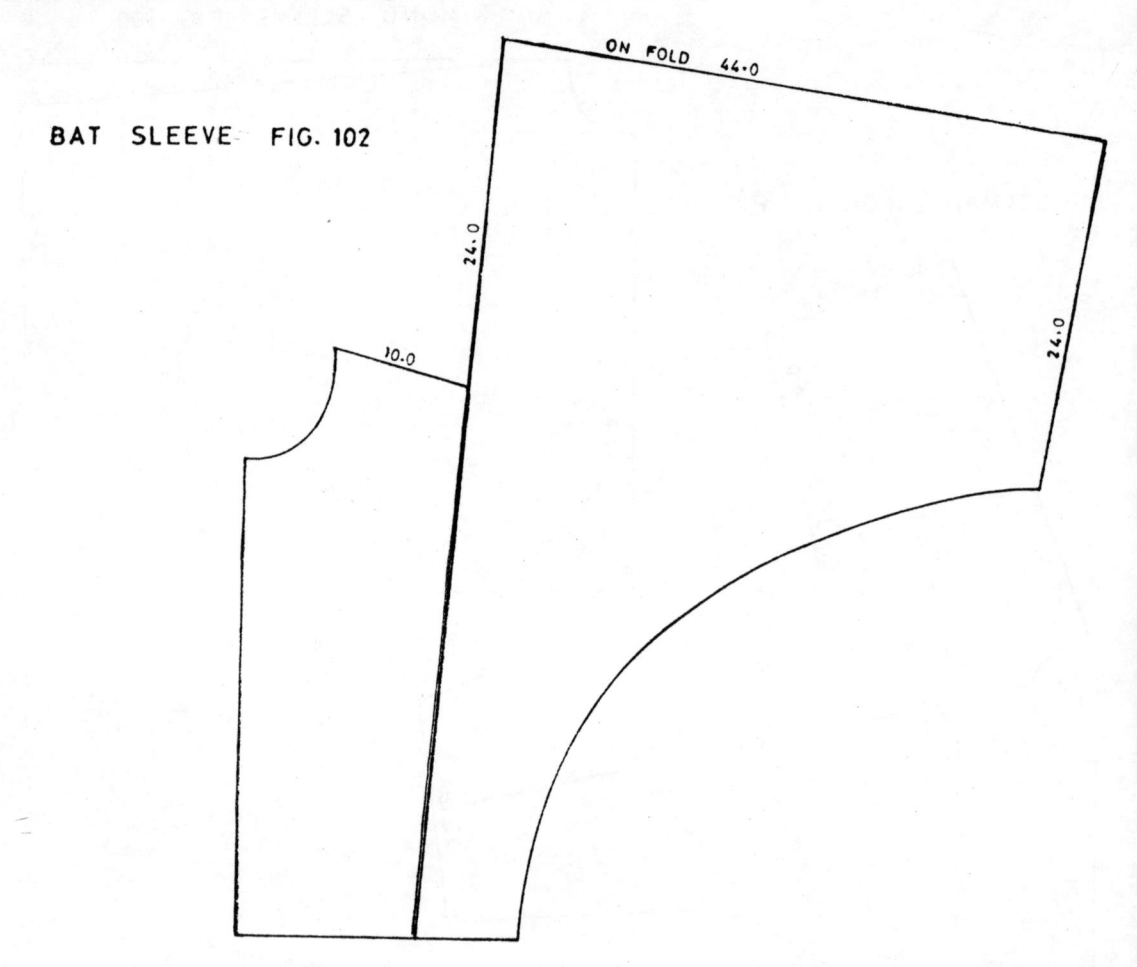

BAT SLEEVE FIG. 102

Sleeves have to be finished at the lower end. Sleeves may be simply hemmed or finished with a cuff, a band, or with ruffles and lace. (Fig 103)

Cuffs are of different shapes and widths and some of these are explained below, with their salient features.

The Lapped Cuff has one end lapped over the other end with the opening along the seamline.

The Shirt Cuff has an underlap and an overlap placket which may be given a straight or pointed-edge finish.

The Art of Sewing

CUFFS FIG. 103

LAPPED CUFF

SHIRT CUFF

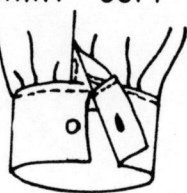

FRENCH CUFF

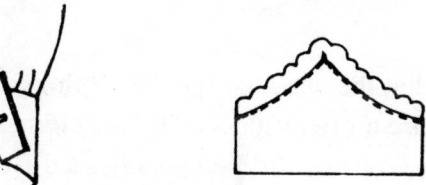

POINTED CUFF WITH LACE

GAUNLET CUFF

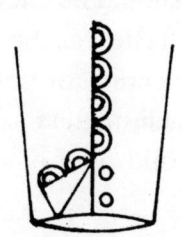

The French Cuff has a double width of cuff which is folded back and generally worn with cuff links.

The Band Cuff may be wide or narrow and is finished without on opening.

The Gaunlet Cuff is a very wide cuff that is fitted and shaped. This is generally fastened with a row of buttons.

The Mock Cuff is like a hem but the hem folds onto the right side and is machined down a little away from the edge. This is commonly used in skirt blouses.

CHAPTER 14
CHILDREN'S CLOTHES

It was not until the 1930's that the need for special clothing for children was recognized. Children from an early age are more influenced by the clothes they wear than is generally realized by adults. Each age group of children attaches a different importance to clothing.

Right from pre-school days, children should be encouraged and allowed to make the final choice of their clothing. A child's taste can be developed and improved in the making of small choices such as the selection of socks, ribbons, handkerchiefs etc. Whereas the parent is concerned about such matters as price, durability, suitability etc. these are not of any importance to the child who is merely concerned about feel and appearance.

Every child is an individual and should be treated as one. At the same time, children should not be forced into wearing clothes that are very different from those worn by others of their age. Remember also, that garments that are too large or those that are handed-down will give a child an inferiority complex.

THE BODICE BLOCK

The bodice blocks for children have been plotted down with the average measurements for the various age groups ranging from infants to the early teens. But since there is little co-relation between age and size, in order to select the correct bodice block, first check the shoulder and chest measurement of the child with that of the bodice block. The shoulder width and the chest measurements vary so slightly within the age group that it can be covered by the amount of ease that has been included in the drafting. The difference is usually in the vertical measurement which can be increased easily without changing the draft outline.

Adapting the basic bodice block is easy when there are no darts and no darts are required for children till the age of thirteen years. After fourteen years of age the teen generally fits into the adult blocks. A size 76.0 centimetres (30") or size 82.0 centimetres (32") may be used when stitching garments such as the Princess line that require to be shaped.

For making one-piece garments, the bodice block and the pant draft may be combined together, making sure that the distance from the neckline to the crotch is sufficient to allow for comfort. The actual neck to crotch measurement should be increased by 5.0 centimetres at the waist level, without having to make any alteration to either the bodice or the pant draft.

Children's clothes are the easiest garments to sew. It would be a good idea to first begin by sewing a skirt because it is by far the most simple of garments to stitch and yet includes many sewing construction details such as the waistband, placket and hem.

The only difficult feature is the neckline. It is advisable, therefore, to first try out neck finishes using waste fabric rather than risk the garment. Try simple designs at first, until you have gained confidence in your stitching ability. You can then attempt to tackle more difficult design features such as collars. Sleeves are not a problem in children's clothing since generally puff or raglan sleeves are used, both of which are easy to attach.

INFANTS

In the infant, it is only the sense of touch that functions perfectly from birth. Baby skin being so sensitive, clothes must be soft and pliable to be really comfortable. Hence, soft knitted fabrics have become popular.

Not only must the fabric be soft but the garment well constructed with flat seams. Cotton fabrics are found to be most suited for babies. Synthetic fabrics are not absorbent and cause irritation. For the summer, simple cotton dresses or vests are the most suitable. In the winter, a cotton vest or a straight cotton dress should be worn next to the skin with the wool over it, and never in direct contact with the skin.

Baby dresses should be open fully down the back or the front, depending on whether the baby sleeps on his back or on his stomach. This would make it both easy and convenient to put on and remove. Buttons or tapes on a garment could hurt a baby. Single or double-breasted vests are suitable for the winter as additional protection for the chest. Vests with overlapping shoulders are ideal as they are without any fasteners. Safety pins have made way for velcro as the ideal fastener for baby diapers and vests.

Baby frocks that have gathers at the neck should not have draw strings. Instead, they should be finished with a piping that can be conveniently tied at the back.

Basically, infant clothing should be simple, comfortable and also easy to launder. Babies should be dressed in white or soft pastel colours. A small amount of hand embroidery may be added to make the garment attactive. Frills and laces cater mainly to the mother's satisfaction and can best be avoided.

The Toddler

At this age, clothes have to be designed mainly for protection and comfort. Since the child is learning to sit and stand, creep and crawl, walk and climb, the clothes should allow enough freedom for all these activities.

Since the child is for most of the time on the floor, protection from dirt and the cold floor are essential. Clothes should be so chosen that they are light yet warm. It would be best not to overburden the child with too many garments and restrict its movements.

One-piece jump-suits are excellent, with a patch or padding at the knees for protection while crawling. These should not be too baggy though loose enough to allow for creeping and stretching.

Another important consideration is an opening at the crotch, down to the knee level to permit ease in dressing and undressing and while changing diapers.

Kimono or raglan sleeves are ideal for growth and they also allow for freedom of movement. The neckline should be low in front but not loose enough to fall off the shoulder.

Bear in mind that you should make enough allowance in the neck-to-crotch measurement. The shoulder should have enough fullness worked in across the shoulder blade to allow for spread. The armholes and sleeves should be low and loose. Soft and smooth fabrics that do not collect soil would be ideal for this age.

The Pre-School Child

Unlike the infant and the toddler, comfort is not the most important aspect of clothing for the pre-school child. At the age of 3-4 years, the child's world is rapidly widening and it enjoys being the centre of attraction.

The pre-school child becomes interested in its clothes, noticing other's clothes as well. With attention-seeking being a major occupation at this age, the child learns that one of the easiest ways is through clothes.

Bright colours and their names have been picked up, the favourites invariably being red, yellow, blue and green. With definite likes and dislikes surfacing, the child should be indulged when it comes to selection.

During these years, the child's limbs grow fast, the baby fat is being shed and a waistline is distinguishable. The child can now wear skirts with straps.

Play clothes should dominate its wardrobe. Cleanliness and neatness are not as important as physical activity which is imperative for normal growth.

This is the age when a child learns to dress independently, so the clothes should be so designed that it is not confused needlessly. All clothes should be open in front so that they can be buttoned easily. The use of large-sized buttons will go a long way in assisting the child to button and unbutton easily. Also, elastics and Velcro at the waist of skirts and pants make for easy dressing and undressing, making the child more self-sufficient and confident. When it comes to bows and ribbons, it is yet too early for the pre-school child to manage independently. The armholes and sleeves should be large enough to slip into easily. Shoes should be of the slip-on variety.

In conclusion, it may be said that appropriateness, durability and conformity are more important to adults and adolescents than to the pre-school child.

ELEMENTARY SCHOOL CHILD

One of the most important areas of development in a child aged 6-12 years is social development. Elementary school kids form cliques and gangs and conformity becomes all important.

It is psychologically harmful for the child, as well as false economy, to buy large garments. These tend to make the child appear clumsy and the butt of uncomplimentary comments.

A wise mother should plan growth features in the clothes, keeping in mind that at this age the child grows more in height than in girth.

Allowance for Growth in Height

1. A pinafore dress with adjustable straps and a wide hem.
2. Skirts and trousers that button onto blouses are an easy method that allows for growth. Only the positions of the buttons need to be shifted as required.
3. Dresses designed with tucks and insertion lace.
4. Contrasting bands of fabric added on to skirts and dresses to form interesting detail.

Allowance for Growth in Girth

1. Raglan sleeves
2. Elastic at waist and sleeves.

THE YOUNG ADOLESCENT

Adolescence is a period of tremendous change. The teenager caught between childhood and adulthood, has to go through a phase of adjustment.

During the early phase of adolescence, the body contours begin to take shape. For the female adolescent, the bust begins to develop as also an increase in the size of the abdomen. As a consequence, a certain degree of self-consciousness is aroused. Selection of garment design is thus invariably made to camouflage both the bustline and the abdomen.

Parents are no more the significant adults to whom the child could readily look to for advice in all matters including clothing. A sense of insecurity pervades the teenager's life and conformity becomes the best recourse. Clothes, being the easiest way to express conformity, become very important. The peer group takes on added significance. Adolescents want to dress like their peers so as to gain ready acceptance to a particular group, gang or clique.

The older adolescent is more stable, and the need for group approval reduces. A sense of individualism, without the fear of rejection, grows. Thus the adolescent who was once a conformist may well turn to becoming a budding fashion innovator.

Average Lengths for Dresses

Size	Age	Waist Length cms	inches	Dress Length cms	inches
I	6 months	9.0*	3½*	35.0	13¾
II	1 year	16.0	6¼	40.0	15¾
III	2-4 years	20.0	7¾	46.0-50.0	18-19½
IV	5-6 years	23.0	9	52.0-59.0	20½-23¼
V	7-8 years	27.0	10½	64.0-76.0	25-30
VI	9-11 years	32.0	12½	82.0-87.0	32-34
VII	15-16 years	36.0	14	89.0-92.0	35-36

* Chest level.

Fabric requirement (in metres)

Age	Simple Dress	Trouser/Pyjamas and Salwar	Nightdress
Infant	0.50	-	-
6 months	0.75	0.80	1.25
1 year	1.00	1.00	1.25
2 years	1.25	1.25	1.50
3 years	1.25	1.25	1.75
4 years	1.40	1.50	1.75
5 years	1.40	1.50	2.00
6 years	1.50	1.75	2.25
7 years	1.50	1.75	2.50
8 years	1.50	1.75	2.75
9 years	1.75	2.00	2.75
10 years	1.75	2.00	2.75
11 years	2.00	2.00	2.80
12 years	2.25	2.25	2.80
13-15 yrs	2.50	2.25-2.50	3.00

These are average measurements. Since the height is not dependant on age and the dress lengths also vary, it is advisable to calculate as per the requirement of the style and the individual.

Calculating Fabric Requirement

Before purchasing fabric, it is necessary to have an estimate of the length of fabric required.

Fabric requirement can be calculated as twice the dress length plus one sleeve length, allowing extra fabric for seams and hem. In the case of infants, one dress length is sufficient.

An extra length of fabric is required for designs such as pleated skirts, wrap-over skirts and double breasted garments. Extra fabric is also required to match checks and stripes and for uni-directional prints.

While buying expensive fabric, place your pattern cuttings on a sheet of paper or any length of fabric having the same width of the fabric you wish to buy, then measure the required length.

SHORTS   FIG 119

The measurements that are provided in this draft are for the age group of 5-6 years.

This draft can be cut along the line AB and fullness may be added for bloomers having elastic at the waist and at the leg opening.

It may also be adapted to the Romper or Sunsuit by adding a bib and a strap. The bib can be cut in any shape desired and should reach up to the chest level. The straps should be crossed at the back and buttoned in front at the bib.

The method given can be followed for children between the age of two and ten years.

FIG. 104 INFANT'S DRESSES

A LINE DRESS

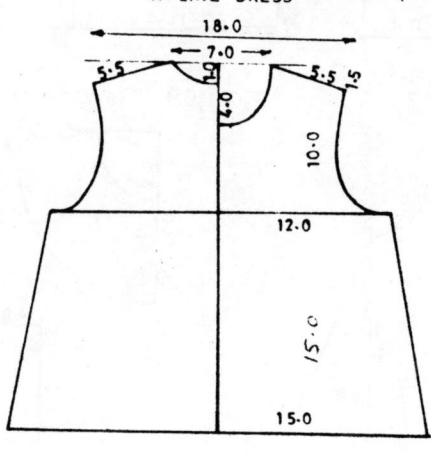

FIG. 105 GATHERS AT FRONT NECK

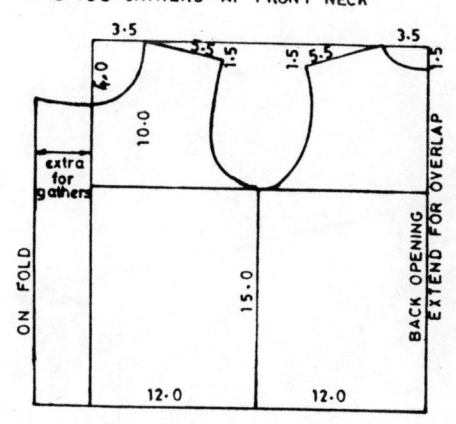

FIG. 106 DRESS WITH YOKE AND GATHERS

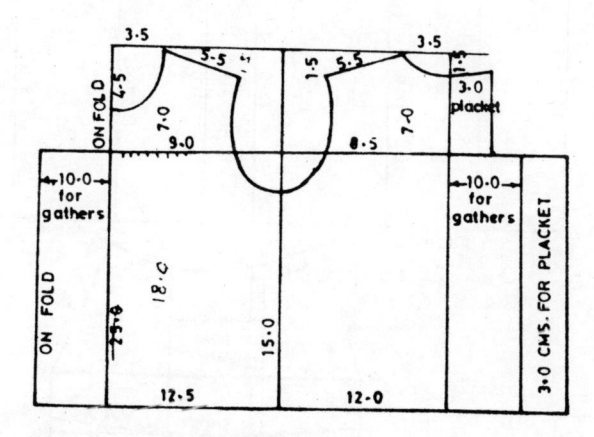

FIG. 107   SIZE 1   6 MONTHS

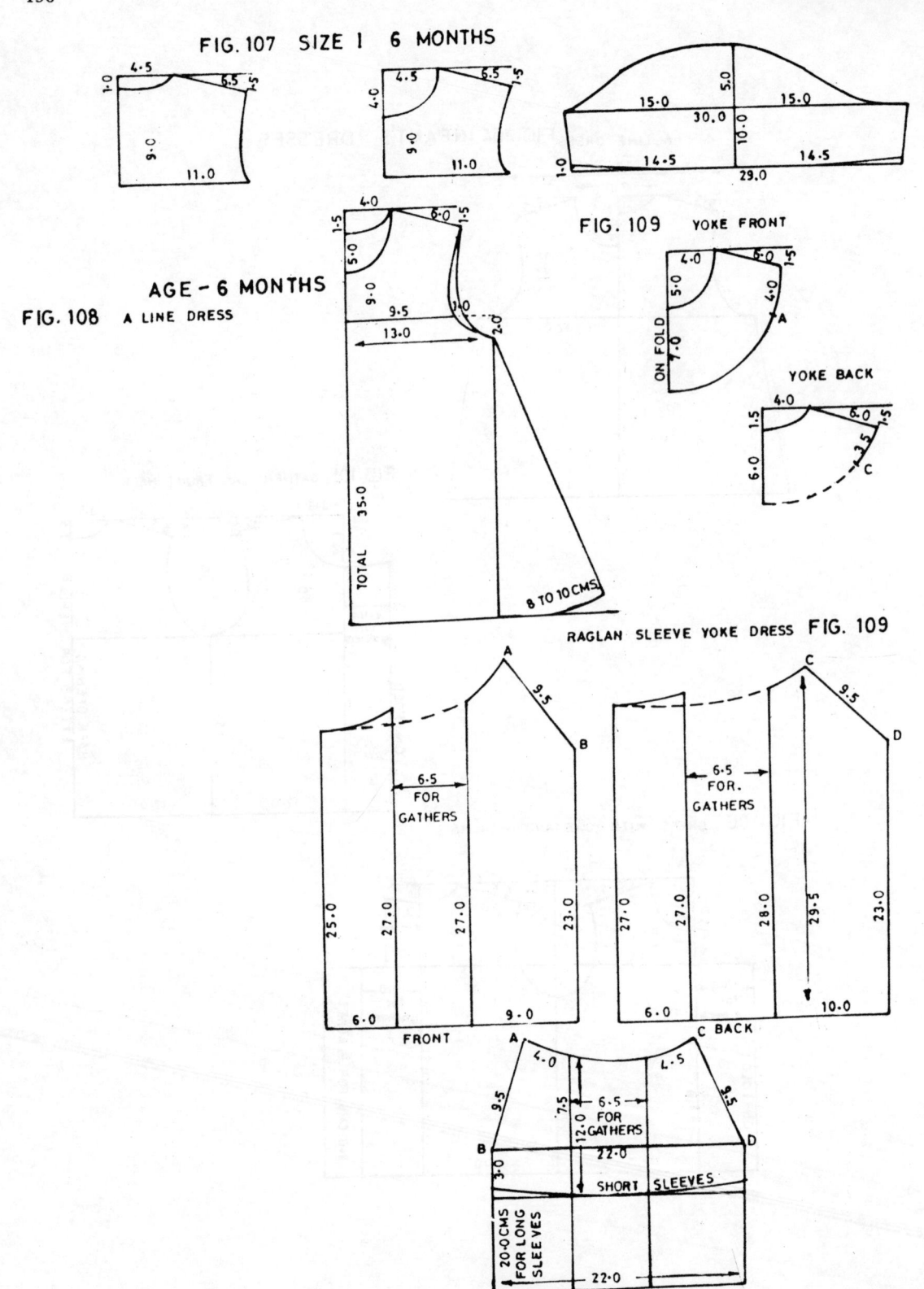

FIG. 108   A LINE DRESS   AGE – 6 MONTHS

FIG. 109   YOKE FRONT

YOKE BACK

RAGLAN SLEEVE YOKE DRESS   FIG. 109

FRONT

BACK

SHORT SLEEVES

20·0 CMS FOR LONG SLEEVES

The Art of Sewing

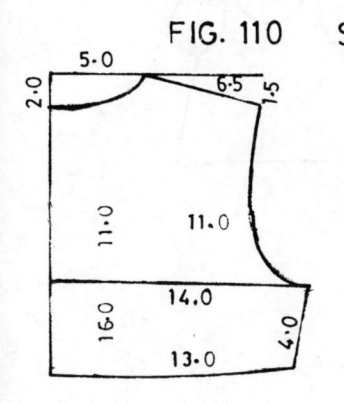

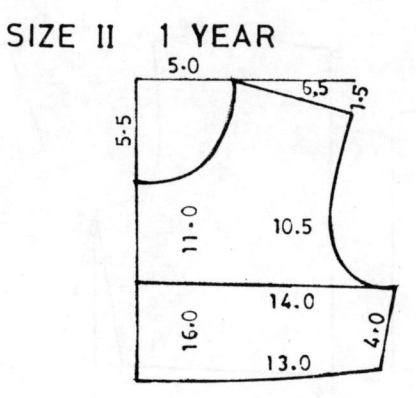

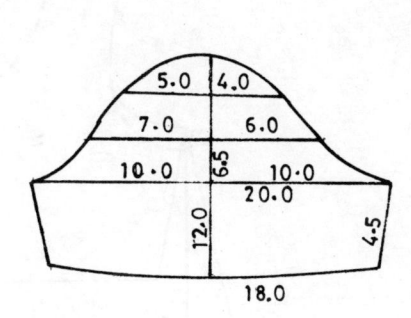

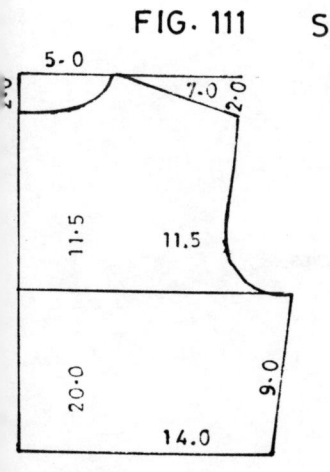

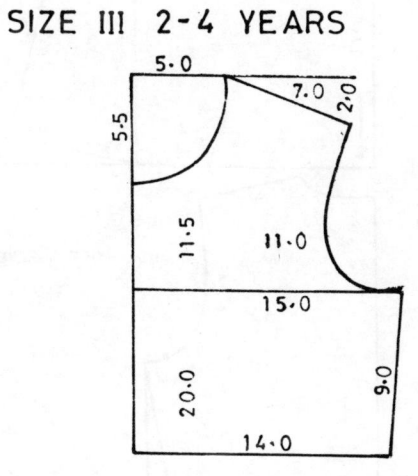

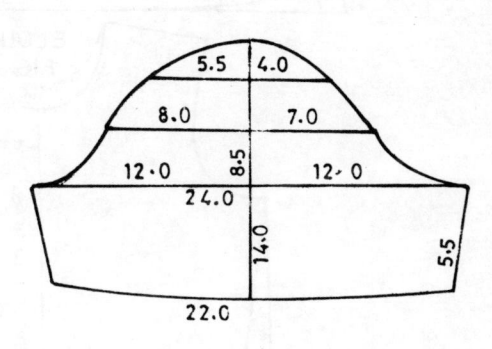

FIG. 110   SIZE II   1 YEAR

FIG. 111   SIZE III   2-4 YEARS

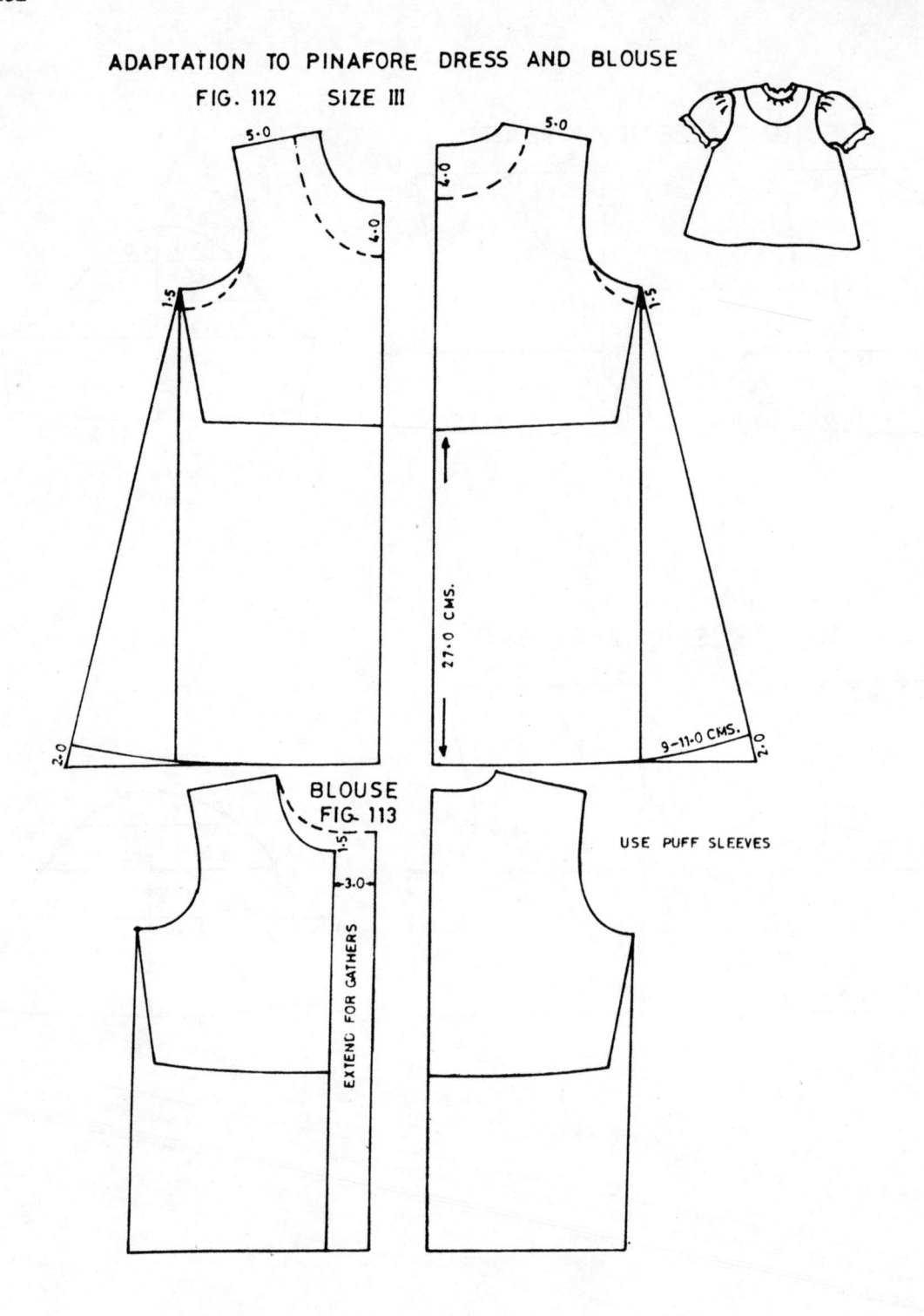

ADAPTATION TO PINAFORE DRESS AND BLOUSE
FIG. 112   SIZE III

5.0
4.0
1.5
27.0 CMS.
9-11.0 CMS.
2.0

BLOUSE FIG. 113

1.5
3.0
EXTEND FOR GATHERS

USE PUFF SLEEVES

The Art of Sewing   133

ADAPTATION   FIG. 114   FIG. 116

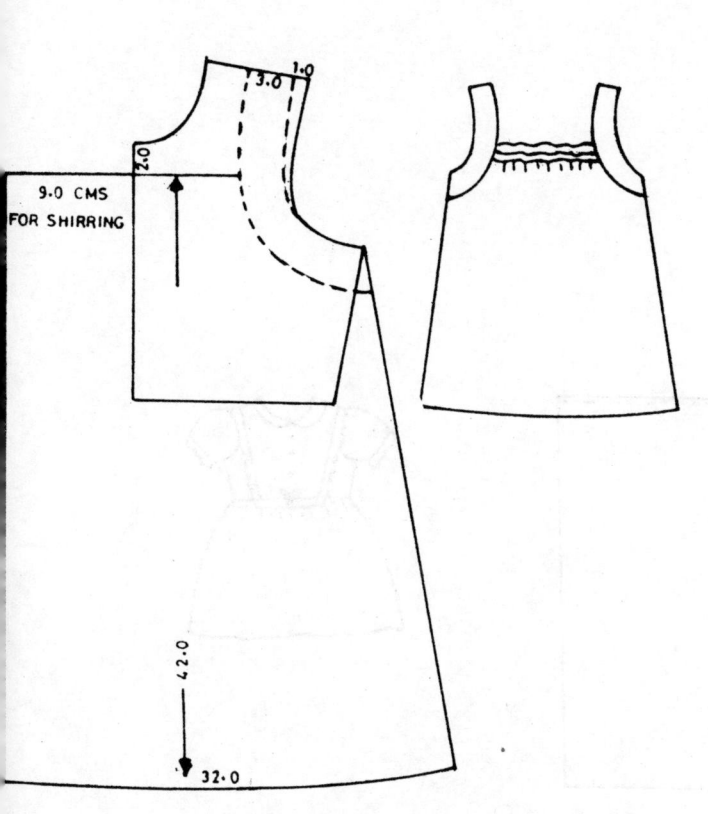

3.0 1.0   2.0

2.0
9.0 CMS
FOR SHIRRING

                                                            6.0   6.0

42.0

                                                      EXTEND
                                                        FOR
                                                      GATHERS

32.0

                                                      ON FOLD

FIG. 115   A COATIE

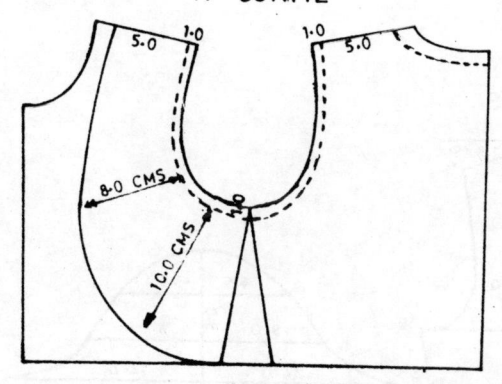

5.0 1.0   1.0 5.0

8.0 CMS

10.0 CMS

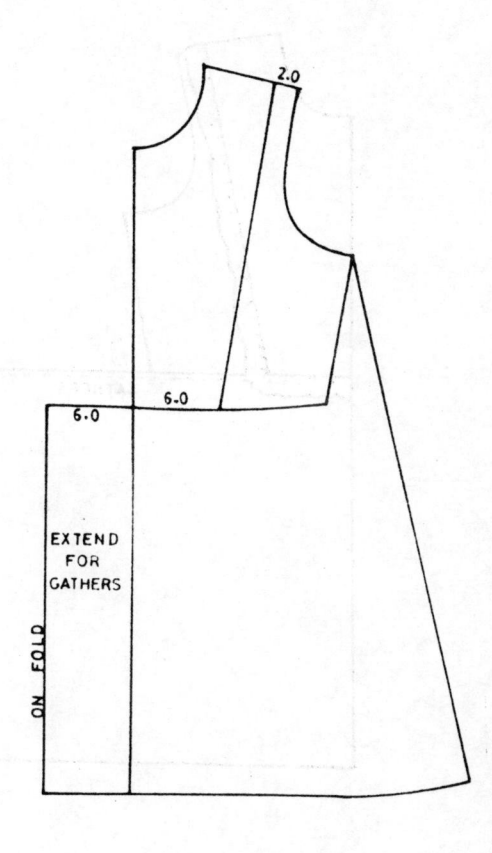

FIG. 117

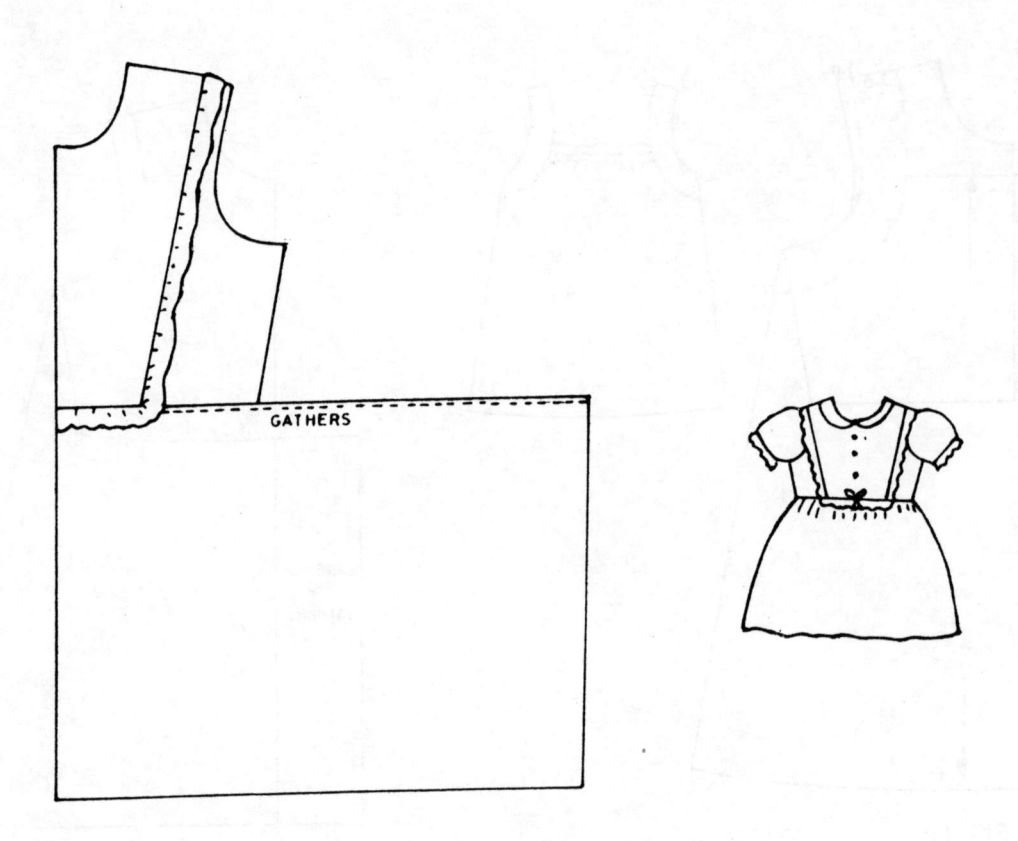

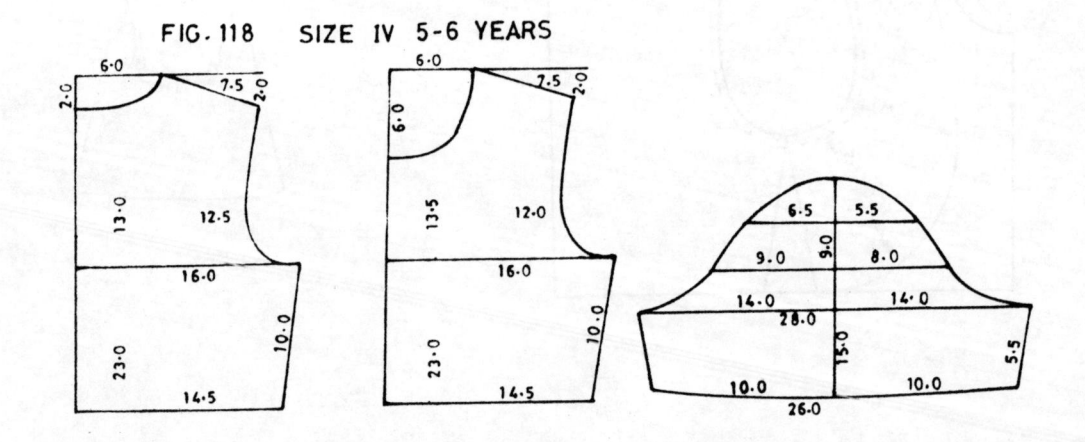

FIG. 118   SIZE IV   5-6 YEARS

The Art of Sewing

FIG. 119 SHORTS   AGE 5-6 YEARS
FOR BLOOMERS CUT ALONG AB AND INCREASE 8·0 TO 10·0 CMS.

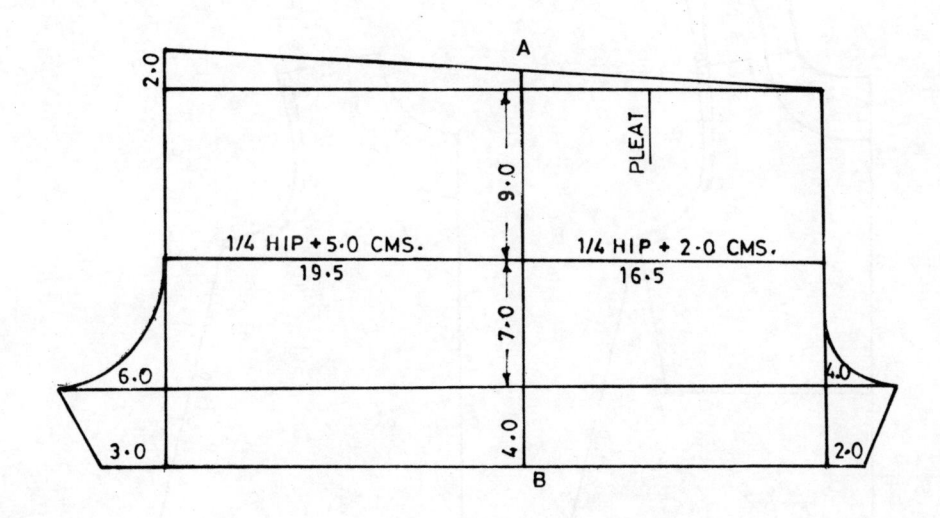

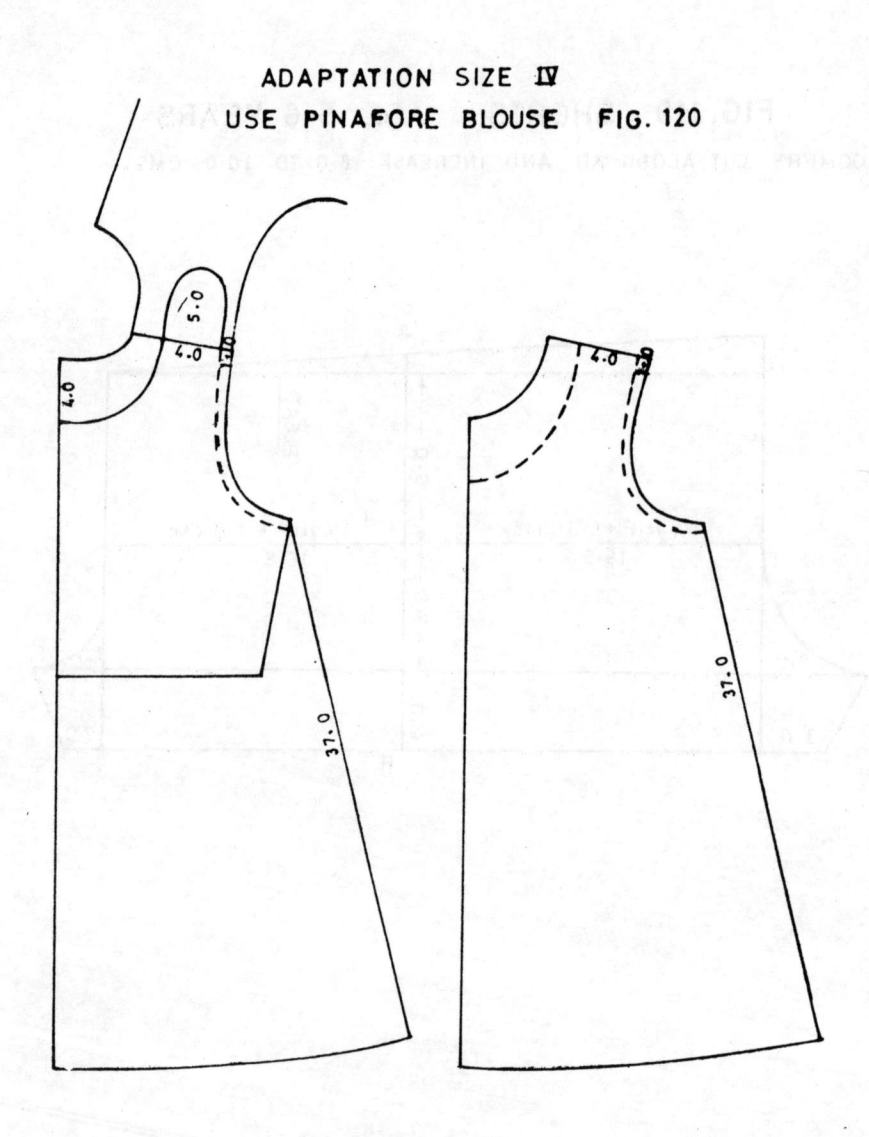

ADAPTATION SIZE IV
USE PINAFORE BLOUSE FIG. 120

The Art of Sewing 137

ADAPTATION SIZE IV
USE PINAFORE BLOUSE FIG. 121

6.5
CUTTING LINE
8.0

6.5
CUTTING LINE
8.0

45.0 CMS.

ON FOLD
30.0

↓ ADD FOR HEM

CUT TWO LENGTHS OF FABRIC FOR SKIRT. FRONT AND BACK
LACE OR FABRIC FRILL MAY BE USED. AT THE EDGE OF BODICE.

SIZE V 7-8 YEARS FIG 122

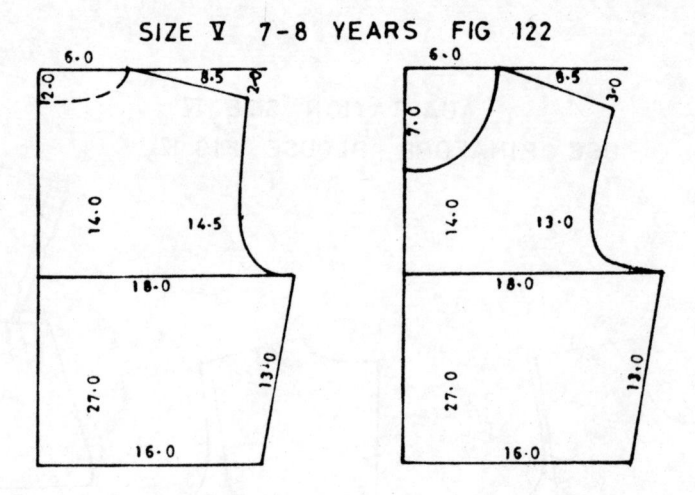

CHILDREN'S PYJAMMAS FIG. 123

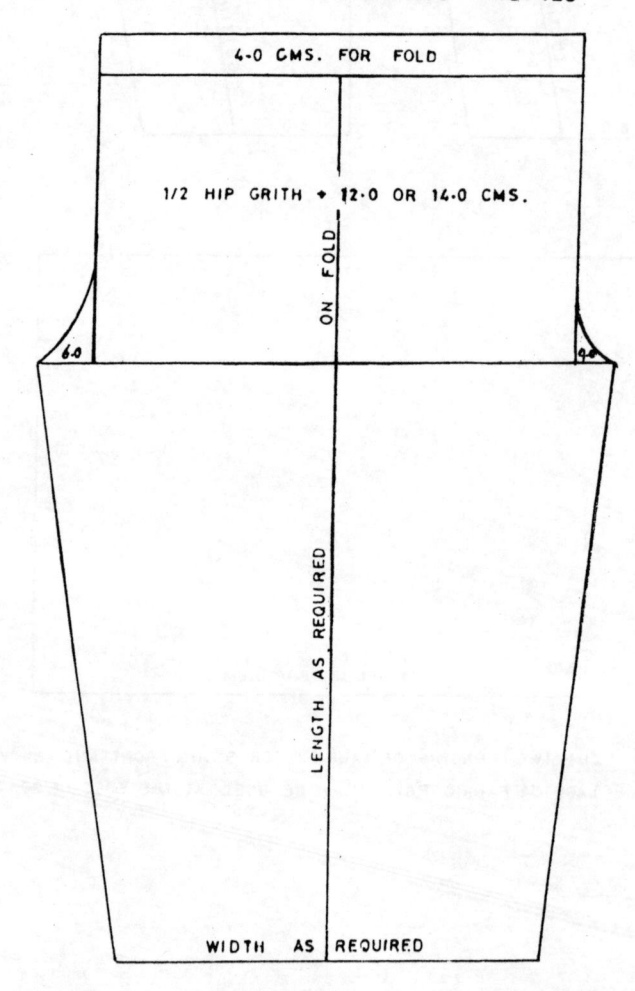

The Art of Sewing   139

SIZE VI 9 - 11 YEARS FIG. 124

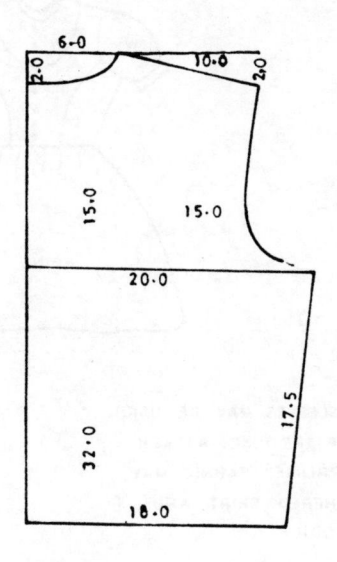

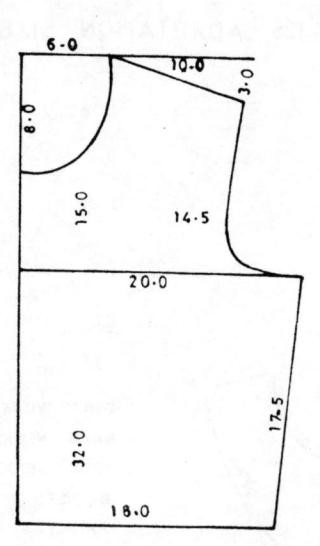

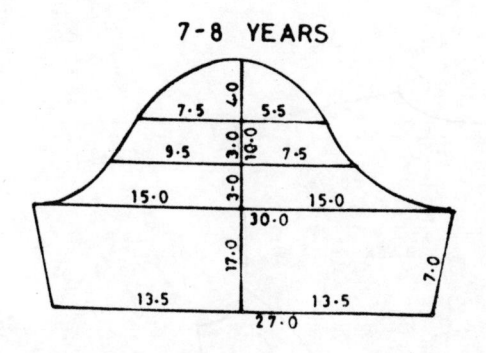

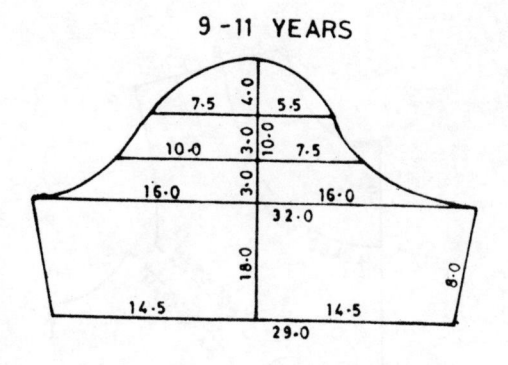

140 The Art of Sewing

FIG. 125 ADAPTATION SIZE VI

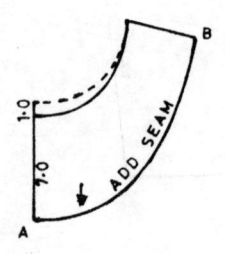

WHITE YOKE AND SLEEVES MAY BE USED. RAISE NECKLINE OF THE YOKE. ATTACH YOKE AB TO AB. PRINTED FABRIC MAY BE USED FOR GATHERED SKIRT AND PRINCESS LINE BODICE.

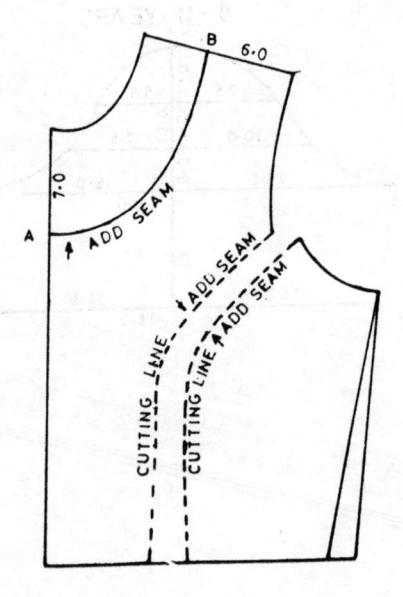

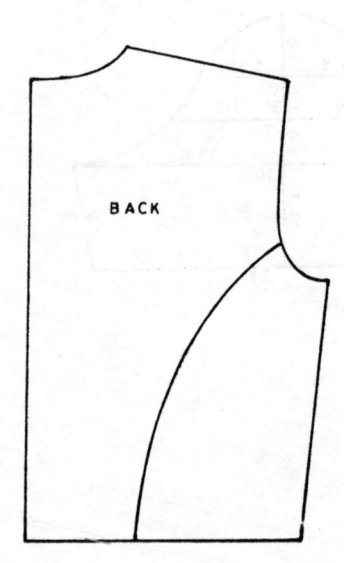

SIZE VII   15-16 YEARS   FIG. 126

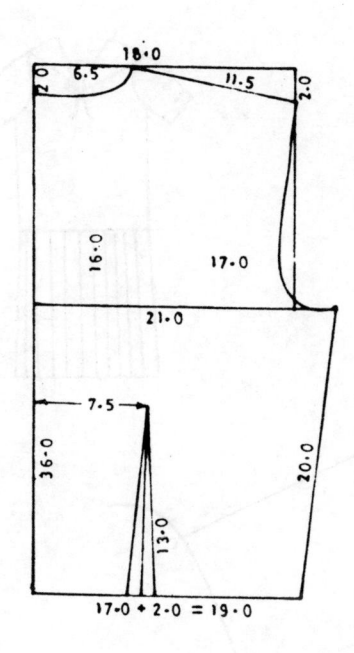

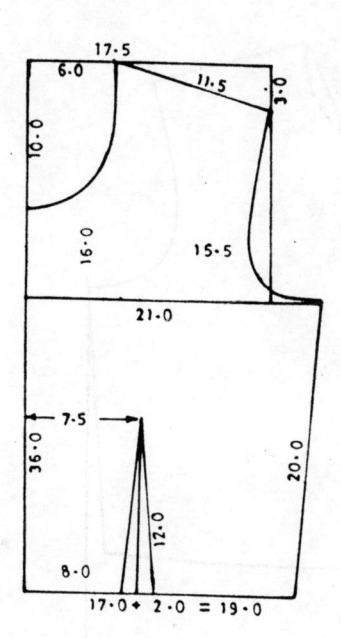

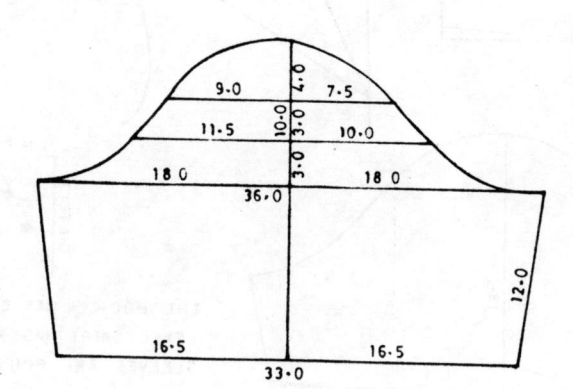

ADAPTATIONS FROM THE BASIC BLOCK TO DESIGNS FIG. 127 SUITABLE FOR AGES 10-16

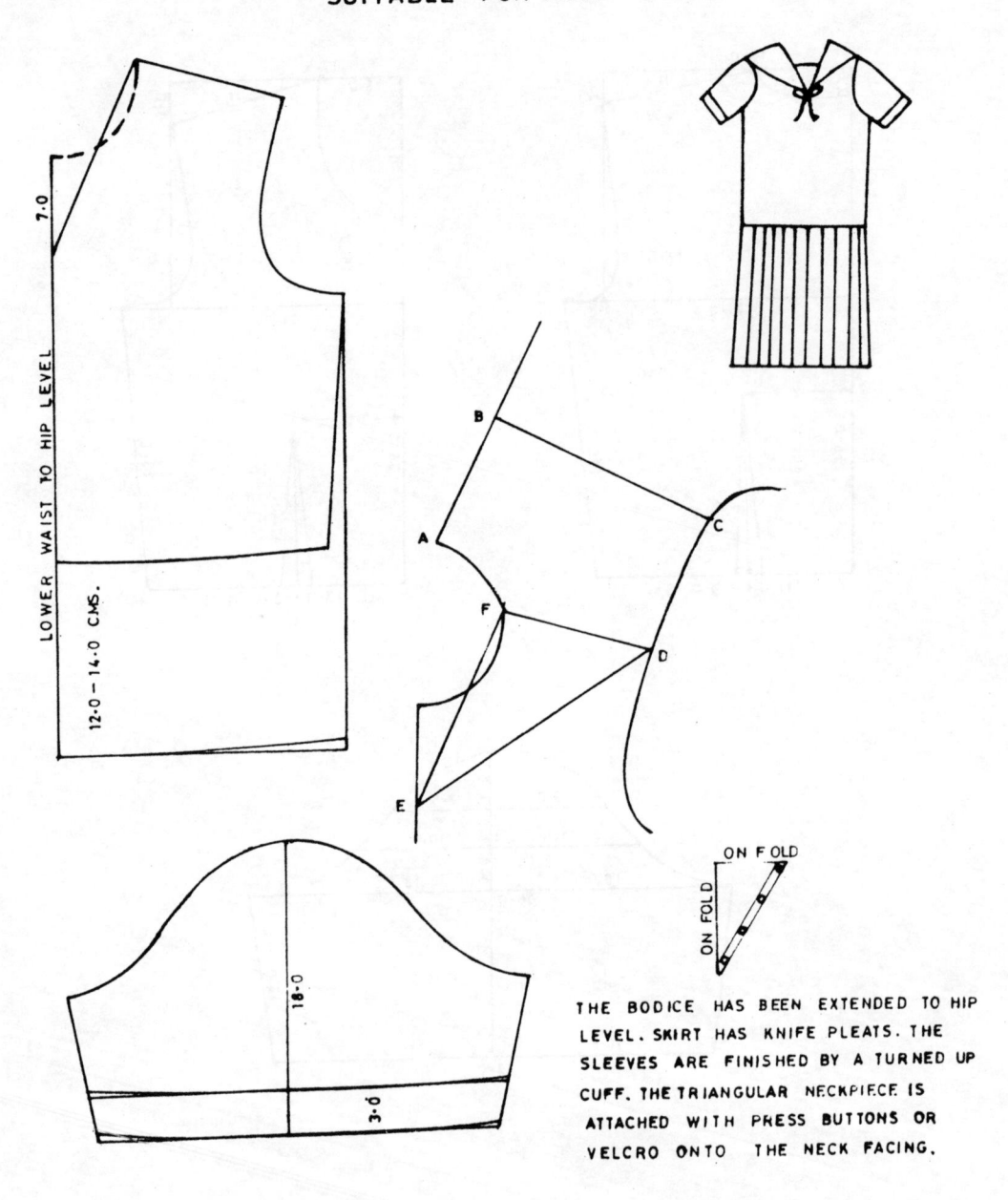

THE BODICE HAS BEEN EXTENDED TO HIP LEVEL. SKIRT HAS KNIFE PLEATS. THE SLEEVES ARE FINISHED BY A TURNED UP CUFF. THE TRIANGULAR NECKPIECE IS ATTACHED WITH PRESS BUTTONS OR VELCRO ONTO THE NECK FACING.

CHAPTER 15

DRAFTING FOR THE ADULT

The adult bodice blocks provided in this book are drawn to scale for the various bust sizes ranging from 76.0 centimetres (30") to 97.0 centimetres (38"). All the measurements marked on the drafts are in centimetres. The drafts provided do not include seam allowances. The seam allowances that are generally given are 1.5 centimetre at the shoulder seam, 0.5 centimetre at the neckline, 0.5 or 1.0 centimetre at the armhole and 2.0 to 3.0 centimetres at the side seam.

The size range 76.0-97.0 centimetres can belong to any age group between sixteen and sixty years. It would be interesting to note that except for the dart positions, only the waist girth and the lower arm girth vary with age. The waistline and the arm girth alterations are simple. All that has to be done is to either take in or let out the side seams at these positions.

After selecting your size, try out a sleeveless bodice blouse on a closely woven muslin fabric. Leave enough seam allowance at the shoulder, armhole and side seam to be able to make alterations if any are required. The stitching should be done by hand to make it easy to alter. Use a double strand of thread for the basting so that the seams are held firmly. Methods of alterations have been shown in Chapter 10. Once a perfectly fitted toile is ready, is can be used to adapt to any garment and style. Since the adaptations cannot be provided for all sizes, size 86.0 centimetres (34") has been selected, as a large majority fit this size. So those whose bust measures 86.0 centimetres, may use the adaptations given in this book exactly as they are.

The two sets of basic bodice blocks provided for each size are the basic bodice block which has two darts and the sari blouse draft with four darts to give a closer fit. The basic bodice block has a wider shoulder and a lowered armhole and can be adapted to other

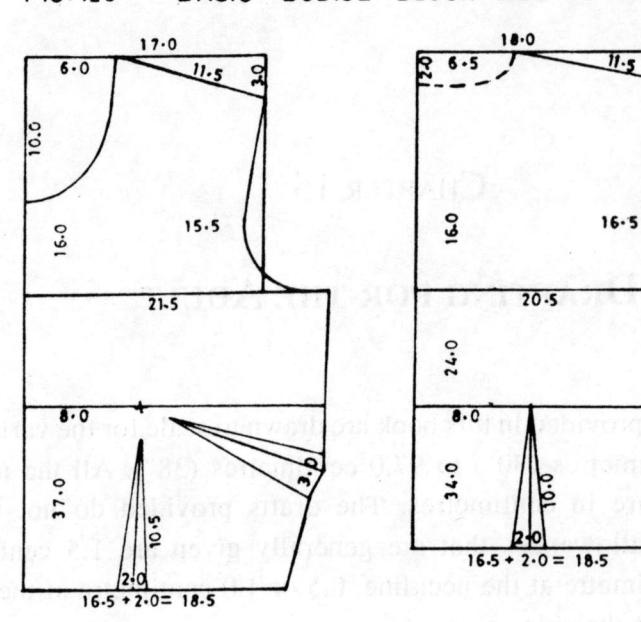

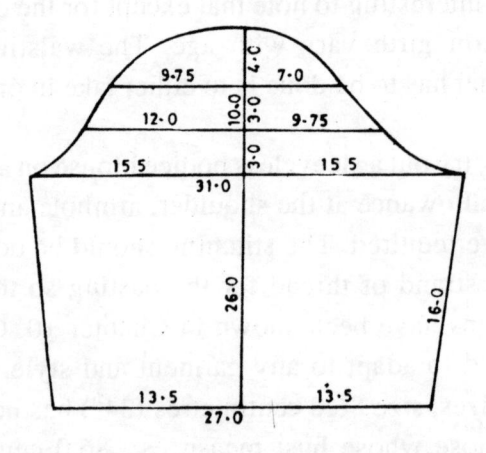

FIG. 128   BASIC BODICE BLOCK SIZE 76·0 CMS.(30")

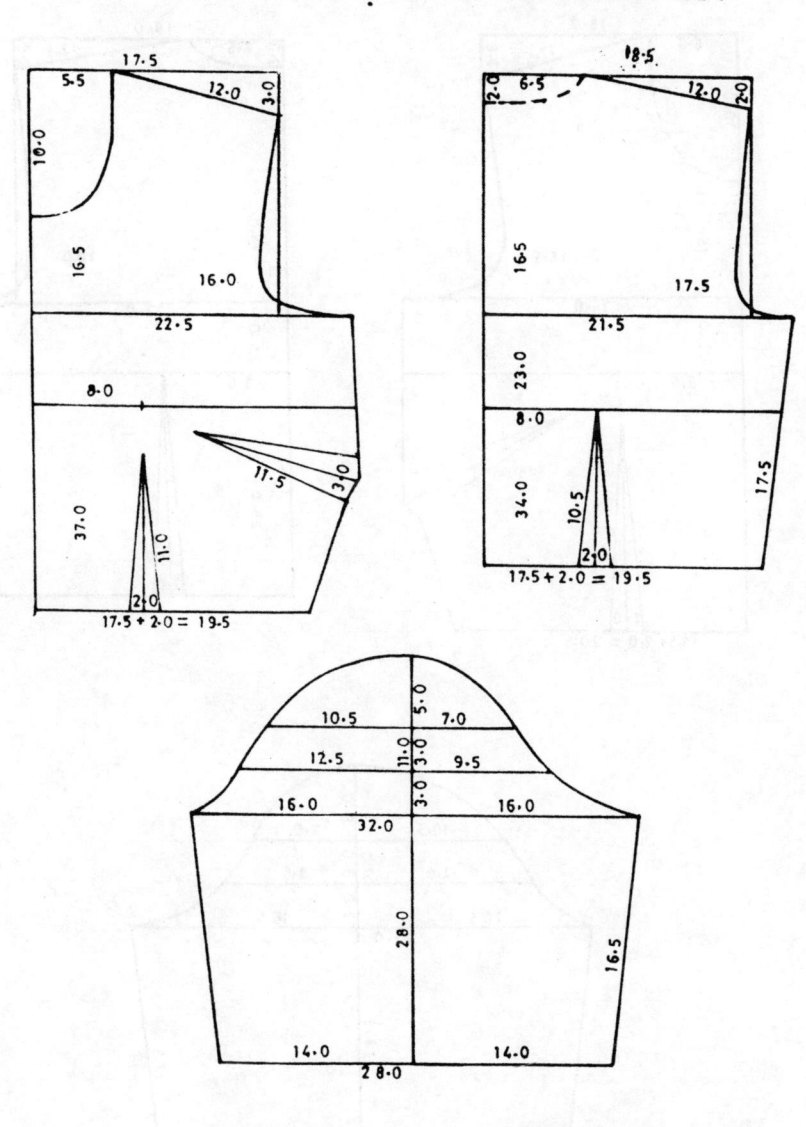

FIG 129   BASIC BODICE BLOCK SIZE 82 CMS. (32)

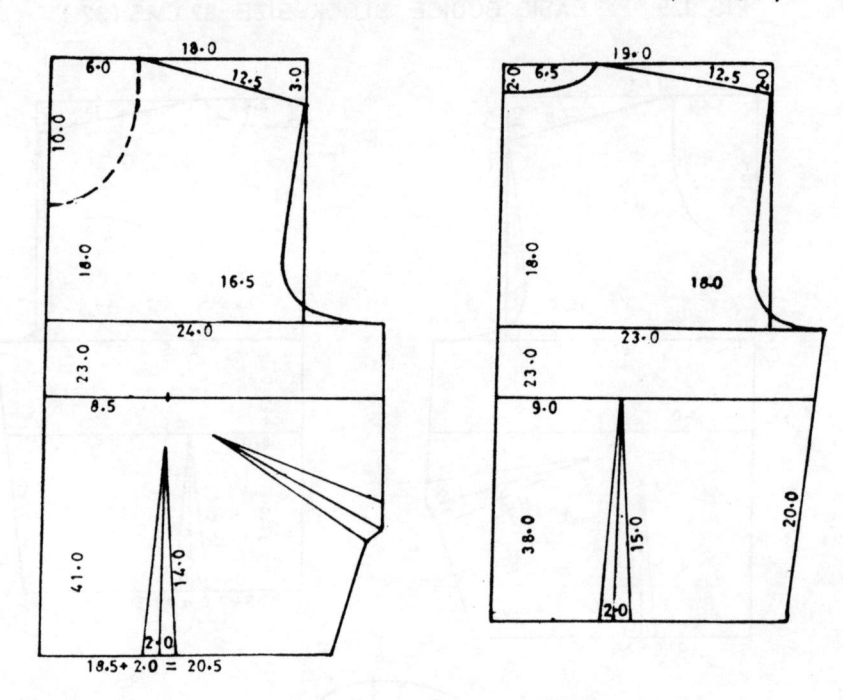

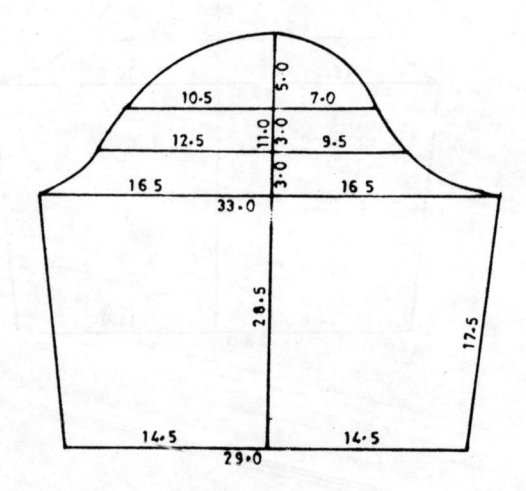

FIG. 130   BASIC BODICE BLOCK SIZE 86·0 CMS. (34")

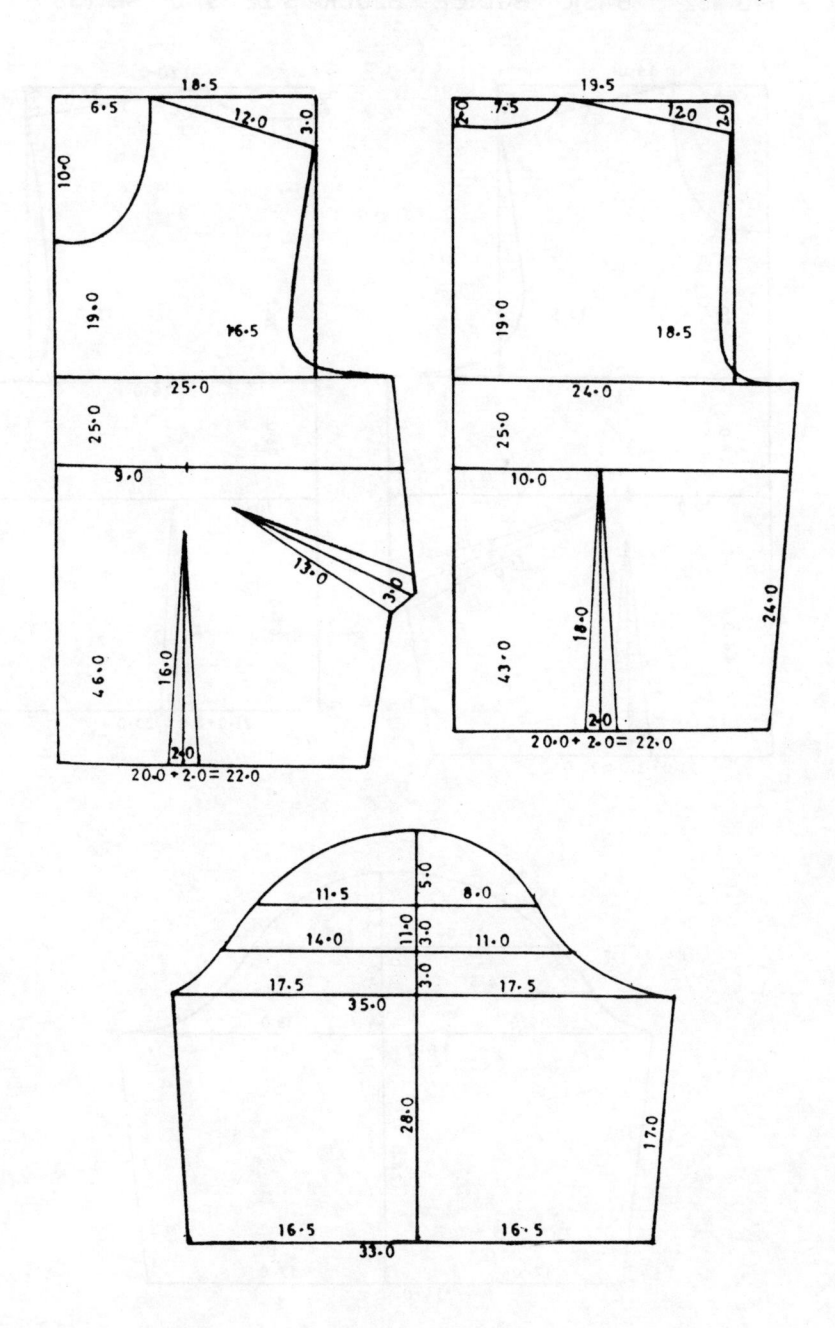

FIG. 131 BASIC BODICE BLOCK SIZE 92·0 CMS. (36")

FIG. 132   BASIC BODICE BLOCK SIZE 97·0 CMS. (38")

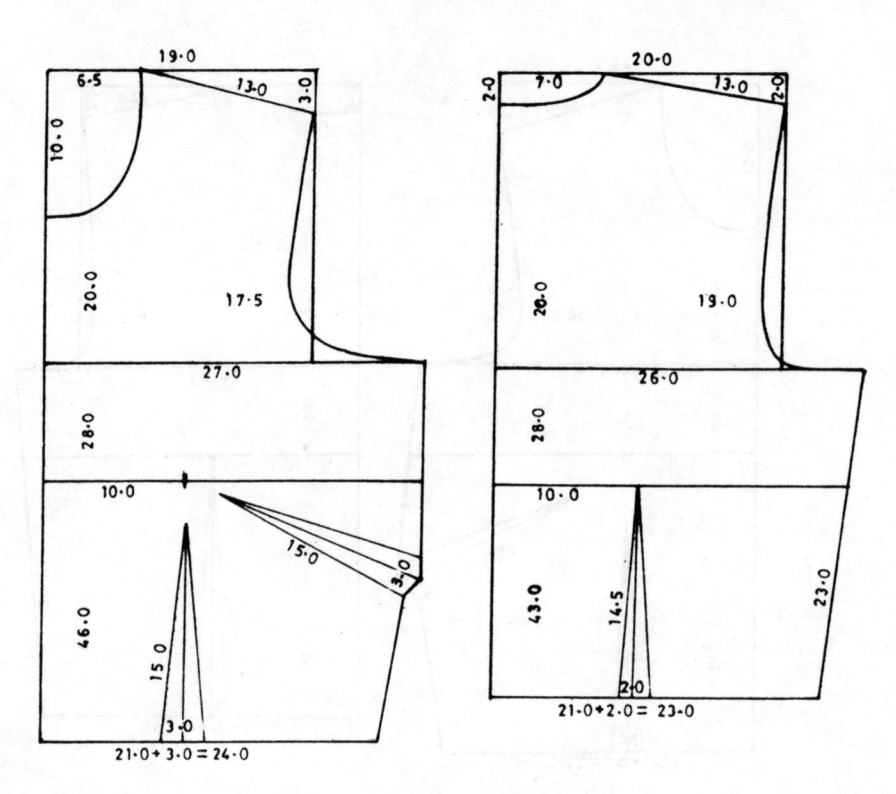

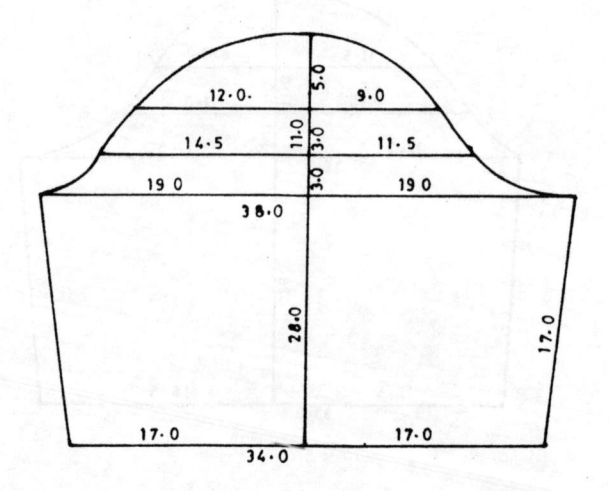

garments such as the skirt blouse, dress, kurta and night clothes. The basic drafts for the trousers, skirt and the sari petticoat have also been included.

MEASUREMENT CHART (CMS)

Bust size	30"	32"	34"	36"	38"	40"	45"
Highest shoulder to armpit level	15.5	16.5	17.0	18.0	19.0	19.0	20.0
Highest shoulder to bust level	22.0	23.0	24.0	25.0	28.0	28.0	34.0
Highest shoulder to waist level	35.0	37.0	39.0	40.0	42.0	42.0	45.0
Shoulder to shoulder (front)	32.0	33.0	34.0	35.0	36.0	36.0	38.0
Shoulder to shoulder (back)	34.0	35.0	36.0	37.0	38.0	38.0	42.0
Across chest (front)	29.0	30.0	31.0	32.0	33.0	33.0	35.0
Across chest (back)	33.0	34.0	34.0	35.0	36.0	36.0	40.0
Girth at bust	76.0	82.0	87.0	92.0	97.0	102.0	115.0
Girth at waist	60.0	64.0	68.0	72.0	76.0	86.0	98.0
Girth at hip	82.0	87.0	92.0	97.0	102.0	107.0	119.0
Shoulder width	11.5	12.0	12.0	12.5	13.0	13.0	14.0
Sleeve girth at armpit level	26.0	27.0	28.0	29.0	32.0	34.0	40.0
Round arm girth	24.0	25.0	26.0	27.0	30.0	33.0	36.0
Sleeve length	25.0	25.0	26.0	26.0	27.0	27.0	28.0

CHAPTER 16

ADAPTING TO NEW STYLES USING THE BASIC BODICE BLOCK

The basic bodice block can be successfully adapted to meet the characteristic design requirements of various styles such as the princess line, yoke line with gathers, etc. New lines or styles are created by either shifting of the darts, or by converting them partially or fully to form gathers, pleats or tucks; or by taking them into seams, without altering the basic fit of the bodice. The shifting of darts to any position can be achieved simply by slashing at the new position and closing the dart that is to be shifted. A space is thus formed at the new position, equal to the one which has been deleted.

The basic block has two darts, one at the waist and the other at the side seam.

Fig. 133(a) shows the shifting of the side seam dart to form a single waist dart. Slash at the centre of the waist dart, then fold and close the side seam dart. Thus the dart width of the side seam has been added to the waist dart. The inner lines show the original dart and the outer lines show the wider new dart.

Similarly Fig. 133(b) shows the shifting of the waist dart to form a single side seam dart.

Fig. 133(c) shows the shifting of both the basic darts to form a single dart at the new position i.e. the shoulder line. Slash from the shoulder seam to the bust point and then close both the waist and side seam dart to give a single, wide shoulder dart.

Fig. 133(d) shows the shifting of the side seam dart to the shoulder line.

Fig. 133(e) shows the shifting of the side seam dart to the armhole.

The method shown in Fig. 133(d) and 133(e) are further used to convert into the princess style. The princess line has a seamline running from the shoulder or the armhole

The Art of Sewing

FIG. 133   SHIFTING OF DARTS

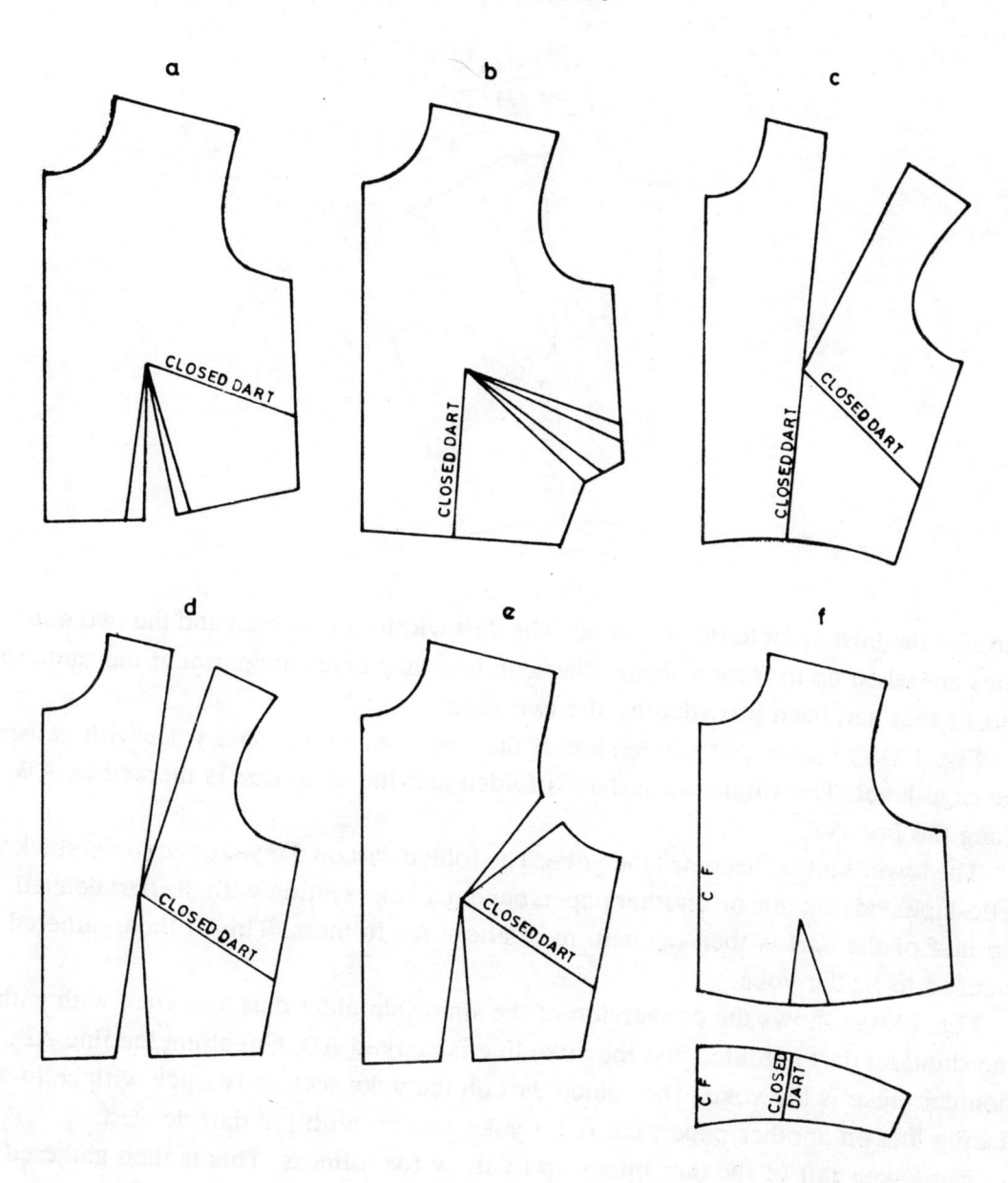

a   b   c

d   e   f

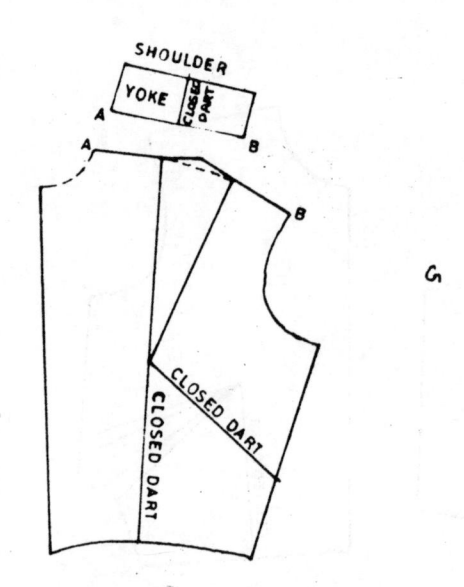

through the bust point to the waistline. The dart widths are deleted and the two outer dart lines are taken up to form a seam. The seamline thus gives the garment the same shape and fit that had been provided by the two darts.

Fig. 133(f) shows that conversion of the single waist dart to a yoke with gathers at the cage level. The single waist dart is folded and the yoke line is marked as AB. Cut along the line AB.

The lower section becomes the yoke. The folded dart on the yoke section is stuck with cello-tape. Placing this on another paper, cut out a yoke section with the dart deleted. The top half of the dart is then opened up to allow for fullness. This is then gathered and attached to fit the yoke.

Fig. 133(g) shows the conversion of the single shoulder dart to a yoke with gathers. The shoulder dart is folded and the yoke line is marked AB. Cut along the line AB. The shoulder piece is the yoke. The folded dart on the yoke section is stuck with cello-tape. Placing this on another paper, cut out a yoke section with the dart deleted.

The lower half of the dart opens up to allow for fullness. This is then gathered and attached to fit the yoke.

Chapter 17

The Sari Blouse

The sari blouse is a garment that most people find rather complex to sew at home though it can be mastered with practice.

Since the sari blouse is a closely fitted garment, a good fit becomes very essential. It is necessary therefore, to stitch exactly on the marked seamlines. Even the slightest irregularity will appear magnified in the finished garment.

There are three areas that call for very special care and attention, namely, the neckline, the sleeves and the shoulder seam. The shoulder seam, since it is easily visible, should be stitched exactly on the seamline and any deviation will mar the appearance.

The neckline finish too, is very important and care should be taken to see that it does not get stretched. So, as soon as the neckline has been cut, a row of stay-stitches should be run at a distance of 0.5 centimetre from the neck edge. The bias binding should be attached with great care, making certain that it is even all through. The sleeve should not appear pulled or stretched nor should there be too many crease lines. A few crease lines, however, are inevitable because of the ease that is added to give freedom of movement. The ease added to the sleeve should be distributed evenly. The centre line of the sleeve should be in line with the shoulder seam.

All darts should be pointing towards the pivot point or the highest bust point. Darts which point either higher or lower can mar the fit of the garment. The armhole and waist darts are curved to allow for the hollow at the armpit and cage, respectively.

The measurements that are required to draft the sari blouse are as follows:

1. Shoulder to shoulder (front)
2. Shoulder to shoulder (back)
3. Shoulder width

4. Across chest width (front)
5. Across chest width (back)
6. Bust point to bust point
7. Highest shoulder point to armpit level
8. Highest shoulder point to bust level
9. Highest shoulder point to waist level
10. Girth at bust level
11. Girth at waist level
12. Sleeve length
13. Cap length
14. Arm girth at armpit level
15. Arm girth at the required sleeve length position.

The Art of Sewing 155

FIG. 134   PRINCESS LINE JACKET

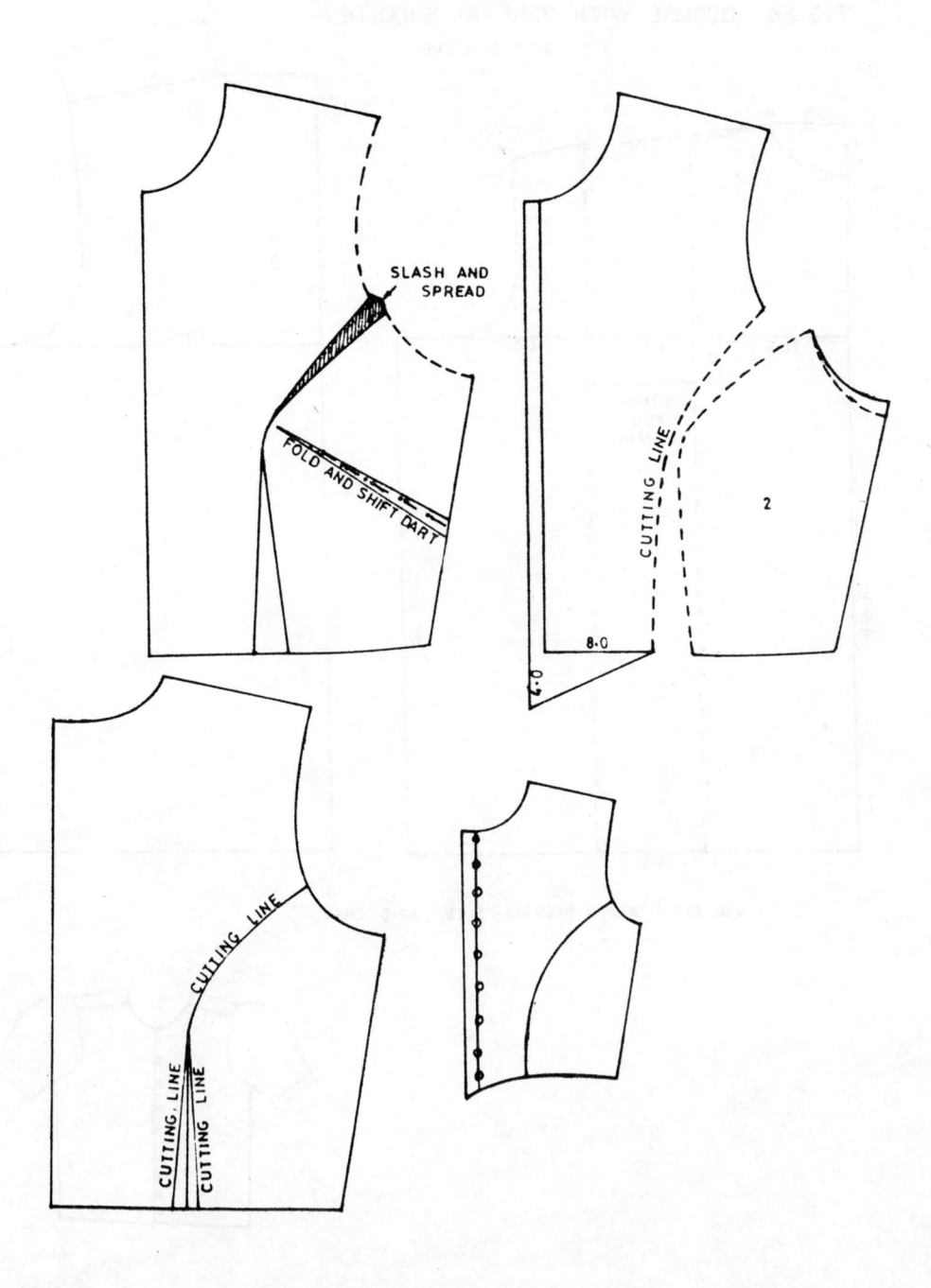

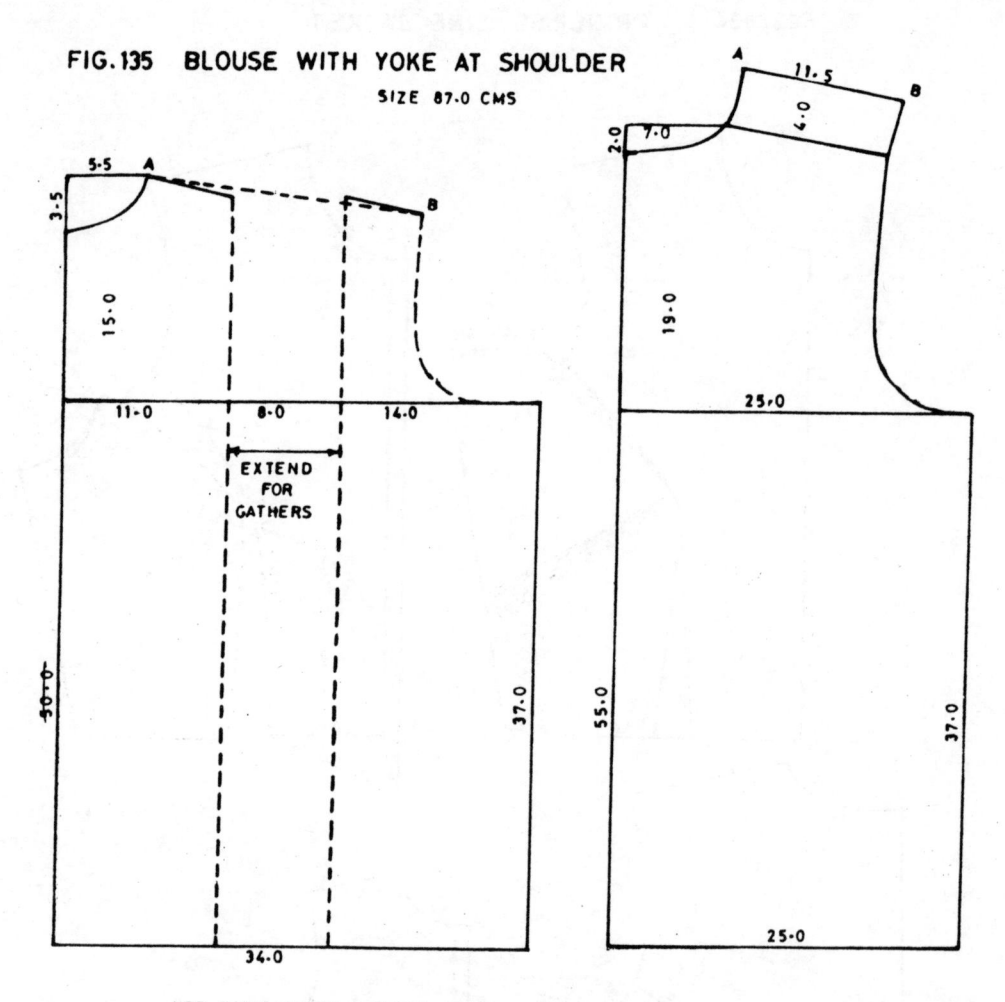

FIG. 135 BLOUSE WITH YOKE AT SHOULDER
SIZE 87.0 CMS

USE BASIC BLOCK SLEEVES SIZE 86.0 CMS.

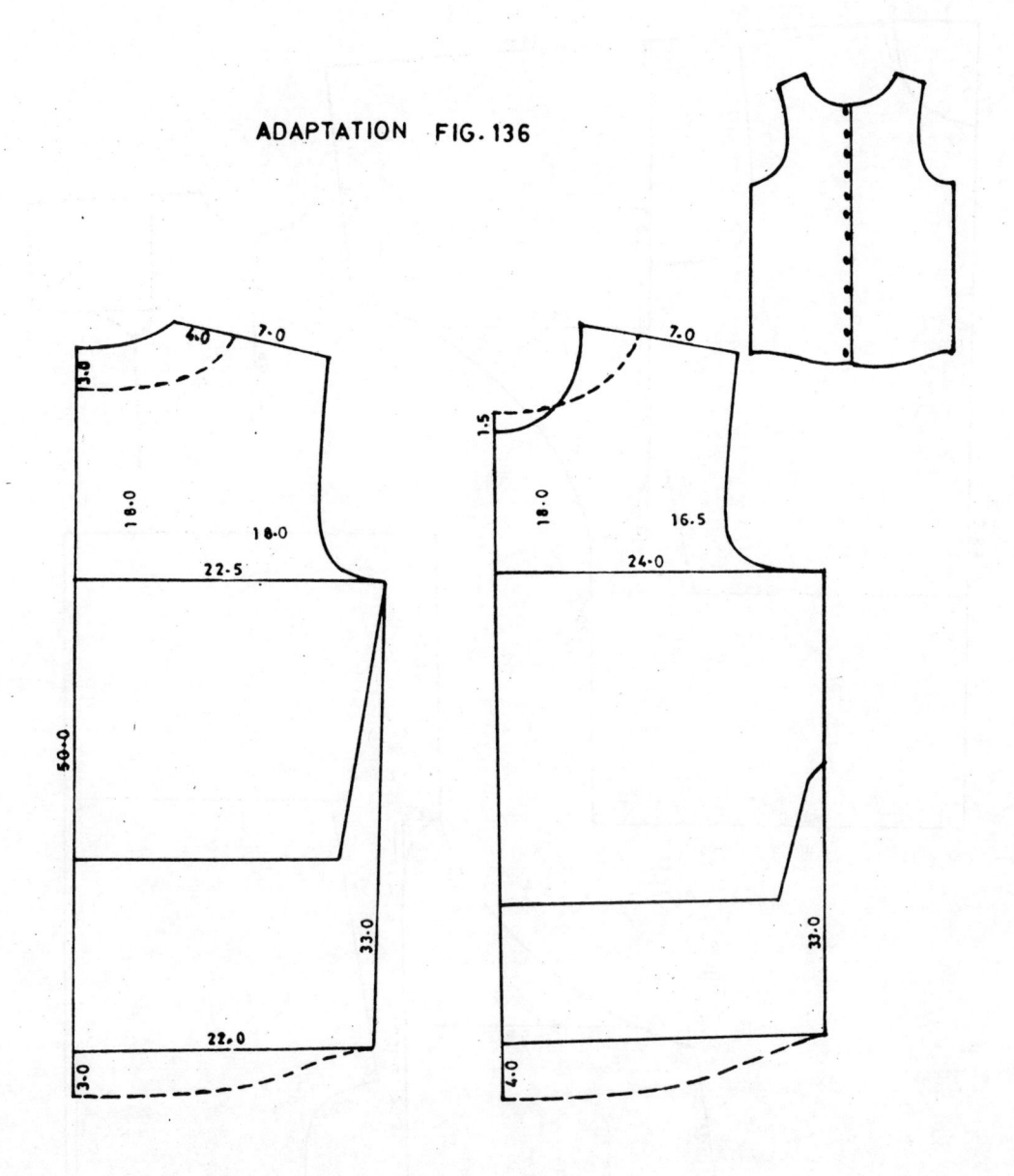

ADAPTATION FIG. 136

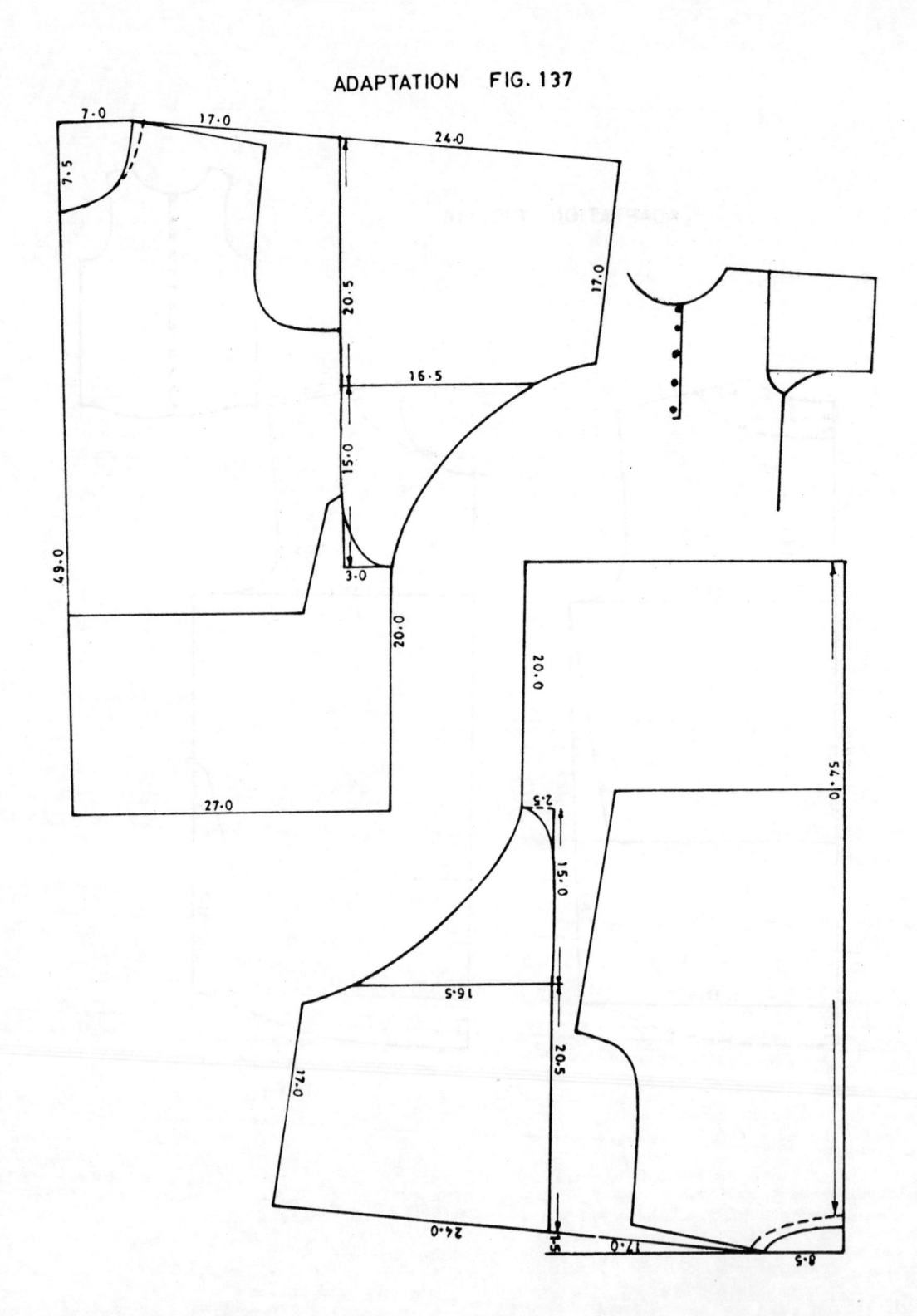

ADAPTATION   FIG. 137

The Art of Sewing

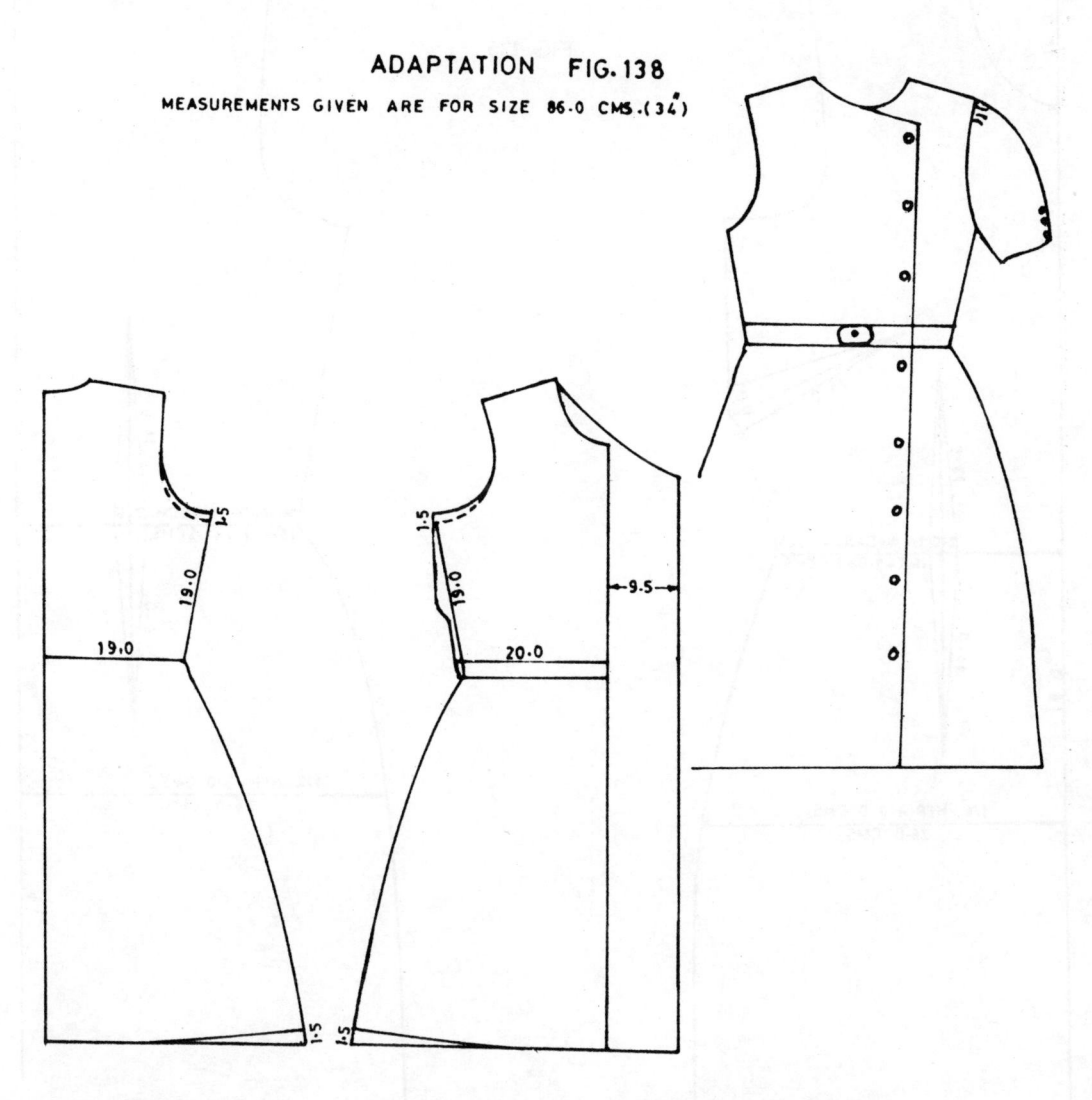

ADAPTATION FIG. 138
MEASUREMENTS GIVEN ARE FOR SIZE 86.0 CMS. (34")

THE FRONT AND BACK WAIST LENGTHS HAVE BEEN KEPT EQUAL, SINCE THE DARTS HAVE BEEN DELETED. ARMHOLE LINE HAS BEEN LOWERED BY 1.5 CMS. CENTRE FRONT LINE HAS BEEN EXTENDED 9.5 CMS. FOR OVERLAP.

ADAPTATION OF THE BASIC BODICE TO THE TRADITIONAL FITTED KAMEEZ
MEASUREMENT GIVEN ARE FOR SIZE 87.0 CMS. LENGTH 100.0 CMS.

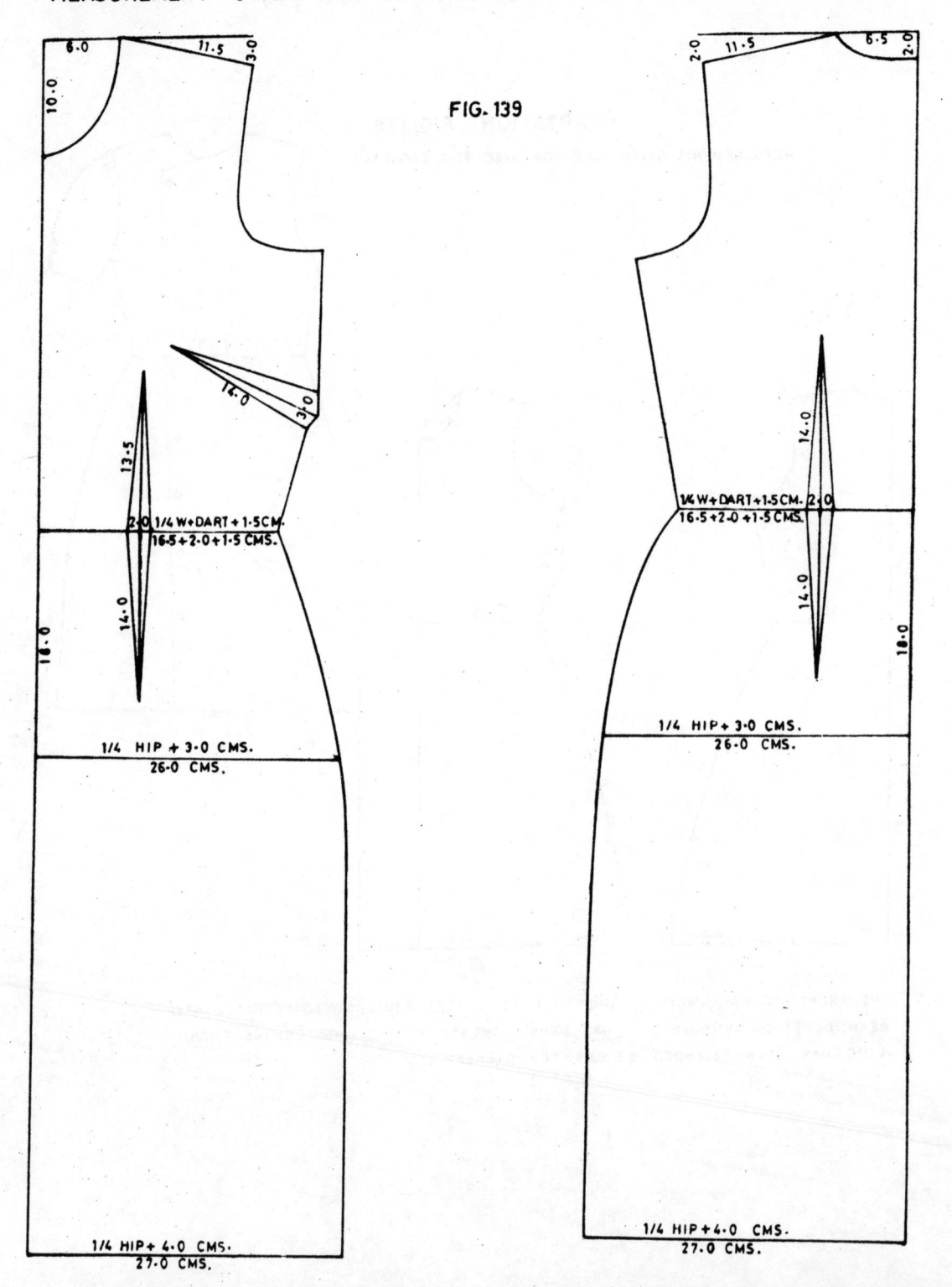

FIG. 139

ADAPTATION FIG 140

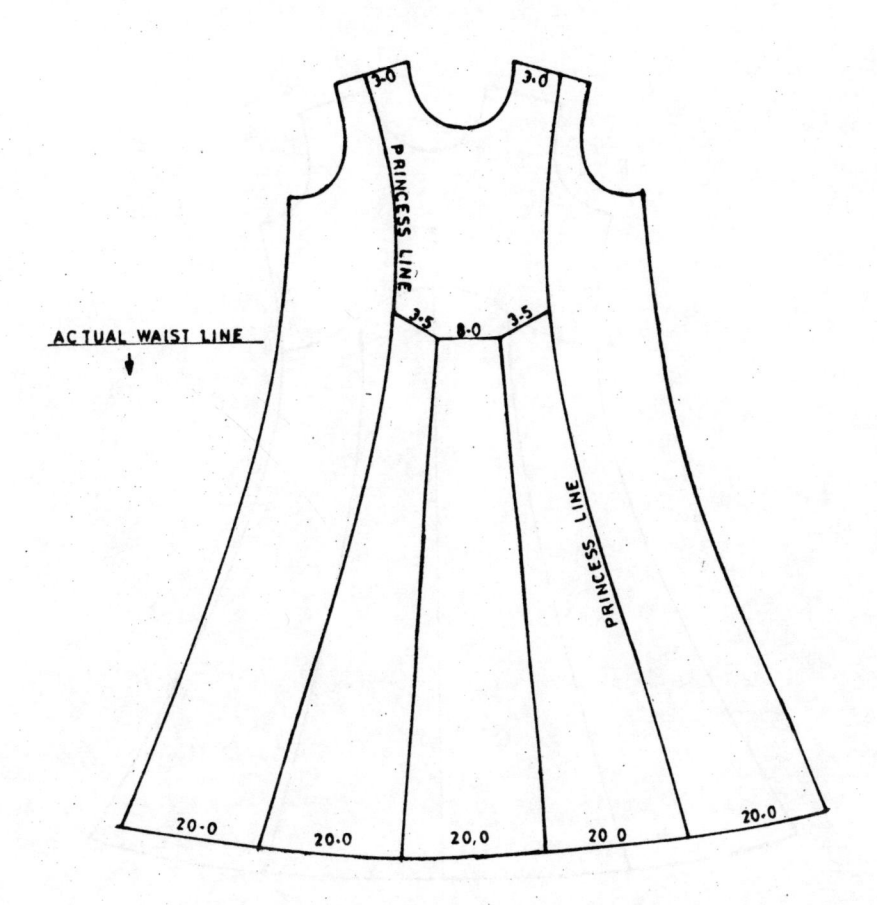

ACTUAL WAIST LINE

FOLLOW PRINCESS LINE ADAPTATION ON PAGE FIG

ADAPTATION   FIG. 141

THE WAIST DART IS CLOSED AND CONVERTED INTO PRINCESS LINE BELOW THE YOKE.
THE WAIST DART HAS BEEN CONVERTED INTO GATHERS ABOVE THE YOKE.
A AND B ARE 4.0 CMS. ABOVE THE ACTUAL WAIST LINE
C IS 18.0 CMS. BELOW THE NECK LINE.

The Art of Sewing

FIG. 142   ADAPTATION

164 The Art of Sewing

FIG. 143   VARIATION OF FIGURE 142

CURVE THE VERTICAL SEAMS AT THE WAIST LINE TAPERING OUT AT BOTH ENDS AS SHOWN. THIS ALLOWS FOR SHAPING IN AT THE WAIST LINE CHANGING THE SILHOUETTE COMPLETELY.

The Art of Sewing

FIG. 144 KALIDAR OR LUCKNOW KURTA

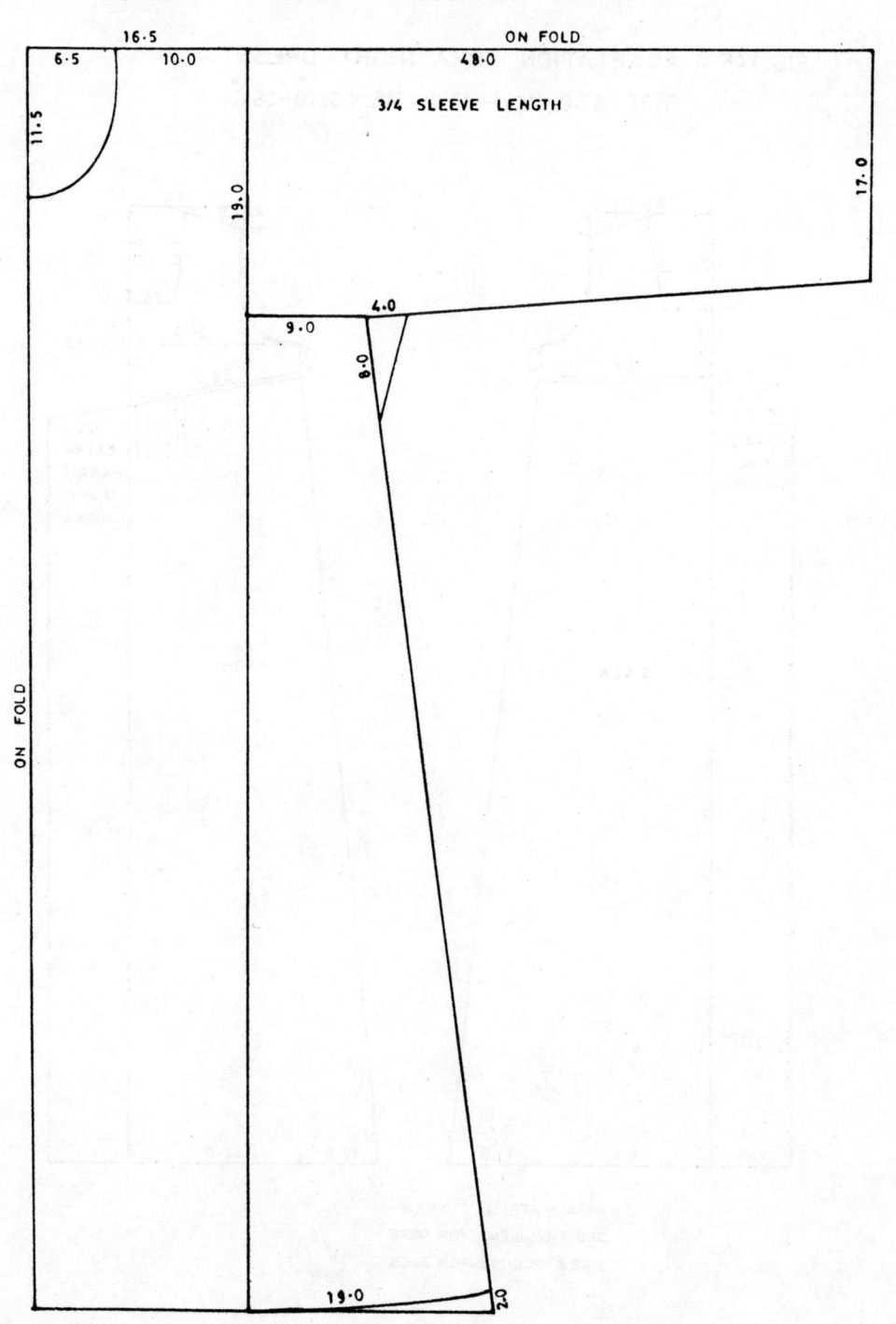

3/4 SLEEVE LENGTH

FIG. 145   ADAPTATION TO A NIGHT DRESS
SIZE 82.0 CMS. – 92.0 CMS. (32.0" – 36.0")

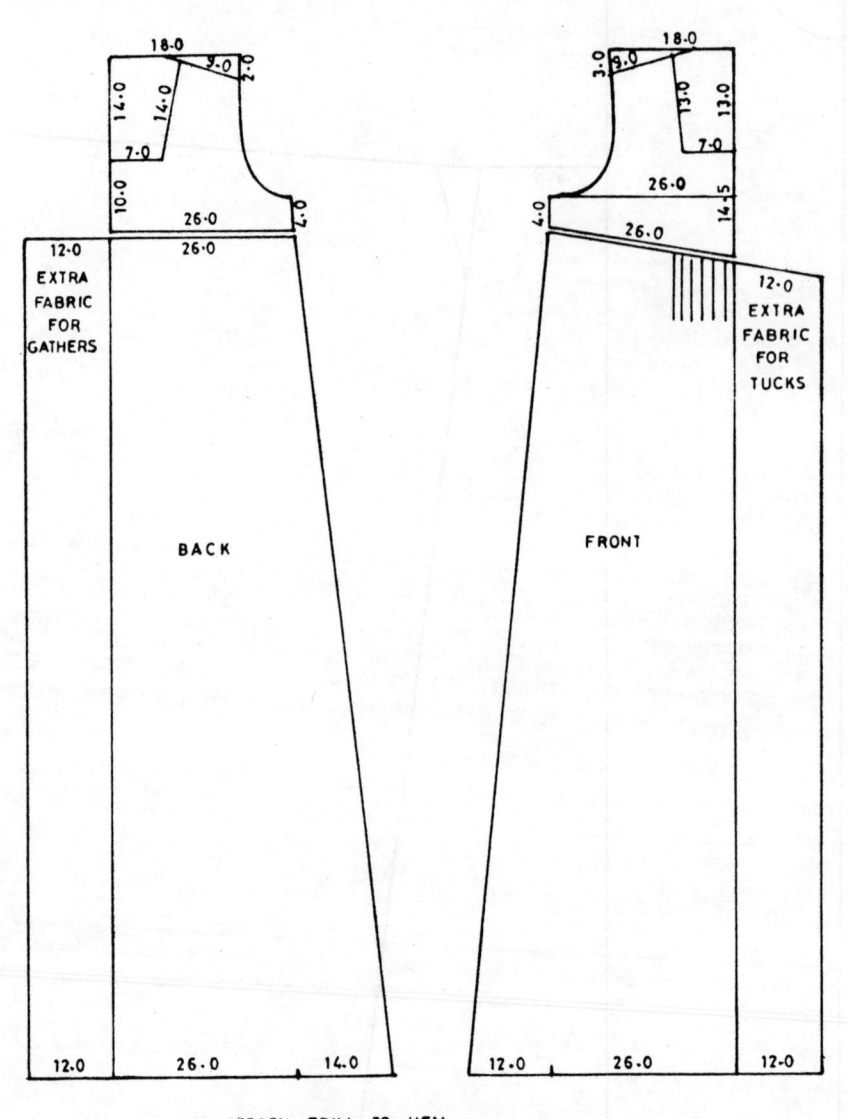

BACK

FRONT

ATTACH FRILL TO HEM
20.0 X 175.0 CMS. FOR FRONT
20.0 X 175.0 CMS. FOR BACK

The Art of Sewing

FIG. 146 KAFTAN—TO FIT SIZE 92·0–102·0 CMS. (36"–40")

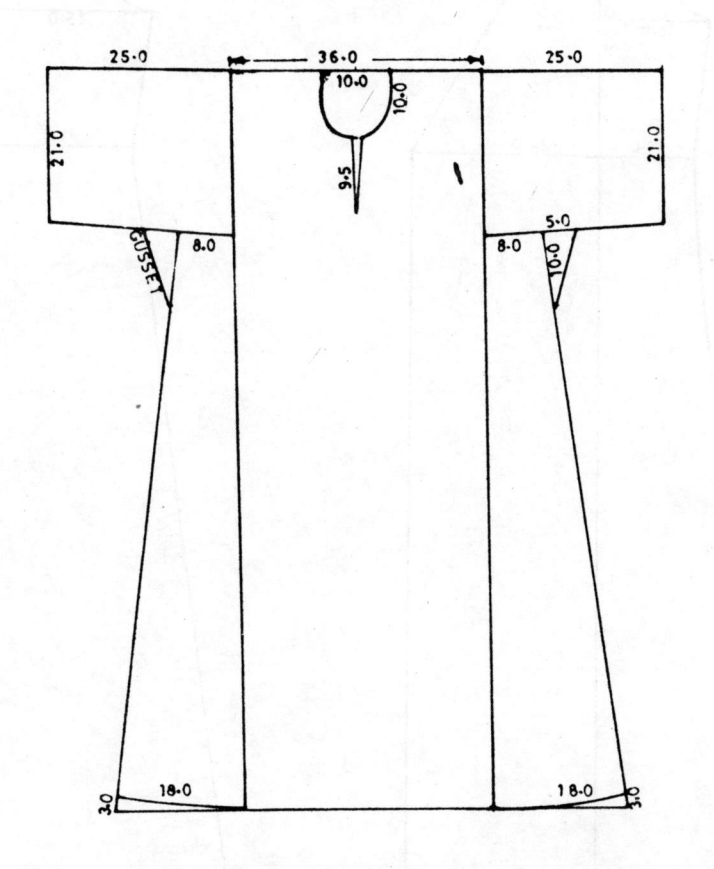

FIG. 147   DRESSING   GOWN   SIZE   36"- 40"

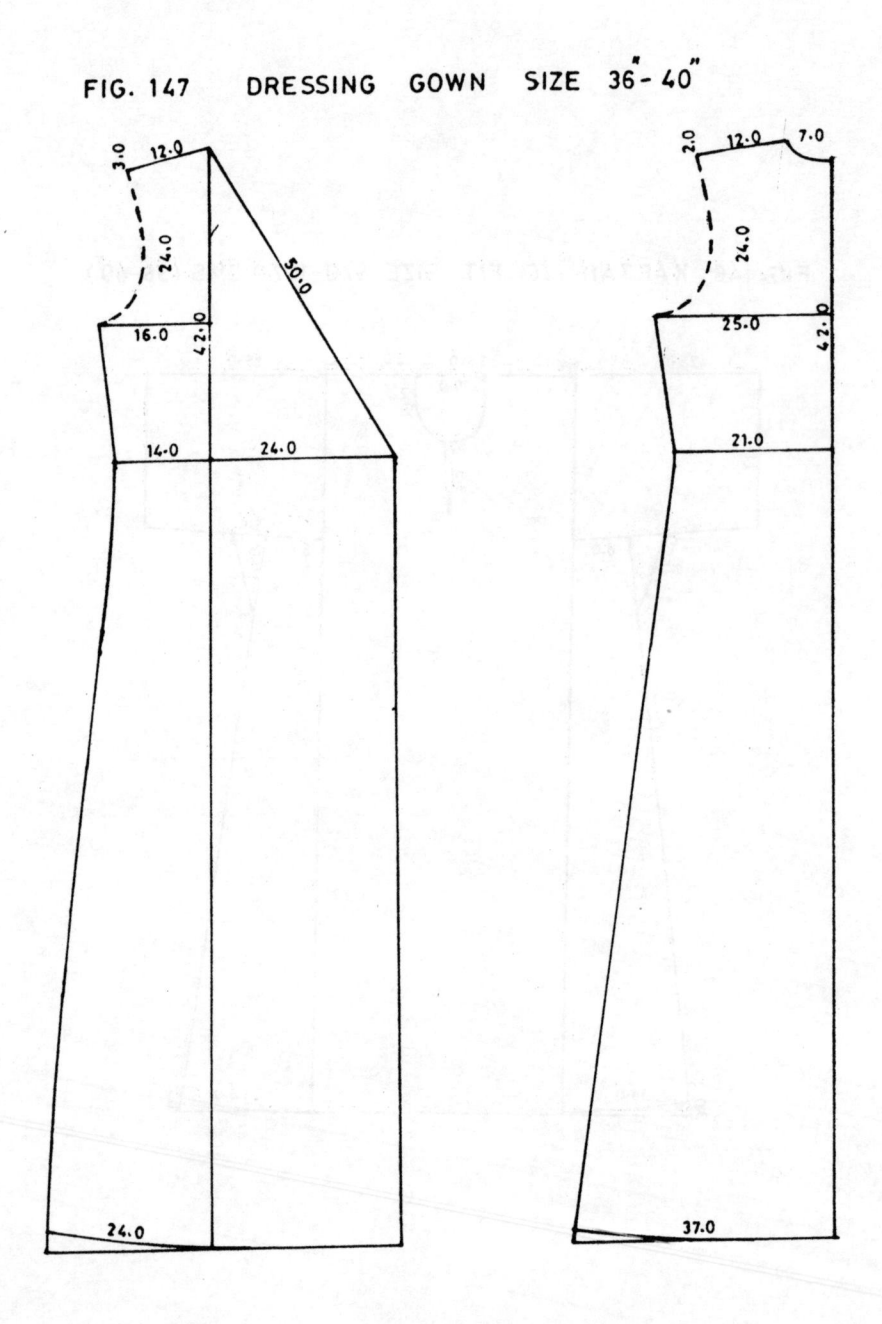

The Sari Blouse Draft (Fig. 148)

Front

Draw a vertical line AI.
AI is the blouse length as measured from the highest shoulder point to the waist level.
The waist level is usually taken about 5.0 centimetres above the actual waist line.
On the line AI mark E as the armpit level and G as the bust level.
Mark C at a distance of 3.0 centimetres above E.
Draw horizontal lines at A, C, E, G and I.
AB = 1/2 of the shoulder to shoulder measurement.
B to B_1 = 3.0 centimetres (shoulder slope).
Join B_1 to a point A_1 on the line AB such that B_1A_1 is equal to the shoulder width.
AA_2 = Neck depth.
Join A_1A_2 to mark the neckline curve.
CD = 1/2 the across chest measurement.
EF = 1/4 bust girth + 2.5 centimetres for ease.
GK = 1/2 the measurement bust point to bust point.
Join B_1D and F to mark the armhole curve.
IJ = 1/4 waist girth + 0.5 centimetres for ease + 4.0 centimetres for the width of the waist dart.

Mark darts as shown in the diagram. All darts should point towards the bust point marked as 'K' and should end 2.0 to 3.0 centimetres away from K.
Fold the side seam dart and draw a straight line joining F to J. FJ is the side seam line.

FIG. 148   SARI   BLOUSE   DRAFT

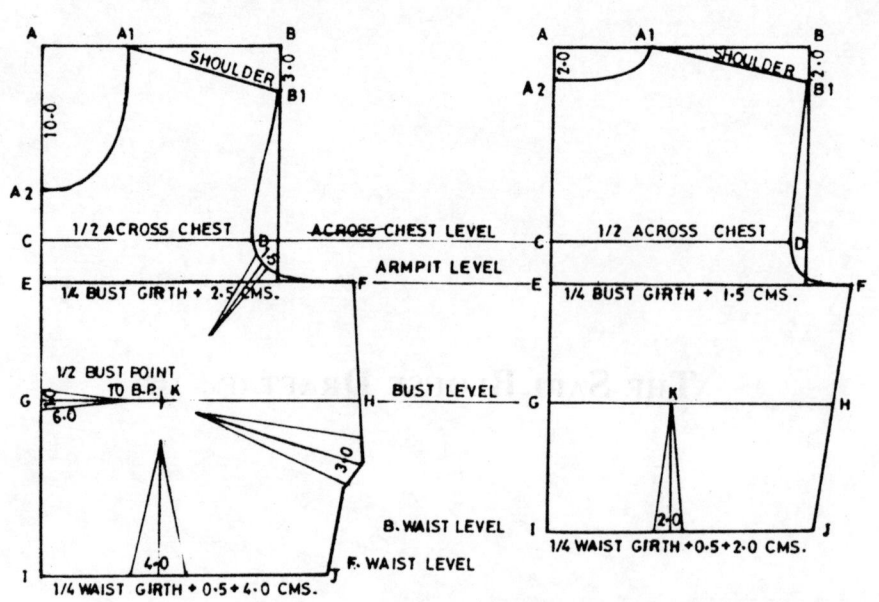

BACK LENGTH IS 3.0 CMS. LESS THAN
THE FRONT LENGTH TO ALLOW FOR THE
3.0 CMS. SIDE SEAM DART AT THE FRONT

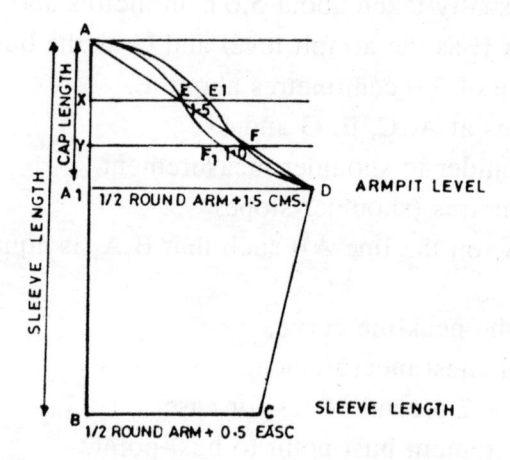

BACK

AI is the back bodice length which is taken 3.0 centimetres less than the front bodice length to allow for the 3.0 centimetres side seam dart at the front.

Draw horizontal lines at C, E, G and I as was done for the front draft.

AB = 1/2 of the shoulder to shoulder measurement.

BB_1 = 2.0 centimetres (shoulder slope).

B_1A_1 = shoulder width equal to that of the front.

Since the shoulder to shoulder measures more at the back than at the front and since the shoulder widths have to be equal, the back neck width will automatically become wider than the front neck width to allow for the difference.

AA_2 = 2.0 centimetres (neck depth).
The neck depth is taken as 2.0 centimetres for all the adult sizes for a close neckline.
CD = 1/2 of the across chest measurement.
EF = 1/4 bust girth + 1.5 centimetres for ease.
GK = 1/2 of the measurement bust point to bust point.
Join B_1D and F to mark the armhole curve.
IJ = 1/4 waist girth + 0.5 centimetre for ease + 2.0 centimetres for the width of the waist dart.
Join FJ to mark the side seam.
Check and match the side seam of the back to that of the front bodice.
Draw a line from the point K to the waistline.
Mark 1.0 centimetre of either side of this line at the waistline. Mark the 2.0 centimetres waist dart from these points to the point K.

SLEEVE

AB = Required sleeve length.
AA_1 = Cap length generally taken as 10.0 or 11.0 centimetres.
A_1D = 1/2 Round arm at the armpit level + 1.5 centimetre for ease.
BC = 1/2 Round arm + 0.5 centimetre for ease.
Mark X and Y as shown.
AX = 4.0 centimetres.
XY = 3.0 centimetres.
Draw horizontal lines at X and Y.
YA_1 = 3.0 centimetres.
Draw a line joining AD.
Mark E and F where AD intersects the horizontal lines X and Y.
EE_1 = 1.5 centimetre.
FF_1 = 1.0 centimetre.
Join DC to mark the side seam.

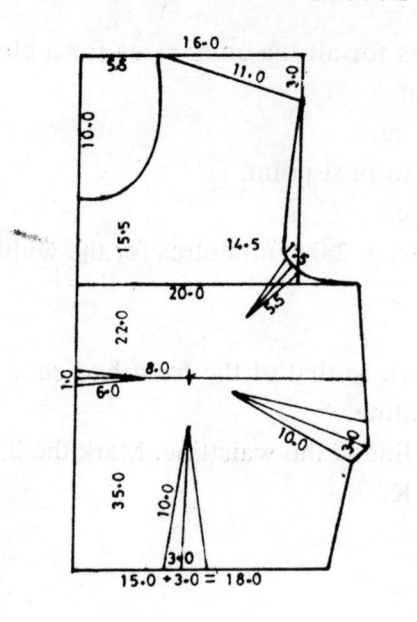

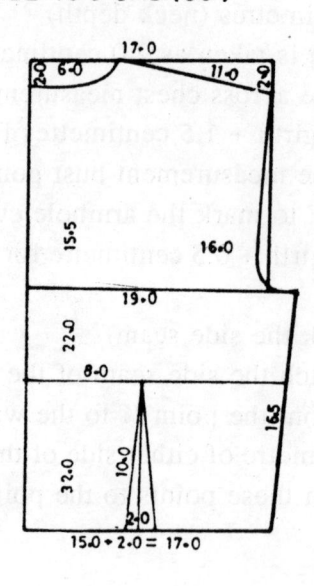

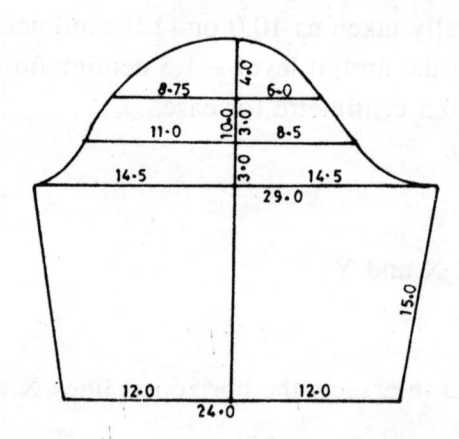

FIG. 149   SARI BLOUSE SIZE 76·0 CMS. (30")

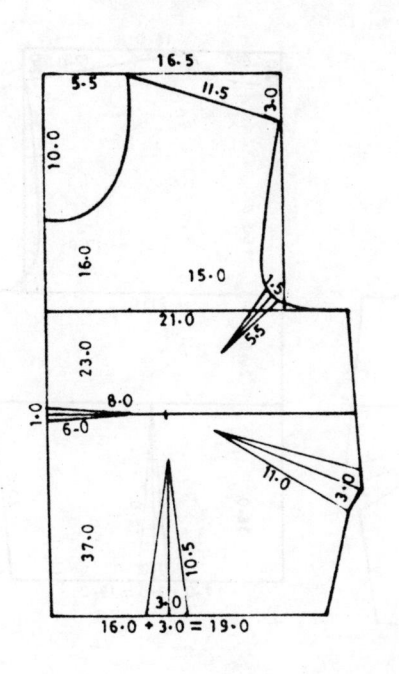

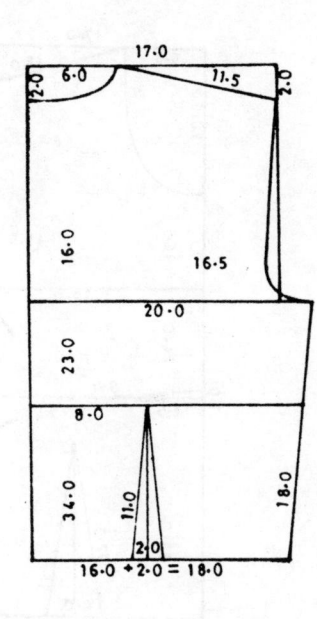

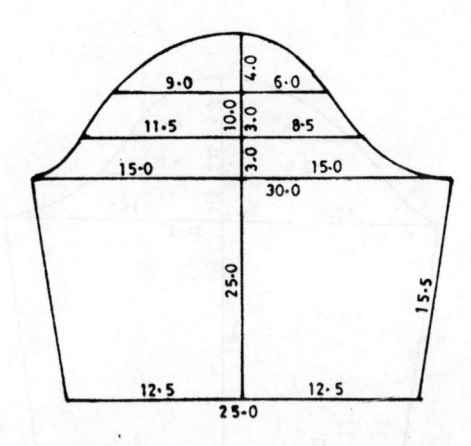

FIG. 150 SARI BLOUSE SIZE 82.0 CMS. (32")

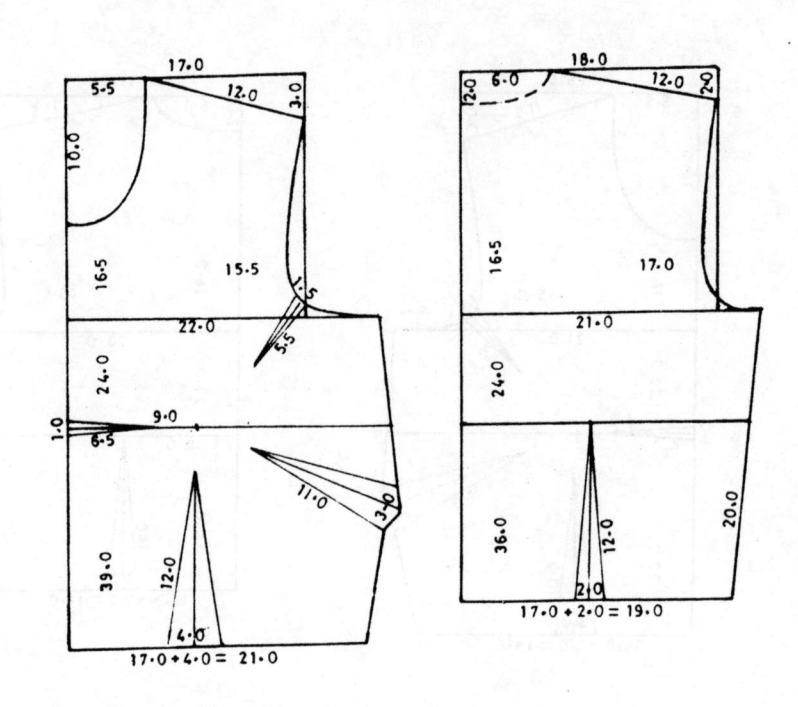

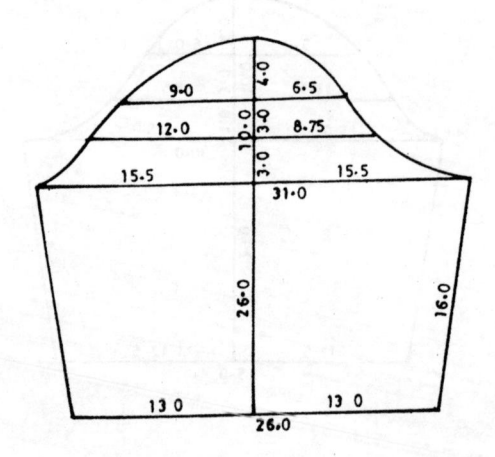

FIG. 151   SARI BLOUSE SIZE 86.0 CMS.(34")

The Art of Sewing 175

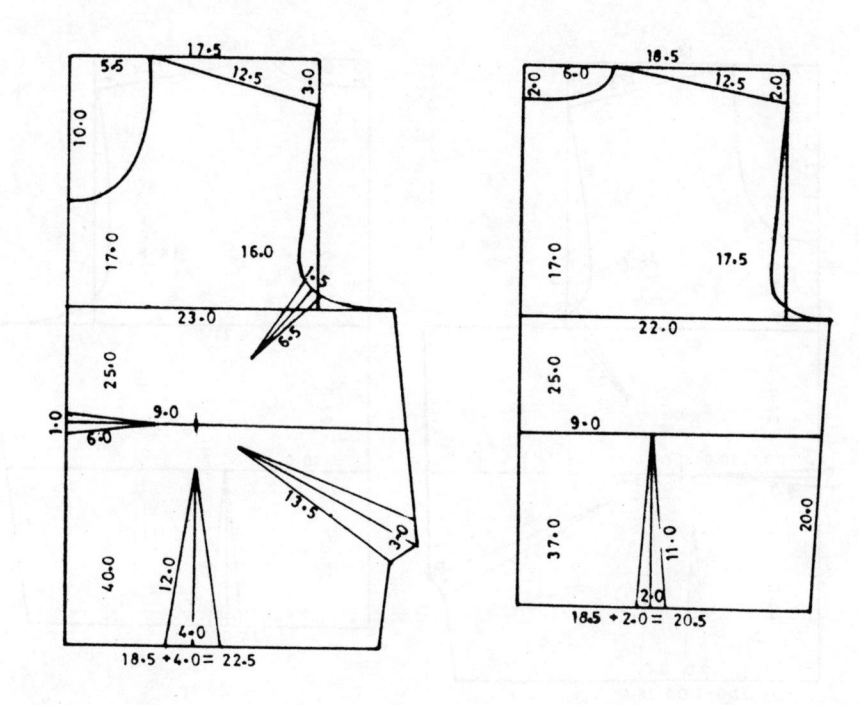

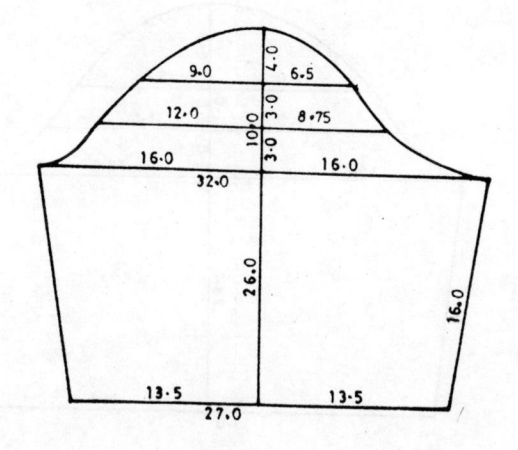

FIG. 152 SARI BLOUSE SIZE 92·0 CMS.(36")

FIG. 153   SARI BLOUSE SIZE 97·0 CMS. (38")

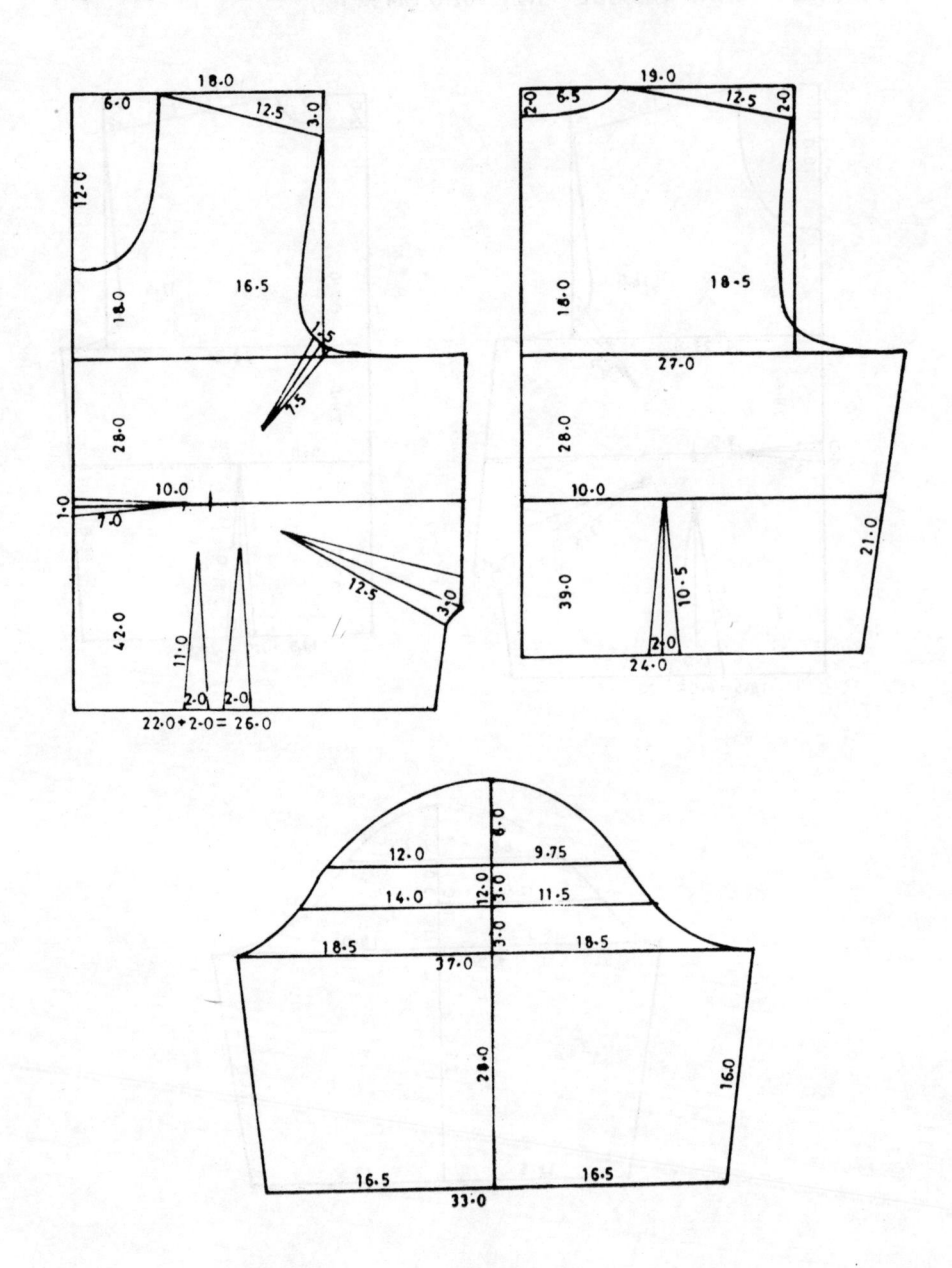

Instructions for sewing the sari blouse

1. The neckline should be stay-stitched.

2. Tack or baste all darts from the tapered end to the base, making sure to match the dart lines on both sides.

3. Machine the darts from the base to the tapered end. After machining each dart, raise the presser foot leaving about 2.0 centimetres of loose thread, then clip the thread. The thread may be knotted at the dart end but this is not absolutely necessary.

    The armhole dart should be double machined as this dart tends to rip open due to the movement of the arm. The darts should be sewn tapering gradually to ensure a smooth finish without any ugly bulges.

4. All darts have to be pressed.

5. The armhole, sideseam and centre front darts are faced downward towards the waistline. The waistline darts, at the front and back, should face the centre front and centre back, respectively. The front waistline dart should be flattened at the centre because it is wide and should not be turned in one direction. Wide darts may be trimmed and finished with zig zag sewing.

6. Next the front button, bands are attached. The upper or right hand side placket strip should be 3.0 centimetres wide. This is turned back and edge-machined. It is then hemmed. The lower or left hand side placket strip should be 6.0 centimetres wide and this is folded into half so as to extend by 2.5 centimetres. This placket is then machined.

7. The shoulder seams are then joined. The seam on either side should be opened and finished with zig zag machining. The seams have to be pressed flat thereafter.

8. The neckline is finished with a facing or bias piping. The bias strip should be 2.0 centimetres wide and should be attached beginning at the right front of the blouse. Whilst attaching a bias facing, place the neckline flat and baste; ease the facing with your hand at the curves. For a V-shaped neckline, a small pleat has to be given at the centre front line of the left section of the blouse where the neckline joins the centre front line in an L-shape.

9. Hem the two sleeves to avoid attaching the wrong sleeve to the wrong armhole. Place both sleeves folded and facing one another to ensure this.

10. The sleeves are attached with the sleeve armsyce about 2.0 to 3.0 centimetres larger than the garment armhole. Ease the sleeve armsyce to fit the armhole. When attaching the sleeve, match the centre of the sleeve to the shoulder line. The seam edges are then finished with zig zag machine stitching.

11. Join the side seams of the sleeve and bodice starting from the sleeve end to the armhole and then down to the waistline on the right side of the garment at a distance of 0.5 centimetre.

12. The waist facing is attached from one end to the other, leaving 1.0 centimetre at the centre front edges for folding in and taking a tiny pleat at the two side seams. Next, turn the facing out and press and finally, edge-stitch the facing. Fold the facing down onto the blouse and hem in place.

13. The garment is then turned to the wrong side and machined on the actual side seamline. The French seam makes for easy alternation of side seams by taking an additional seamline on either side of the original seam so as to loosen or tighten the garment as and when required.

14. Finally, press the garment well, using a steam iron.

Chapter 18

The Skirt

The basic skirt sloper is a plain fitted skirt with darts at the waist. The basic skirt has a total ease of 4.0 centimetres at the waist. While taking measurements for the skirt, note that the waist measures more at the lower end of the waistband than at the top. If the waistband is narrow it can be cut in a single piece, the length equal to the waist girth, but if the waistband is more than 4.0 centimetres wide, it should then be cut with seams at the sides or at the centre back to allow for shaping.

The measurements required for drafting the basic skirt sloper are:

1. The length from waist to hip
2. Length of the skirt
3. Waist girth
4. Hip girth.

Drafting instructions: Fig. 154 - To fit hip size 92.0 cms and waist size 66.0 cms.

Front

AB = Required skirt length minus 4.0 centimetres for the width of the waistband.
D is marked 14.5 centimetres below A on the line AB.
Draw horizontal lines at A D and B.
AC = 1/4 waist girth + 2.0 centimetres for the front waist dart.
DE = 1/4 hip girth + 2.0 centimetres for ease.
BF = DE + 1.0 centimetre.

FIG. 154 BASIC SKIRT DRAFT

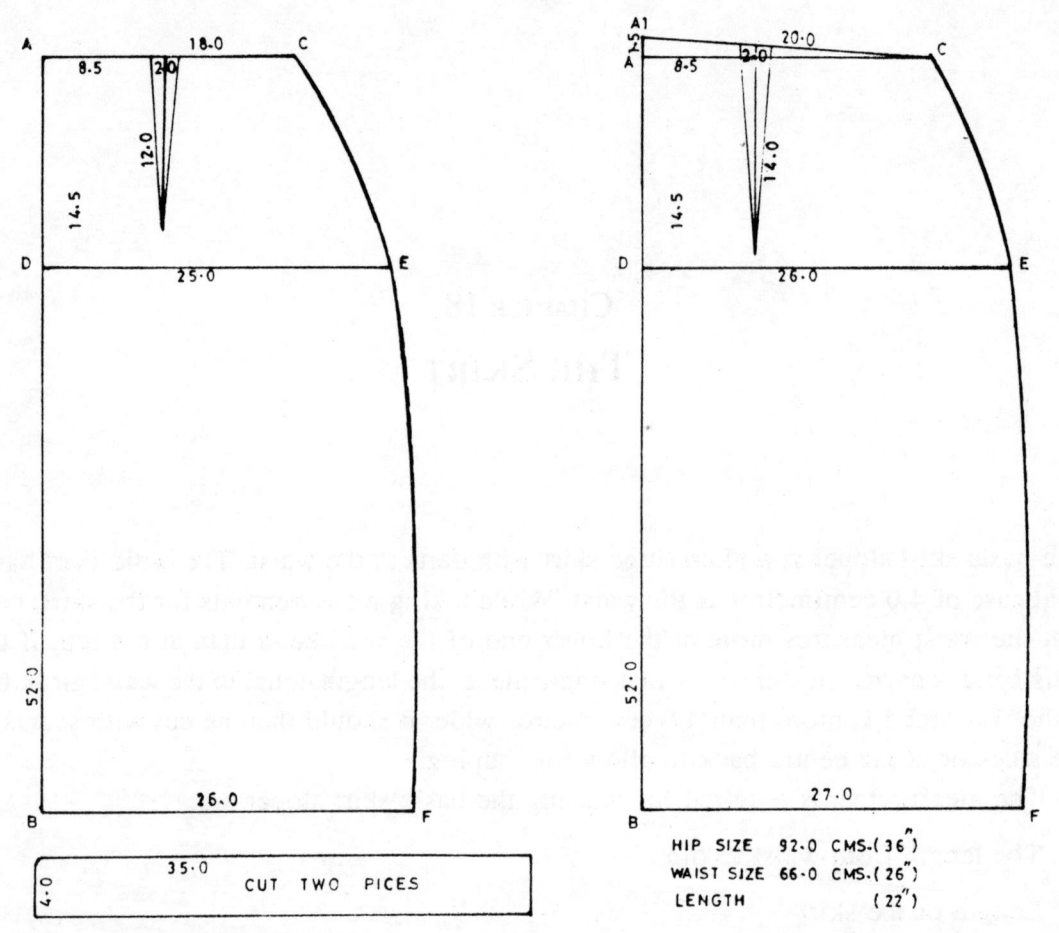

Join C and E with a curve and extend to F.
CEF is the side seam.

Mark the 2.0 centimetres waist dart at a distance of 8.5 centimetres from A. The dart length = 10.0 to 12.0 centimetres.

BACK

AB = Required skirt length minus 4.0 centimetres for the width of the waistband.
Mark a point A_1 1.5 centimetre above A.
D is marked 14.5 centimetres below A on the line AB.
AC = 1/4 waist + 4.0 centimetres (2.0 centimetres for the dart width and 2.0 centimetres for ease).
Join A_1 to C with a straight line.
DE = 1/4 hip girth + 3.0 centimetres.

BF = DE + 1.0 centimetre.
Join C to E with a curve and extend to F.

Mark the 2.0 centimetres waist dart at a distance of 8.5 centimetres from the point A_1 on the line A_1C. The length of the dart is 12.0 to 14.0 centimetres.

WAISTBAND

Width of the waistband = 4.0 centimetres.
Length of the waistband = waist girth + 2.0 centimetres for ease + 2.0 centimetres for the button placket extension.

Skirts are of many types. The width of the fabric influences the skirt design. Extra wide fabric is required for a skirt that is cut on the bias grain of the fabric. Flare can also be introduced in the skirt in the form of gathers and pleats and additional flare can be added in the form of panels and gores. The skirt draft can be combined with the bodice draft to make a dress. There is such a wide variety of skirts from the fitted and shaped skirt to the fully flared umbrella skirt.

THE PLAIN GATHERED SKIRT

The plain gathered skirt may be made from two lengths of fabric, one for the front and one for the back. The waistband and plackets may be cut widthwise from one end of the fabric.

THE UMBRELLA SKIRT

The full umbrella skirt requires a large width of fabric, varying with the length of the skirt. If the fabric is only 36 inches wide, a half umbrella skirt can be made with seams at the side or at the centre front and back, joining the two half circles to form a full circular skirt.

Full Umbrella Skirt (Fig. 155): An umbrella skirt is cut on bias and is a full circular skirt having no seams. Fold the fabric on the bias by holding one end of the fabric and folding the fabric width onto the selvedge. The bias or crosswise grainline is then further folded into half. There are four folds of cloth now, in the form of a triangle.

When the fabric width is 36 inches or 90.0 centimetres, the triangular piece measures 63.6 on both the equal sides and the third side measures 90.0 centimetres. When the fabric width is 45 inches or 114.0 centimetres, the two equal sides measure 80.6 centimetres and the third side 114.0 centimetres.

The waist curve is obtained by calculating the radius of the waist girth using the formula:

Radius = Circumference divided by 2π

Having thus calculated the radius, the waist curve is obtained by marking off a circular quadrant as shown in the diagram by using the calculated radius of curvature.

For example: If the waist girth or circumference is 66.0 centimetres, then the radius of curvature is $\dfrac{66}{2} \times \dfrac{7}{22} = \dfrac{21}{2} = 10.5$ cm.

FIG. 155   FULL UMBRELLA SKIRT

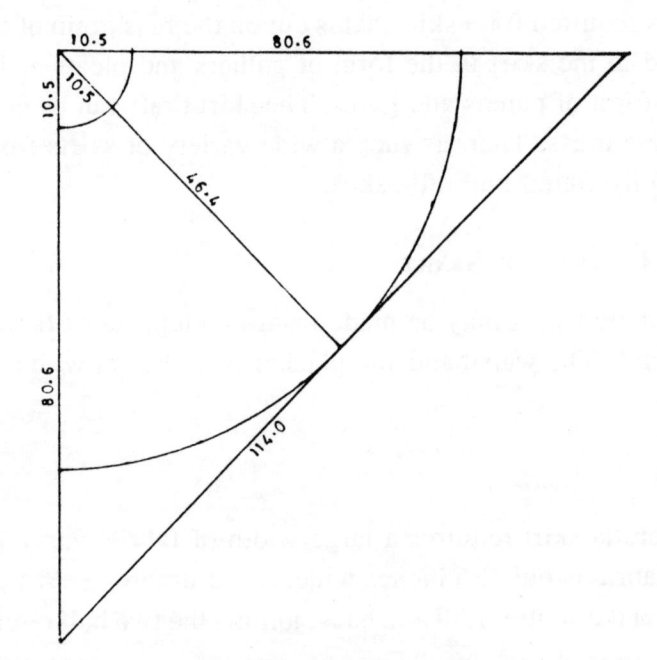

Half Umbrella Skirt (Fig. 156): For the half umbrella skirt, the fabric is folded only once on the bias. The fabric now is in two layers. When the width of the fabric is 114.0 centimetres or 45 inches, the two equal sides measure 114.0 centimetres and the third side measures 161.2 centimetres (Fig. 156).

The radius of the waist girth, which was calculated earlier as being 10.5 centimetres, has to be doubled for a half circular skirt. Mark this curved line as shown in the diagram. Measure to the end of the fabric and mark a curve radially. This gives the skirt length. When the fabric width is 45 inches or 114.0 centimetres, then a full umbrella skirt will give a length measuring 46.4 centimetres of 18¼ inches, whereas a half umbrella skirt will give a skirt length of 92 centimetres or 36 inches.

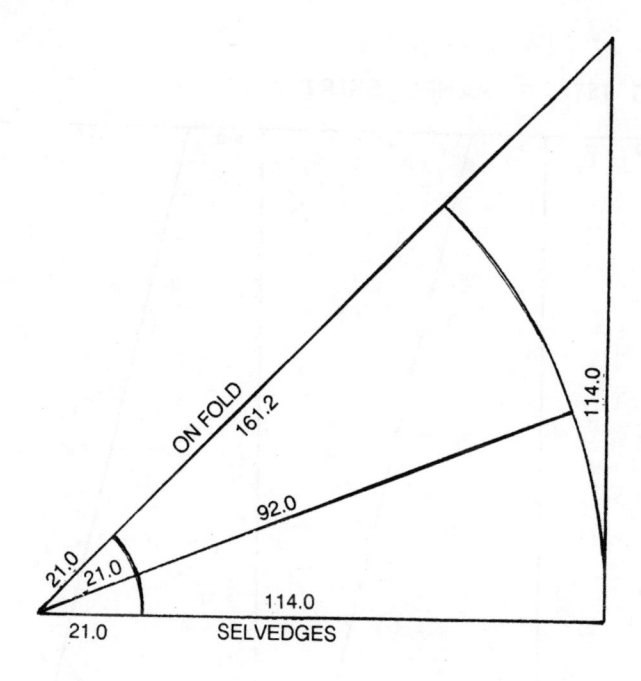

FIG. 156   HALF UMBRELLA SKIRT

The Panel Skirt (Fig. 157): The panel skirt is flared at the hem and tapers towards the waistline. The waist girth is divided by the number of panels required. Each panel will thus be equal at the waistline. At the hemline, the panel can measure twice or thrice as much as at the waist, depending on the width of the fabric.

A panel can be made only in self-coloured fabric or one having an all-directional print, as the panels are placed facing in both directions alternatively. When joining the panels be sure always to join one straight edge to a slant edge. The hemline will therefore be irregular and will have to be curved to perfection.

GORED SKIRT (Fig. 158)

A gored skirt is fitted upto the hipline and flares out to the hemline. The basic skirt sloper with a waist dart can be adapted to the gored skirt.

Lengthen the waist dart to the hipline. Draw a vertical line from the tip of the waist dart to the hemline. Slash this line from the hemline to the hip level and close the waist dart. The slashed line will then flare out by itself. At the side seam, an additional flare is added, as illustrated. Join the side seam to the extended hemline. The gores are then joined together. The straight seams are taken at the centre front and centre back and the curved seams at the two sides.

FIG. 157   PANEL SKIRT

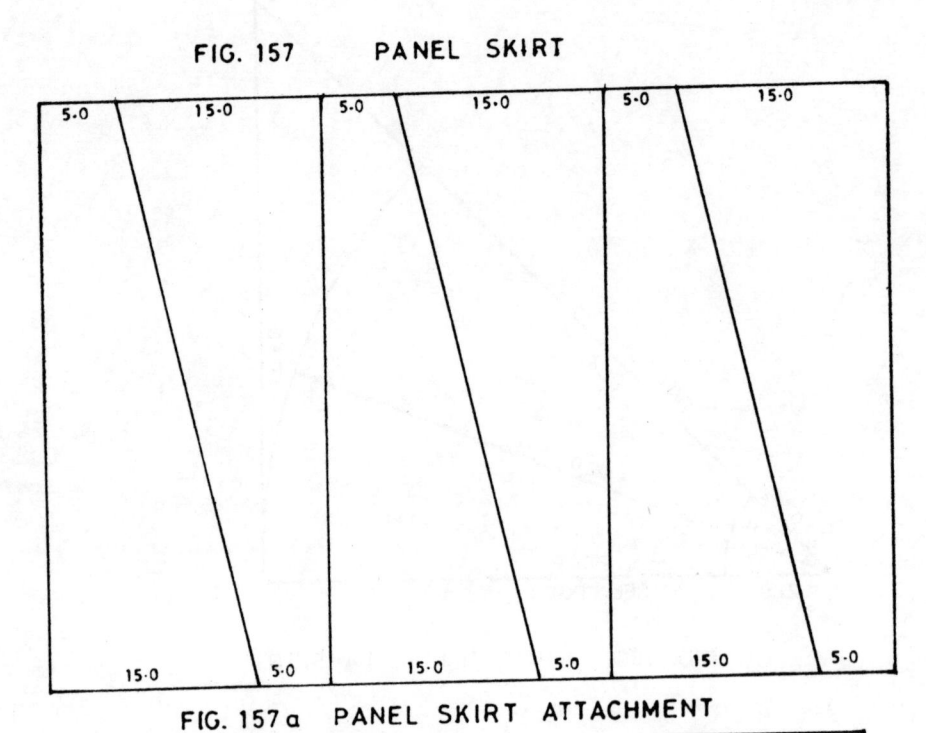

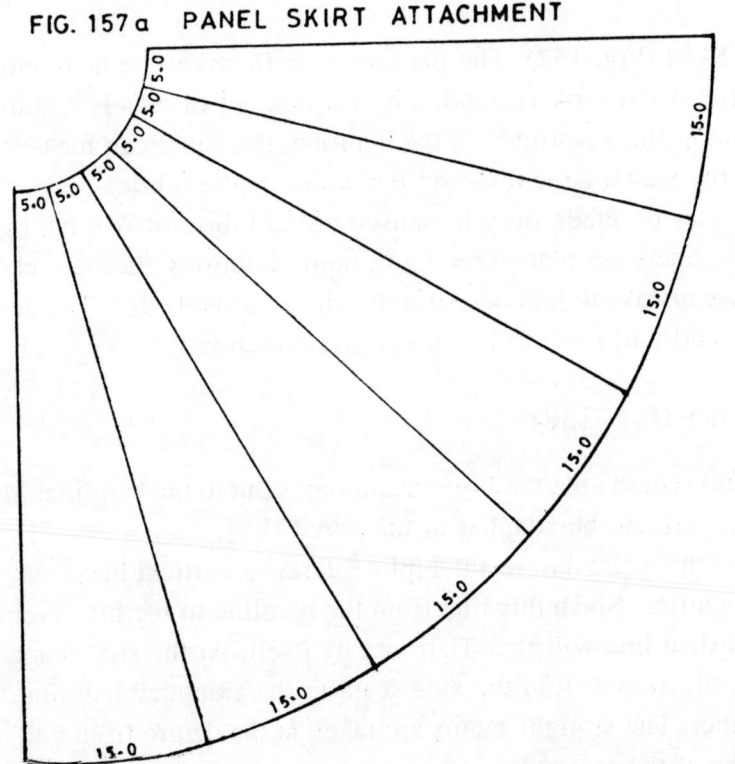

FIG. 157a   PANEL SKIRT ATTACHMENT

The Art of Sewing

FOUR GORE SKIRT FIG. 158

CUT FOUR PICES

DART CLOSED

SLASH AND SPREAD

0.5

6.0

BASIC SKIRT SLOPER

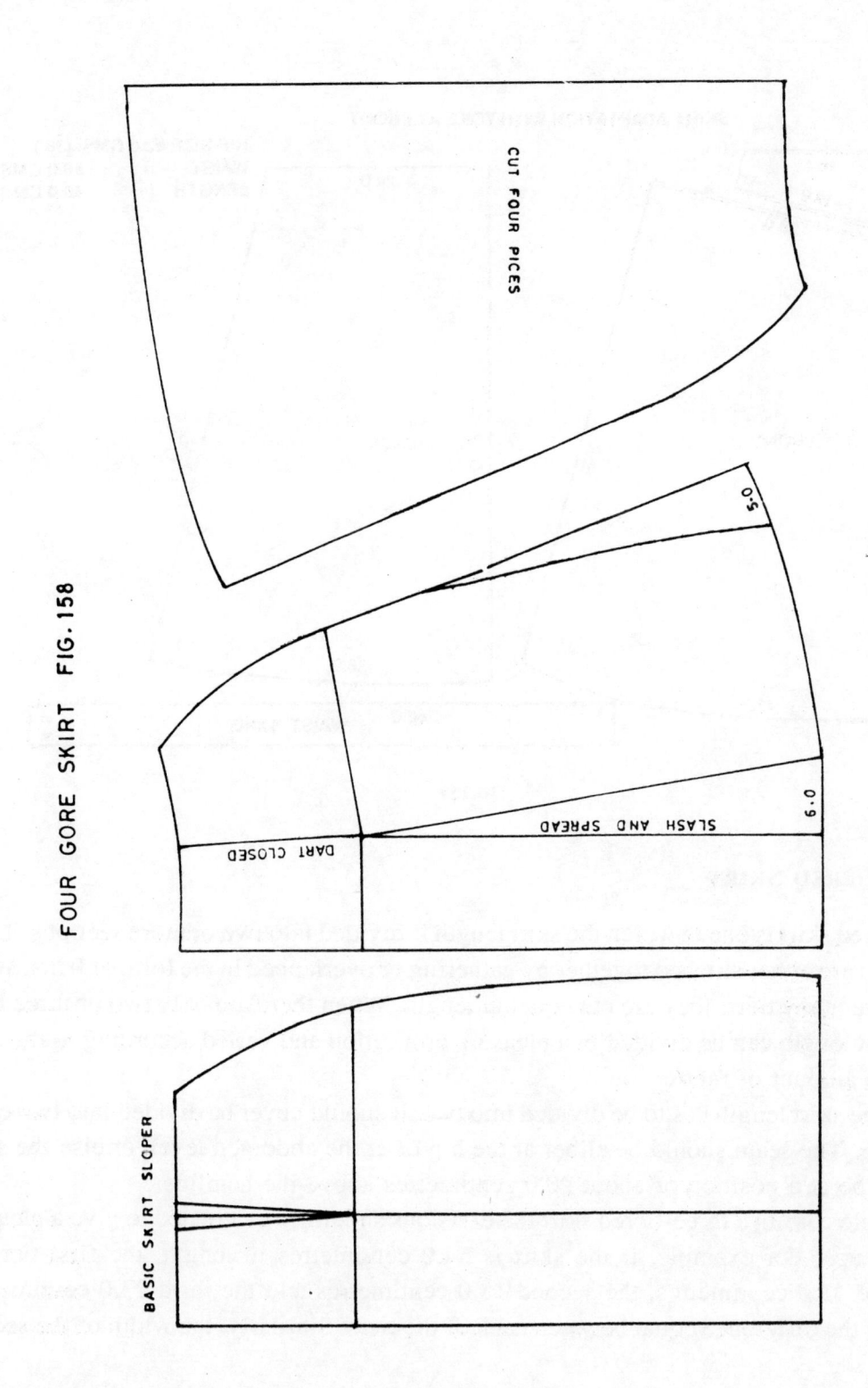

SKIRT ADAPTATION WITH YOKE AT FRONT

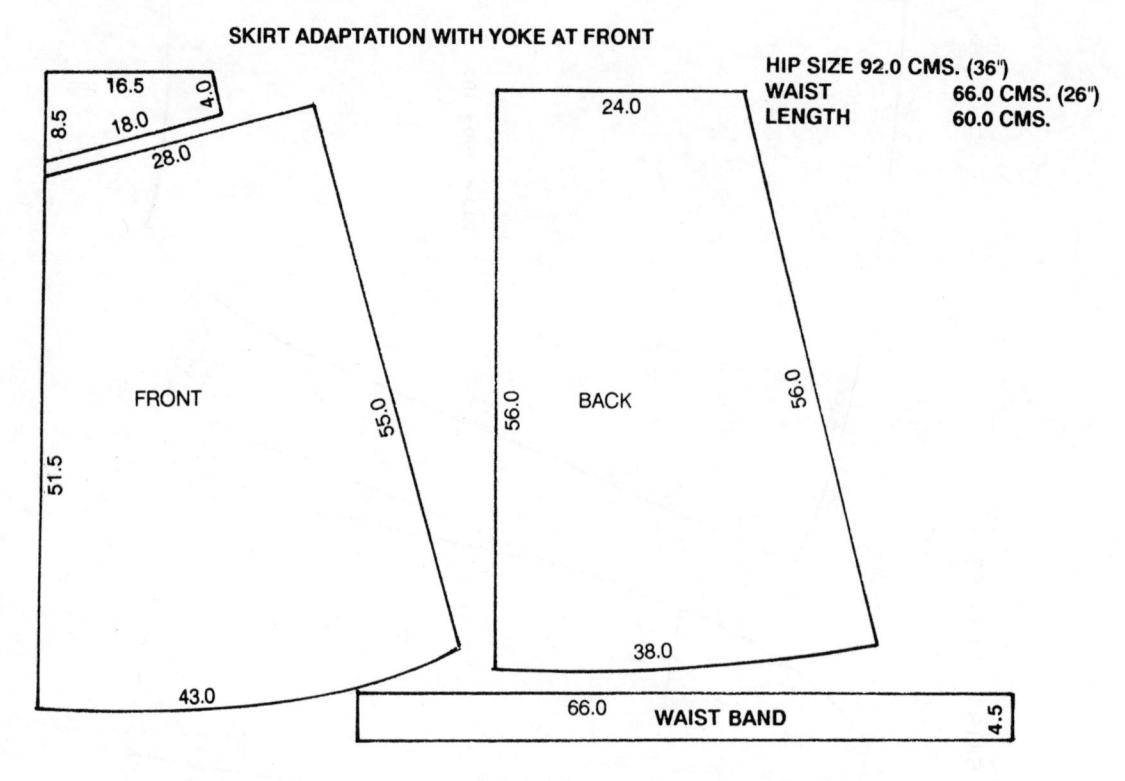

HIP SIZE 92.0 CMS. (36")
WAIST 66.0 CMS. (26")
LENGTH 60.0 CMS.

FIG.159

THE TIERED SKIRT

The tiered skirt is one in which the skirt length is divided into two or more sections. These sections are either stitched together by gathering or overlapped in the form of frills. When there are many tiers, they are cut equal in length. When there are only two or three tiers, the skirt length can be divided in a pleasing proportion and varied according to the style and the amount of fabric.

If the skirt length has to be divided into two, it should never be divided into two equal sections. The seam should be either at the hip or at the abdomen level, or else the seam should be at a position of about 20.0 centimetres above the hemline.

While cutting a three-tiered skirt the divisions should be calculated to give a pleasing appearance. For example, if the skirt is 54.0 centimetres in length, the first tier can measure 13.0 centimetres, the second 18.0 centimetres and the third 23.0 centimetres, making the difference equal between each of the tiers. Similarly, the width of the second tier has to be atleast 25.0 centimetres more than the one immediately above it to allow for gathers.

PLEATED SKIRTS

Refer pages 46-47

A CULOTTE OR THE DIVIDED SKIRT

This is divided at the centre by the introduction of a crotchline. This skirt is generally used as sportswear. It is also popular as casual wear for girls.

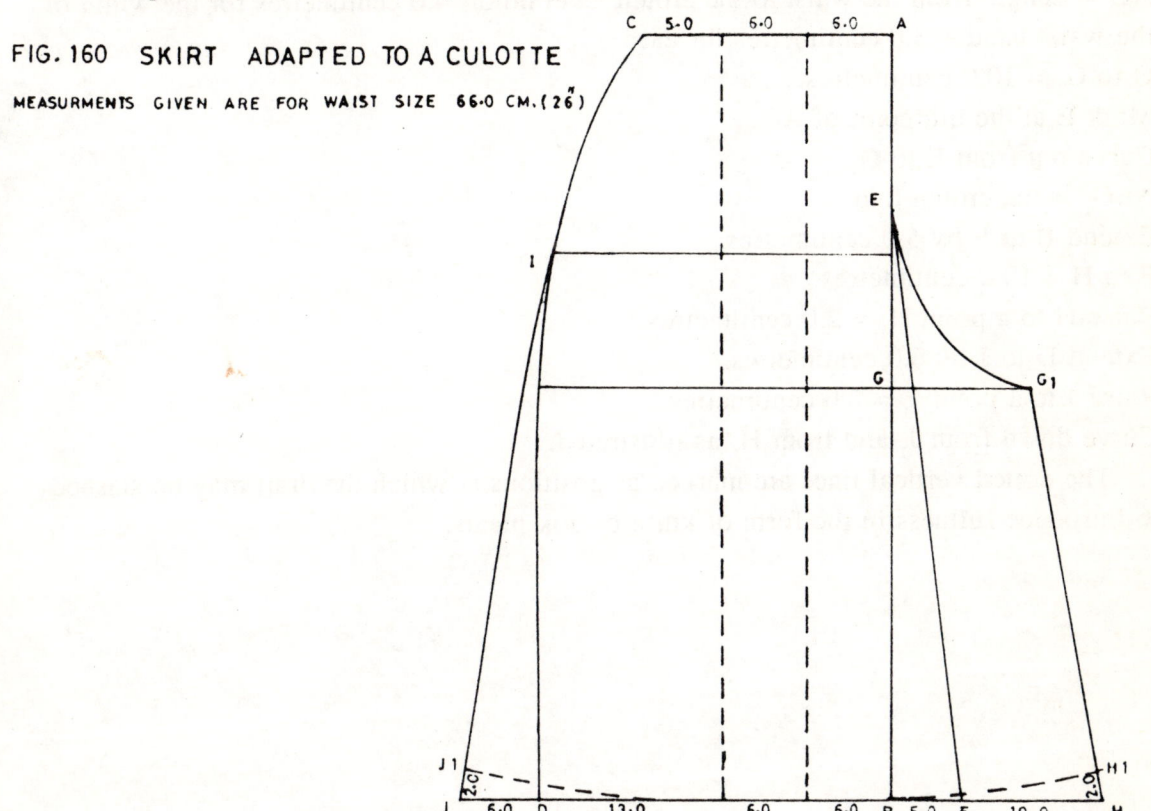

FIG. 160 SKIRT ADAPTED TO A CULOTTE
MEASUREMENTS GIVEN ARE FOR WAIST SIZE 66.0 CM. (26")

The measurements in this draft (Fig. 160) are given to fit a waist size of 66.0 centimetres (26"). The divided skirt is loose at the hip level and can fit a hip size of 87.0 to 92.0 centimetres (34" to 36").

The measurements required to draft are:
1. Waist girth
2. Hip girth
3. Length from waist to hip level

4. Length from waist to crotch level
5. Required length.

Trace out the basic skirt sloper and mark the outline as ABDC.
Mark I at the hip level.
CI = Length from the waist to the hip level minus 4.0 centimetres for the width of the waistband.
Mark G at the crotch level.
AG = Length from the waist to the crotch level minus 4.0 centimetres for the width of the waist band + 3.0 centimetres for ease.
G to G_1 = 10.0 centimetres.
Mark E at the midpoint of AG.
Curve out from E to G_1.
AEG_1 is the crotch line.
Extend B to F by 5.0 centimetres.
F to H = 10.0 centimetres.
Raise H to a point H_1 = 2.0 centimetres.
Extend D to J by 6.0 centimetres.
Raise J to a point J_1 = 2.0 centimetres.
Curve down from J_1 and from H_1 as illustrated.

The dotted vertical lines are marked as positions at which the draft may be slashed to introduce fullness in the form of knife or box pleats.

CHAPTER 19

THE SARI PETTICOAT

This draft (Fig. 161) is for a two-piece sari petticoat. These are comfortable without being too bulky, having fewer seams than the six-piece petticoat.

AB = Full length including hem width minus 3.0 centimetres for the waist band.
AE = 18.0 centimetres.
AC = 1/4 waist + 4.0 centimetres for ease + 2.0 centimetres for dart width.
EF = 1/4 hip + 8.0 centimetres for ease.
BD = EF + 11.0 centimetres for flare at the hem.
Raise D by 2.0 centimetres to D_1.
Join C F D_1 for the side seam.
Mark the waist dart as shown.

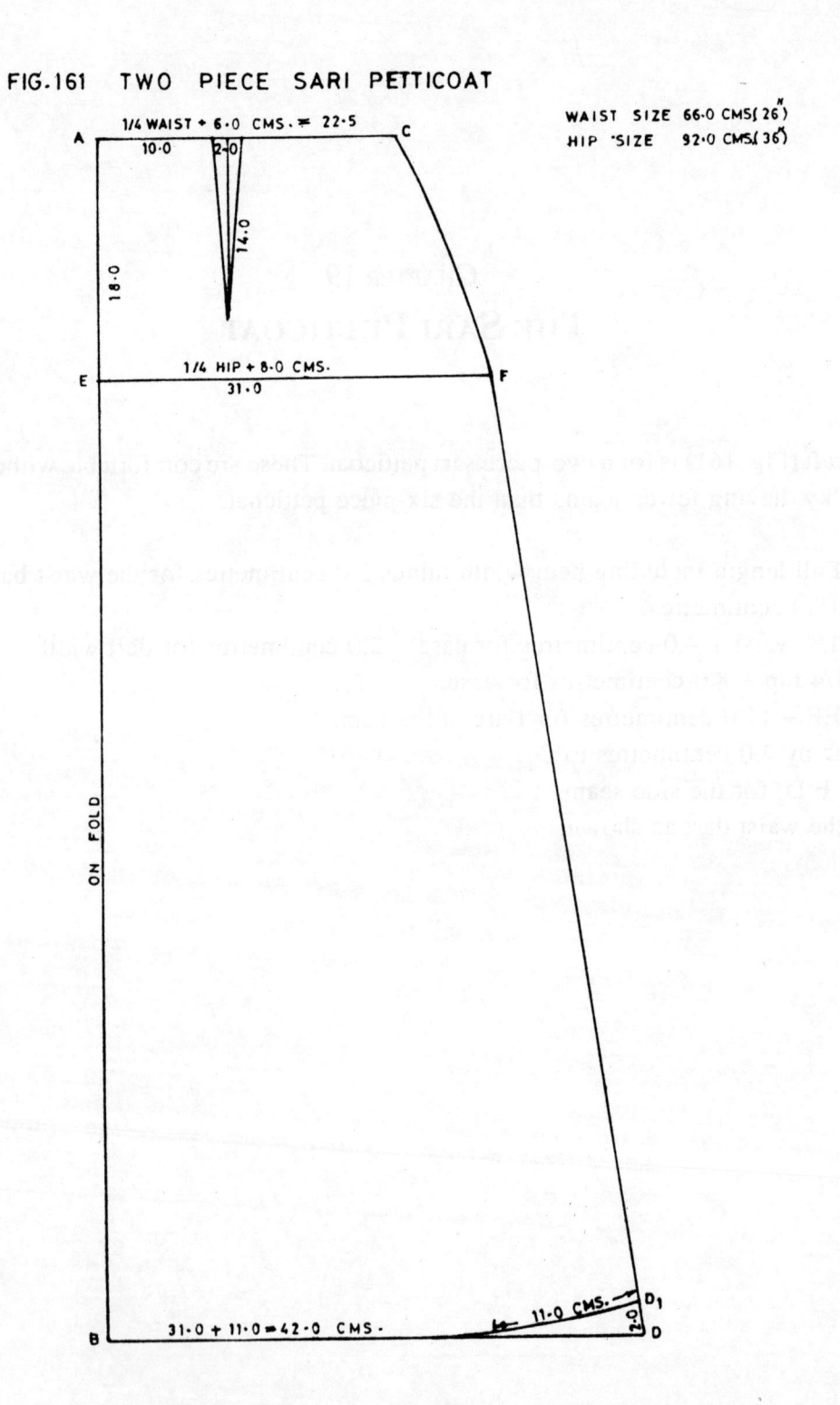

FIG. 161 TWO PIECE SARI PETTICOAT

WAIST SIZE 66.0 CMS (26")
HIP SIZE 92.0 CMS (36")

Sari Petticoat Measurement Chart

Waist Girth in inches	Waist Girth in centimetres	With ease	Hip Girth in inches	Hip Girth in centimetres	With ease
26	66.0	73.0	36	92.0	102.0
27	69.0	76.0	37	94.0	104.0
28	71.0	79.0	38	97.0	107.0
29	74.0	81.0	39	99.0	109.0
30	76.0	83.0	40	102.0	112.0
31	79.0	86.0	41	104.0	114.0
32	81.0	88.0	42	107.0	117.0
33	84.0	91.0	43	109.0	119.0
34	86.5	93.5	44	112.0	122.0
35	89.0	96.0	45	114.5	124.5
36	91.5	98.5	46	117.0	127.0
37	94.0	101.0	47	119.5	129.5
38	96.5	103.5	48	122.0	132.0

Length inclusive of belt width

Height	Height in centimetres	Length in inches	Length in centimetres
5'1"	155.0	37	94.0
5'2"	157.5	38	96.5
5'3"	160.0	39	99.0
5'4"	162.5	40	101.5
5'5"	165.0	41	104.0
5'6"	167.5	42	106.5
5'7"	170.0	43	109.0
5'8"	172.5	44	112.0

Chapter 20
The Salwar

The salwar draft (Fig. 162) is inclusive of seam allowances. The bottom width is deliberately cut larger to allow for shaping as shown in the diagram. After the centre section has been joined to the two side sections, measure the required 'pauncha' width adding 4.0 centimetres seam allowance, 2.0 centimetres for each side. Draw a curve and cut along this line. This shaping ensures a good fall.

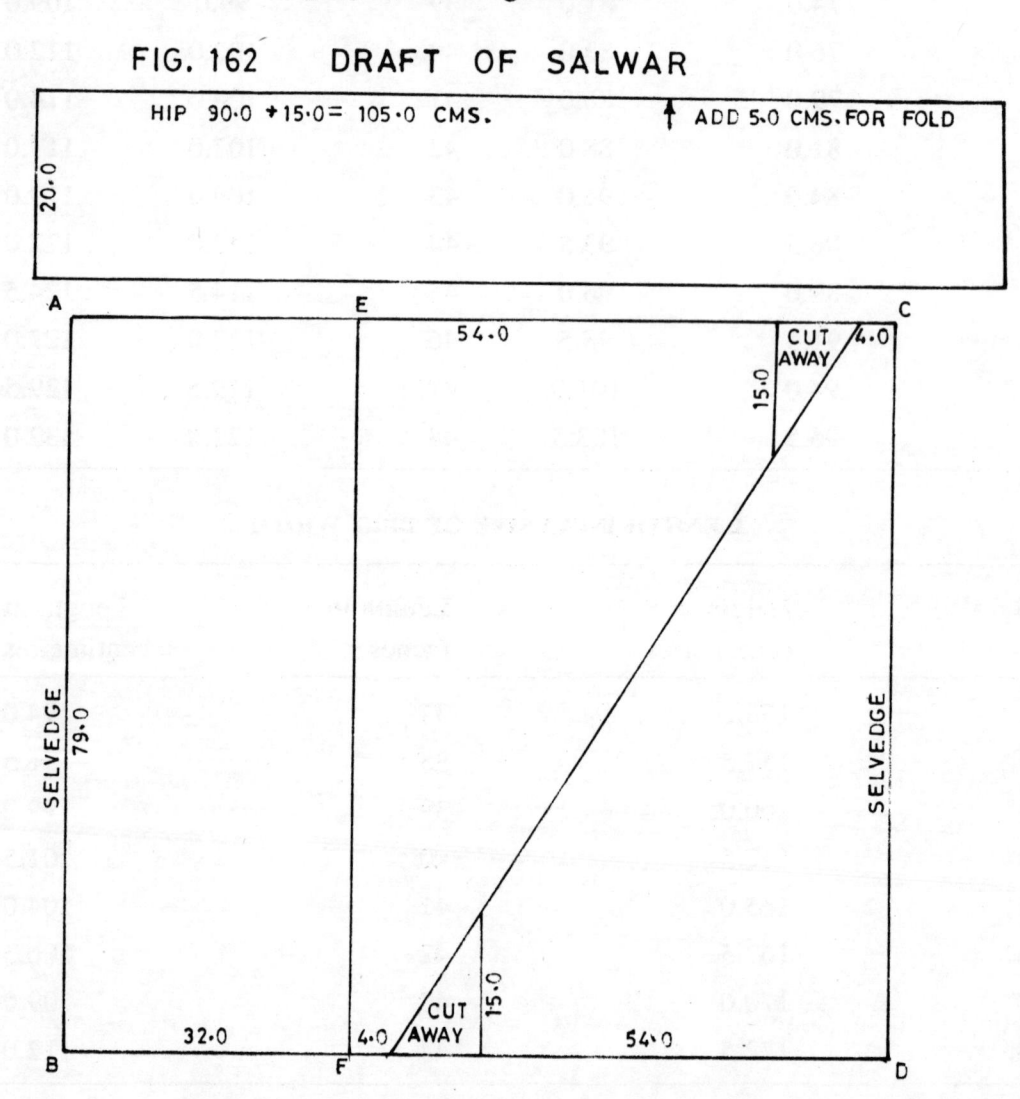

FIG. 162   DRAFT OF SALWAR

The Art of Sewing

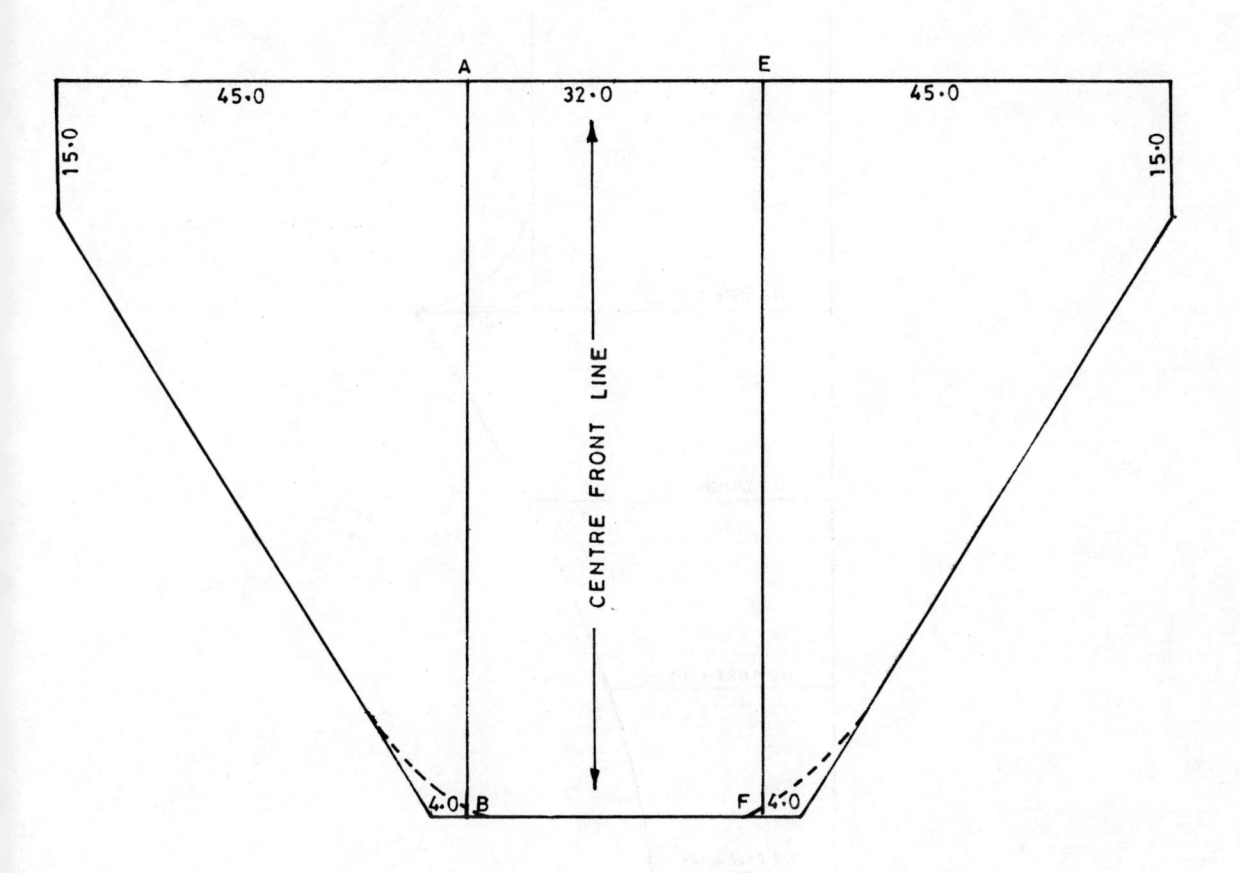

45·0   A   32·0   E   45·0

15·0   15·0

CENTRE FRONT LINE

4·0 B   F 4·0

FIG. 163 DRAFT OF THE CHURIDAR

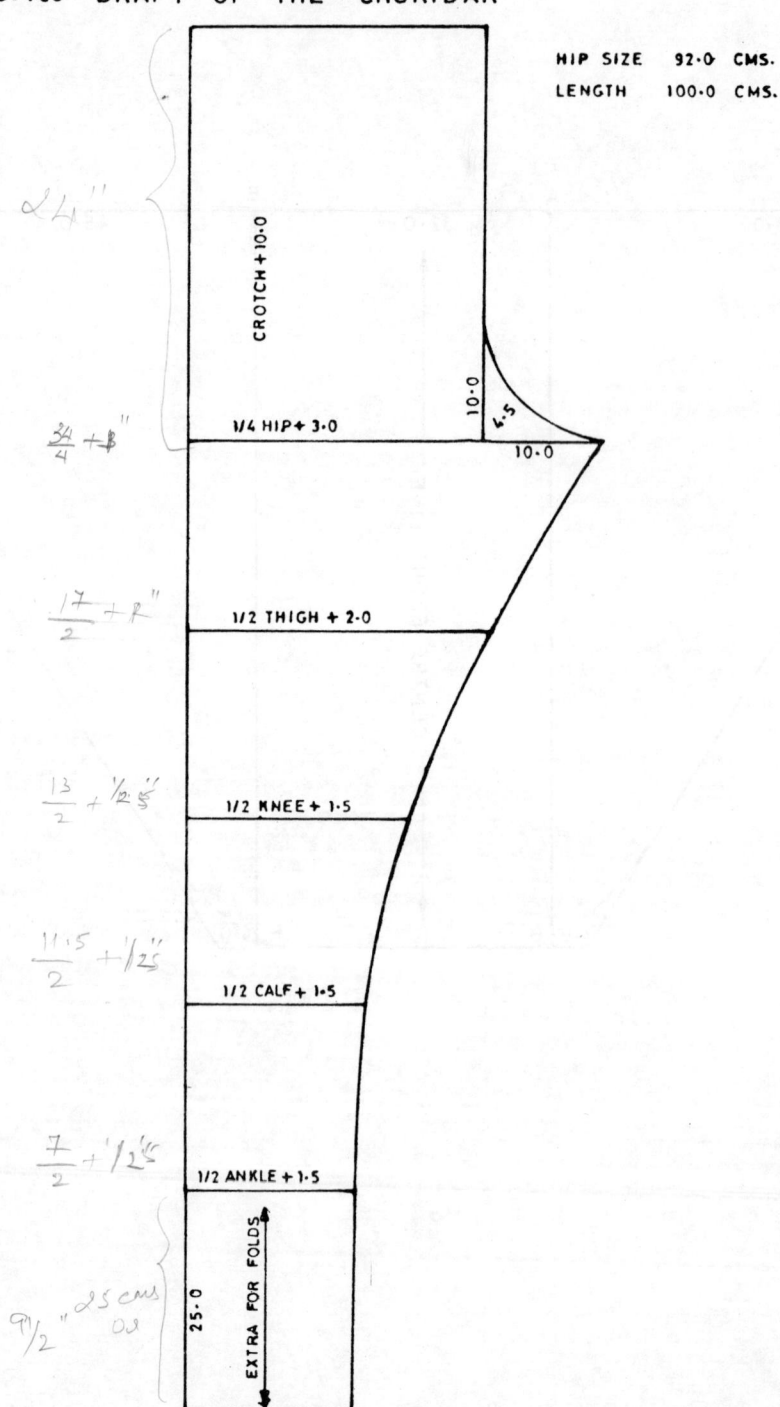

HIP SIZE   92·0 CMS.
LENGTH   100·0 CMS.

CROTCH + 10·0

1/4 HIP + 3·0   10·0   4·5
                 10·0

1/2 THIGH + 2·0

1/2 KNEE + 1·5

1/2 CALF + 1·5

1/2 ANKLE + 1·5

25·0   EXTRA FOR FOLDS

CHAPTER 21

SHORTS

Front

Draw a line AB = Crotch length. 24 cms.

From A, mark a point C = 1/4 waist + 4.0 cms for dart widths. 59 cms +

Mark two darts at a distance of 10.0 and 14.0 cms from A.

Length of the darts = 10.0 cms.

A to A_1 = 1.0 cm. Join A_1 to C.

BD = 1/4 hip + 2.0 cms for ease. 69 cms +

BE = 5.0 cms.

F is 10.0 cms from A.

Draw a vertical line from F to G = Length of shorts. 30 cms.

FIG. 164   SHORTS   HIP SIZE 92·0 CMS.(36") WAIST 70·0 CMS.(27·5")

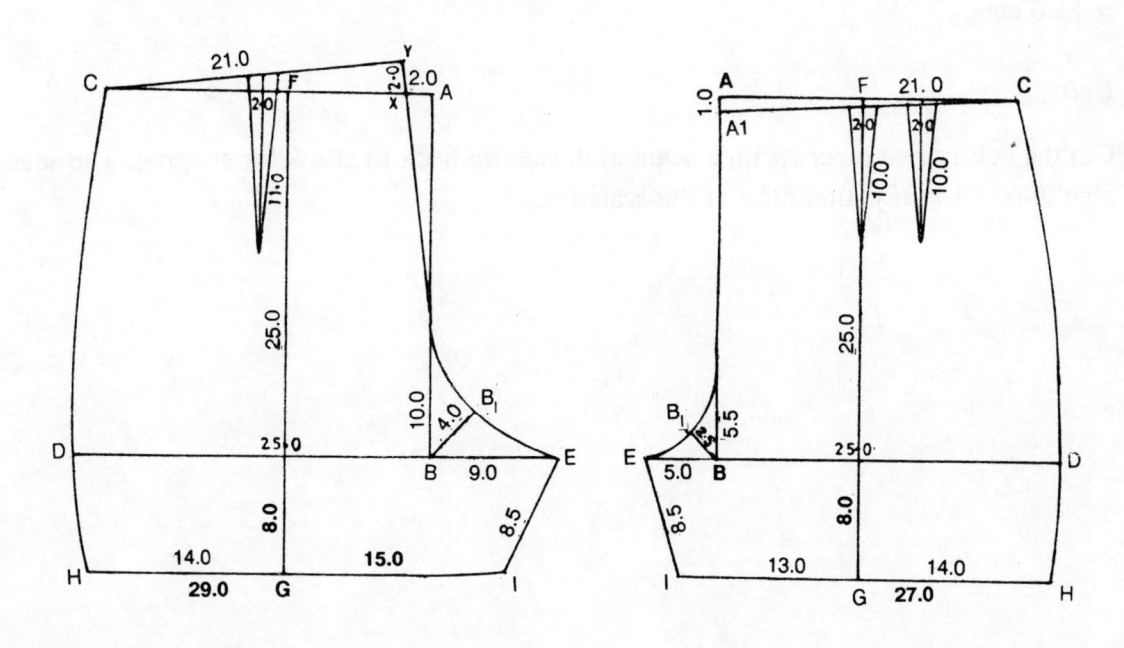

GI = 1/4 Thigh Girth.

GH = 1/4 Thigh Girth + 1.0 cm.

Join CDH with a curved line, using a skirt curve.

Join A_1 to E with a curve.

Back

Draw a line AB = Crotch length.
At A draw a horizontal line.
AC = 1/4 waist girth + 4.0 cms. (2.0 cms for dart and 2.0 cms for shaping in at A)
Mark X, 2.0 cms from A.
X to Y = 2.0 cms.
BD = 1/4 Hip + 2.0 cms for ease.
BE = 9.0 cms.
Mark F, 10.0 cms from A.
Draw a vertical line FG = Length of shorts.
GI = 1/4 Thigh girth + 2.0 cms.
GH = 1/4 Thigh girth + 1.0 cm.
Join CDH with a skirt curve.
Mark a 2.0 cms dart at a distance of 10.0 cms away from Y on the line YC. The dart length = 11.0 cms.

Belt

Cut the belt in two pieces with a seam at the centre back to allow for shaping. The seam also allows for any alteration at the waistline.

Chapter 22

Trousers

Front (Fig. 165)

Draw a line AB = Crotch length minus Belt width.
AD = 1/4 wist + 2.0 centimetres for the waist dart or pleat.
Mark A_1, 1.0 centimetre below A.
Join D to A_1 for the waistline.
BC = 1/4 Hip Girth.
BJ = 5.5 centimetres.
BB_1 = 2.0 centimetres.
Draw a curved line from A_1 connecting A_1B_1 to J.
A_1B_1J = Front Crotch line.
Mark E = 1/2 of CJ.
Draw a vertical line from the waistline AD through E to a point G = Full length minus Belt width.
F = 1/2 of EG - 5.0 centimetres from E.
F to F_2 = 1/2 knee girth.
F to F_1 = 1/2 knee girth + 3.0 centimetres.
The ease at the knee would vary with the style of the trouser.
G to I = 1/2 Ankle girth + 2.0 centimetres.
G to H = 1/2 Ankle girth + 3.0 centimetres.
Join JF_2 to I for the inner leg curve.
Join CF_1 to H with an outward curve for the side seam.

FIG. 165   DRAFT FOR TROUSERS

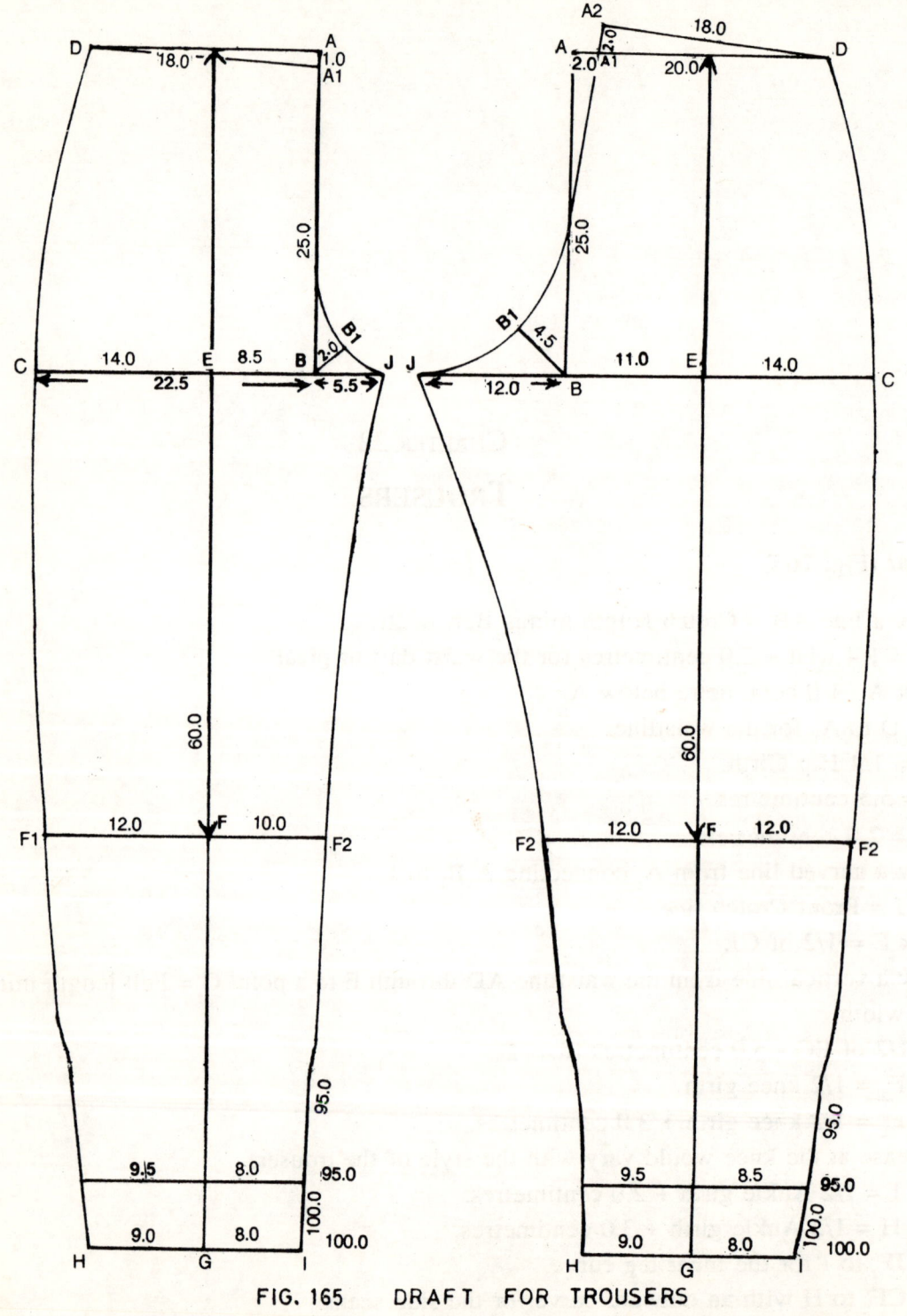

MEASUREMENTS GIVEN ARE FOR HIP SIZE 92·0 CMS. (36″)
WAIST SIZE 66·0 CMS. (26″)

Back

AB = Crotch length minus belt width.
AD = 1/2 waist + 4.0 centimetres (2.0 cms for the dart and 2.0 centimetres to allow for shaping in at A).
AA_1 = 2.0 centimetres. A_1A_2 = 2.0 centimetres.
Join A_2 to D equal to A_1D_1 of the front draft.
BC = 1/4 Hip + 2.0 centimetres.
BJ = 12.0 centimetres.
BB_1 = 4.5 centimetres.
Join $A_2A_1B_1$ to J for the crotch curve.
Mark E from C equal to CE of the front draft.
Draw a vertical line from the waistline through E to G. Equal to full length minus belt width.
Mark F at knee level same as for the front.
FF_1 and FF_2 = 1/2 knee girth + 2.0 centimetres.
GI = 1/2 ankle girth + 2.5 centimetres.
GH = 1/2 ankle girth + 3.5 centimetres.
Join JF_1 to H with an inward curve.
Join DCF_2 to I with an outward curve.

Belt

Cut the belt in two pieces with a seam at the centre back to allow for shaping. The seam also allows for any alteration at the waistline.

Chapter 23
Sewing Tips

1. All seams need double machining. This little extra effort during sewing will ensure that the seams do not rip easily.

2. While sewing the shoulder seams, start from the armhole edge to the neck edge, turn and double-machine the seam, making sure that the second stitch line does not shift from the seamline.

3. All straight seams should be stitched absolutely straight; any irregularities will appear magnified after the garment has been completed.

4. While attaching a facing, keep the workpiece flat on a table.

5. While making gathers, set the machine on the largest stitch size, loosen the top tension slightly and machine two rows, one on the seamline and one 0.5 centimetre above it. Wind the top threads round a pin and pull up to the desired length by the bobbin thread only. Ease the fabric gently while pulling to avoid breaking the thread.

6. While attaching an eased or gathered section of a garment, always keep it on top to ensure evenness and to keep the gathers from shifting.

7. While attaching pockets and while stitching down the pleats, double-machine the edges for reinforcement.

8. While attaching ruffles or lace, provide extra ease at the corners.

9. A curved seam is stitched in the same way as a plain seam but the edges are notched so that the seams may be pressed flat. Curved seams are pressed on a Tailor's Ham so that the curve does not flatten during pressing (Figs. 166a and b).

FIG. 166 a INWARD CURVE

FIG. 166 b OUTWARD CURVE

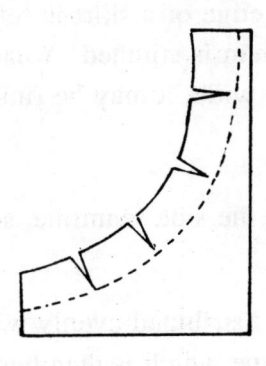

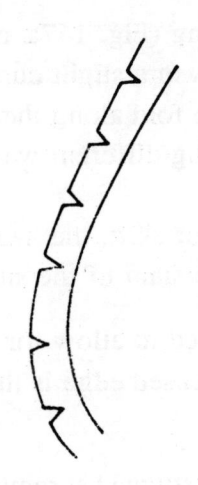

FIG. 167 a   CURVED HEMS

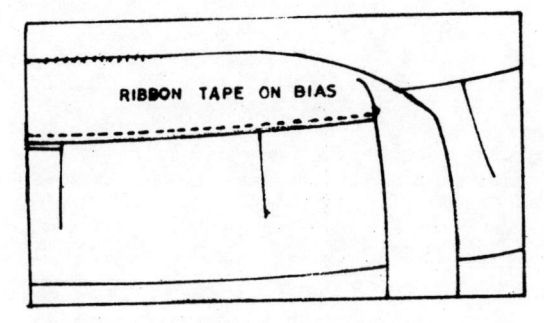

RIBBON TAPE ON BIAS

FIG. 167 b

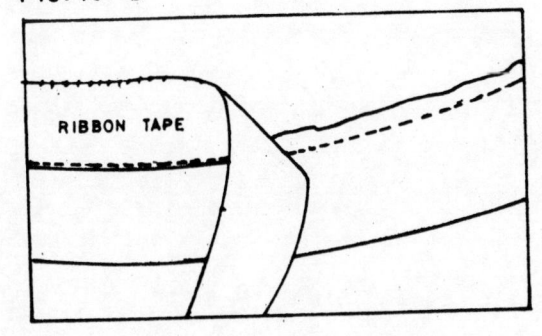

RIBBON TAPE

10. A bias seam must be a sewn with a looser tension to prevent puckering. Never pull edges that are cut on the bias while sewing or they will get stretched permanently. If a straight edge is being attached to a bias edge, have the bias on the underside.

11. While hemming (Fig. 167a and b), remember that the edge of a skirt is seldom straight and even a slight curve will affect the way a hem is stitched. A narrow hem is easy to fold along the curves. When the hem is wide, it may be finished in the following different ways:

For an A-line dress or skirt, the hem is folded before cutting the side seamline, so that the hem matches the slant of the side seam.

The hem edge is eased to allow for the excess amount to be distributed evenly without forming folds. This eased edge is then attached onto a bias tape which is then hemmed onto the garment.

Narrow darts may be stitched at regular intervals along the hem edge. Attach this to a bias tape and then hem into position.

INDEX

A
A-Line, 3
Allowance, 3
Alter, 3
All-in-one Facing, 52
Applique, 3
Armhole, 3
Armscye, 3

B
Back Stitch, 3, 28
Bagging Out, 3
Balance, 97
Bands, 3
Bar, 3
Basque, 3
Basting, 4, 25
Bar-Tacks, 33
Belt Carriers, 35
Bertha, 4
Bias, 4, 53
Binding, 4, 55
Blind Stitch, 4, 32
Bobbin Winder Spindle, 22
Bodice Blocks, 122
Bolero, 4
Bound Seam, 43
Braid, 4
Breakline, 4
Brettelle, 4
Brides, 4
Buckram, 4
Bustle, 4

C
Capsleeve, 5
Cap, 5
Casing, 5, 36
Catch Stitch, 32
Centre Front, 5
Chalk, 17
Chic, 5
Children's Clothes, 122
Chinese Cord, 5
Clip, 5
Closing, 5

Collarette, 5
Collar, 102
   Bertha, 104
   Chinese or Mandarin, 107
   Convertible, 110
   Cossack, 5
   Eton, 7
   Flat, 103
   Mandarin, 10
   Partial Roll, 108
   Peter Pan, 103
   Ring, 11
   Roll, 11, 108
   Shawl, 108
   Shawl, 12
   Straight, 106

Collar draft, 110
Colour, 74
Construction Lines, 5
Corsage, 5
Cord Piping, 5
Costume, 5
Count of Yarn, 5
Cowl, 6
Crease, 6
Crowfoot, 6
Cuffs, 120
Culotte, 6
Cushion or Ham, 20
Co-ordinates, 5

D
Dart, 6
Design Elements, 95
Design Lines, 6
Dickey, 6
Dolman, 6
Double Breasted, 6
Drafts, 101, 143
Draped, 6
Drape, 6
Dressmaker's Carbon, 17
Dressform, 6
Drop, 6

INDEX

Drop Feed Control, 22

E Ease, 6
Edging, 7
Edge stitch, 6
Emery Bag, 7
Empire Line, 6
End, 7
Extension, 7
Eyelet, 7

F Fabric, 65
Fabric Requirement, 127
Fabric Selection, 70
Fabric Selection, 72, 73
Fabric, 65, 68
Facing, 7
Facing, Fitted or Shaped, 50
Faggoting, 7
Fastenings, 7
Fichu, 7
Figure Types, 7
Fish Dart, 7
Fittings, 7, 86
Flap, 7
Flared, 7
Flounce, 7
Flouncings, 7
Fly Front, 7
Fray, 8
French Curves, 19
Frog, 8

G Gathering, 8
Gauging, 8
Gingham, 8
Give, 8
Godets, 8
Gore, 8
Grain, 8
Grey Goods, 8
Gusset, 8

H Halter Neck, 8

Hand Finishing, 8
Harem Trousers, 8
Hem, 8
Hem, Invisible, 9
    Rolled, 11
Hemline, 8
Hemming, 29
Hemming, Invisible, 31
Hinged Bed Plate, 22
Hipsters, 8

I Infants, 123
Insertions, 9
Interfacing, 9, 59
Interlining, 9
Ironing Board, 19 .

J Jabot, 9
Jersey, 9

L Lapel, 9
Layout, 9
Lengths for Dresses, 126
Line, 95
Lining, 9, 57
Loop, 9

M Machine Basting, 9
Machine Faults, 23
Marking, 10
Marking Body Locations, 80
Measurements, 79
Measurement Chart, 149
Measuring Gauge, 16
    Tape, 16
Mitre, 10
Mitring, 33

N Nap, 10
Neckline Finishes, 49
Needles, Hand Sewing, 19
    Machine, 18
Needle Bends or Breaks, 23
Needle Clamp, 22

INDEX

Needle Plate, 22
Needle Skips Stitches, 23
Notch, 10

O
Opening, 10
Overblouse, 10
Overskirt, 10

P
Panel Line, 10
Patterns, 66
Peplum 10
Petticoat, Sari, 189, 191
Peg Top, 10
Picot, 10
Pile, 10
Pinking, 10
Pinking Shears, 17
Pins, 17
Pivot, 10
Pin Cushions, 17
Pin Tucks, 10
Placket, 10, 62
Pleats, 10, 45
   Box, 46
   Inverted, 47
   Kick, 9, 48
   Knife, 9
   Sunburst, 13
Pocket, Patch, 60
Polo Neck, 10
Presser Foot, 22
Pressure Regulating Screw, 22
Princess Line, 11
Proportion, 97
Pre-School Child, 124
Pucker, 11

R
Raglan, 11
Ravel, 11
Redingote, 11
Reinforce, 11
Rever, 11
Rhythm, 97
Ribbon, 11

Rip, 11
Ric Rac, 11
Rosette, 11
Rouleau or Rouleaux, 36
Ruching, 36
Ruffle, 11
Rulers, 16

S
Sag, 11
Salwar, 192
Sari Blouse, 153, 169, 177
Sari Blouse Draft, 169
Sash, 11
Scallop, 11
Scissors or Clippers, 17
Seamline, 12
Seam, 5, 12
   Crossed or Intersecting, 43
   Double Channel, 41
   Faggot, 43
   Flat Fell or Welt, 40
   Flat or Plain, 38
   French, 39
   Lapped, 42
   Mantua, 42
   Piped or Corded, 43
   Shaped, 41
   Slot, 12, 44
Seams and Seam Finishes, 38
Seam Allowance, 12
Seam Finish, 12
Seam Pocket, 61
Seam Rippers, 18
Selvedge, 12
Semi-Fitted, 12
Sewing Construction Details, 25
Sewing Machine, 15
   Care of, 23
   Techniques, 25
   Terms, 3
   Tips, 200
Shank, 12
Shears, 17
Sheath Gown, 12
Shirring, 12

205

INDEX

Shirt Dress, 12
Shirt, Sleeve, 12
Shorts, 128, 195
Shorts Bermuda, 4
Shrink or Shrinkage, 12
Silhouette, 12
Size, 12
Skew, 12
Skimmer, 12
Skirt, 179
   Culotte for Divided, 187
   Full Umbrella, 181
   Gored, 183
   Half Umbrella, 182
   Panel, 183
   Plain Gathered, 181
   Tiered, 186
   Umbrella, 181
Slashed Neckline, 52
Slash, 12
Sleeves, 112
   Bat, 120
   Bell, 4
   Bishop, 115
   Cut, 118
   Dolman, 118
   Kimono, 9, 118
   Leg O'mutton, 9, 116
   Petal, 117
   Puff, 11
   Raglan, 117
   Set-In, 113
   Tailored, 13
   Trumpet, 14
   Virago, 14
Slip, 30
Slorts, Pleated, 187
Smock, 13
Spool Thread Breaks, 23
Stand, 13
Stay, 13
Stay Binding, 13
Stay Stitching, 13
Stiletto, 19
Stitch, Lock, 30

Stitch, Padding, 33
Stitch Length Regulator, 22
Stitch Width Regulator, 22
Straight of Goods, 13

T
Tabard, 13
Tacking Arrowheads, 33
Tack, 13
Take-Up Lever, 22
Taper, 13
Tent, 13
Thimble, 18
Threads, 18
Thread count, 13
Tiers, 13
Toddler, 124
Toggle, 13
Top Stitching, 13
Tracing Wheel, 16
Trapunta, 13
Trimming, 13
Trim, 13
Trousers, 93, 197
Tubing, 14
Tucks, 14
Turtleneck, 14

U
Underlay, 14
Underlining, 14
Understitching, 14
Unit Construction, 14

V
Vent, 14

W
Wadding, 14
Waist bands, 62
Weave, 14
Welt or Slash Pocket, 61
Whip Stitch or Over Sewing, 32
Wrap, 14

Y
Yardage, 14
Yoke, 14

206